Wellness Prescriptions

Simple Steps To A Longer, Healthier Life

Marvin Moe Bell, M.D.

Best of health!
Dr. Moe Bell

BETTER HEALTH BOOKS
Scottsdale, Arizona

Many real-life patient experiences and examples are used throughout this book. All names and some details have been altered to preserve the privacy of the patients.

This book is meant to provide information and encourage a healthy lifestyle, but should not be used as a substitute for the advice of a qualified medical professional.

Second printing
Printed in the United States of America

For information, contact Better Health Books,
Scottsdale, AZ
betterhealthbooks@cox.net

Cover design by Bill Greaves, Concept West

Text design by Michele DeFilippo, 1106 Design

Library of Congress Control Number: 2004096583

ISBN 0-9760695-0-4

Dedicated to Carrie—my wife, best friend, and editor

Table of Contents

Introduction...vii

Part I: Lifestyle

Chapter 1   Good Health Is Mostly Up to You 1
Chapter 2   Diet: A Four-Step Plan to Healthier Eating 13
Chapter 3   Exercise: Getting Active for Health
             and Happiness..31
Chapter 4   Stress: Don't Sweat the Small Stuff.....................47
Chapter 5   Alcohol: Demon Spirits or Elixir of Life? 59
Chapter 6   Smoking: Why to Quit, How to Quit 73

Part II: Heart Health

Chapter 7   Heart Disease: Protecting the Pump 91
Chapter 8   Overweight: The Fight Against Fat...................107
Chapter 9   High Blood Pressure: Don't Blow a Gasket 127
Chapter 10   Cholesterol: Friend and Foe 143
Chapter 11   Diabetes: The Plague of Plenty 159
Chapter 12   Arterial Disease: Avoiding Stroke and
             Other Calamities 177

Part III: Cancer Control

Chapter 13   Controlling Cancer: Healthy Habits
             Can Lower Your Risk...189
Chapter 14   Cervical Cancer: A Success Story 201
Chapter 15   Lung Cancer: A Long Way to Go Baby 213
Chapter 16   Colon Cancer: Of Fiber and Fiber-Optics........223

Chapter 17 Breast Cancer: What Women Need
to Know 235
Chapter 18 Prostate Cancer: Is Ignorance Bliss?................249

Part IV: Active Aging

Chapter 19 The Golden Years: How to
Age Gracefully 261
Chapter 20 Osteoporosis: Give Your Bones a
Break... So They Won't 273
Chapter 21 Arthritis: Coping with Creaky Joints...............289
Chapter 22 Memory Problems: How to Keep from
Forgetting..305
Chapter 23 Advance Directives: How to Guide
Your Final Scene...321

Appendix A: List of Tables and Figures................................331
Appendix B: List of Sidebars...332
References...334
Index 350
About the Author...356

Introduction

*"An ounce of prevention is worth
a pound of cure."*
—Wise proverb

WHY *YOU* NEED THIS BOOK!

Do you worry about terrorist attacks, nuclear accidents, anthrax, smallpox, or the latest epidemic overseas? If so, you are not alone. Most Americans worry a lot about being stricken by things over which they have no control. In reality, however, your risk of illness or death from one of these headline grabbers is extremely low. The greatest killers of Americans actually are tobacco, poor diet, physical inactivity, and alcohol. Fortunately, unlike the headline grabbers, these are things over which you *can* exert control. Though most people don't realize it, *half* of early deaths and chronic diseases in this country could be prevented if all Americans adopted a few good lifestyle habits. This book tells you how.

Americans are barraged with conflicting and confusing health advice in the news, on the Internet and in the bookstores. Do you really need a cholesterol test, mammogram, PSA test, colonoscopy, bone density test, and more? Should you believe current advertisements that say you should have a heart scan, lung scan, or—what the heck—a whole body scan? Are the vitamins, herbs, and other supplements recommended by your local health-food store really good for you? *Wellness Prescriptions: Simple Steps to a Longer, Healthier Life* uses up-to-date medical evidence to answer such questions and empower you to make informed health decisions.

It also tells you how to prevent serious illness; which treatments work best for sicknesses that occur despite prevention efforts; and how to manage chronic conditions like high blood pressure, high cholesterol, diabetes, and arthritis. If you want to improve your health, prevent illness, and increase your chances of living a long life, this book is for you.

PHILOSOPHIC BASIS:

"It is the duty of the physician to prevent disease, relieve suffering, and treat the sick."

—Sir William Osler, father of modern medicine

Modern medicine has generally reversed the order of priorities described by Dr. Osler. Most effort is devoted to diagnosing and treating diseases, rather than preventing them. Dramatic high-tech interventions like artificial hearts, for example, get a lot more attention than lifestyle modifications that can reduce a patient's risk of ever developing heart problems.

Life habits such as smoking, overeating, excessive drinking, inactivity, and getting stressed out take a huge toll on health. From heart disease to cancer to strokes to accidents, the key to prevention is choosing a healthier lifestyle. Some simple changes can improve health and well being dramatically. This book tells you which preventive strategies make sense, which ones don't, and why.

When prevention fails, modern medicine has the ability to detect and treat many diseases at an early stage. New drug treatments, diagnostic tests, and surgical techniques are introduced almost daily. We often equate "new" with "better." Unfortunately, new tests and treatments are often adopted before experience and research teach us which ones help and which ones harm. Just like consumer products, new drugs or medical devices sometimes are banned after widespread use leads to unanticipated problems. This book explains which screening tests and treatments work, which ones don't, and which ones we aren't yet certain about.

The mission of this book is threefold:

- To help you learn as much as possible about how to lower your risk of getting sick.
- To inform you about the pros and cons of screening for diseases before symptoms occur.
- And to advise you on treatments for diseases that occur despite your best preventive efforts.

MEDICAL BASIS:

My advice on prevention relies on "evidence-based medicine," not on celebrity endorsements or the latest health fads. Modern medicine, like our modern world, keeps getting more complicated, and it can be difficult to distill the flood of new medical findings into sensible recommendations. The evidence-based approach is to make a medical recommendation only when there is research to suggest that it is beneficial.

The strongest evidence in medicine comes from "randomized, controlled trials (RCTs)," research studies in which people have been randomly assigned to either a treatment group or a control group. While the study is being conducted, the researchers should not know who is in the treatment group and who is in the control group. RCTs provide the best evidence of whether a treatment or test is beneficial, or whether it causes harm.

Because of the challenges of running experimental studies on people, many research studies are "observational." Observational studies report on groups of people who have been followed over time. The groups can be people with a particular disease who are compared with similar people who do not have the disease, or they can follow a single large group like the residents of Framingham, Massachusetts. Observational studies are not as powerful as RCTs, but they provide helpful insights.

This book is evidence-based whenever possible. I have taken many recommendations from the U.S. Preventive Services Task Force (USPSTF), a government-sponsored panel of experts who review available medical evidence and make recommendations about prevention. Unfortunately, many medical tests and treatments have yet to be studied through RCTs. When there is limited evidence to provide guidance, I rely on expert opinions and recommendations of well-respected organizations such as the American Cancer Society.

In addition to evidence and expert opinions, my advice on healthy living is based on common sense and experience gained during my 20 years of medical practice. As a family doctor, I try to remember the Hippocratic Oath when it says, "First, do no harm." Though I have done my best to use the latest medical evidence in writing this guide, I must remind readers that medicine constantly changes. Please keep an open mind and be aware that new knowledge will continue to further our quest for wellness.

HOW TO USE THIS BOOK:

Wellness Prescriptions: Simple Steps to a Longer, Healthier Life is intended to be an informative, easy-to-understand, practical reference for all adults. The book is divided into four parts: Lifestyle, Heart Health, Cancer Control, and Active Aging. I hope all readers will review Part I on Lifestyle. Those first six chapters contain a crucial message for establishing and maintaining wellness: Each day you make decisions that have a tremendous impact on your well being—from what you eat to how much you exercise to whether you buckle your seatbelt. These choices, which are completely under your control, can help preserve—or destroy—that precious resource, your health.

Readers can pick and choose among topics covered in the other chapters as their interests or health concerns dictate. The first chapter in each part provides an overview, but subsequent chapters are written to stand alone. Key points and advice are highlighted throughout each chapter. I highly encourage readers to look at the book's final chapter on advance directives. It might seem odd in a book on prevention, but making some decisions now about your life's end stage could prevent unwanted interventions later on and provide guidance for family members called upon to make choices on your behalf. I wish you the best of health, and I hope this book will help you turn that wish into a reality.

PART I

Lifestyle

CHAPTER ONE
....

Good Health Is Mostly Up to You

"Let health be represented by the number one. Family, friends, success, can all be represented by the number zero. Without the number one, you have nothing. With the number one, each additional zero increases your happiness."
—Confucius

Why did comedian Bob Hope live to be 100, but actor John Ritter die prematurely in his 50s? Why did Bill Clinton need quadruple bypass at age 58, while Jack LaLanne was going strong at 88? When I was in medical school in 1980, a Surgeon General's report on health promotion and disease prevention offered some powerful insights into causes of premature death and disease.[1] The report estimated that *half* of the early deaths in the United States were caused by unhealthy lifestyles (see figure 1). Genetics, the environment, and lack of medical care shared the blame for the other half. This chapter explores the role of these factors, as well as luck, on health and lifespan.

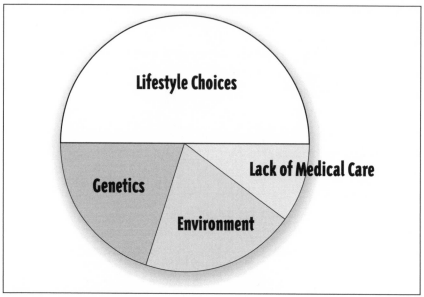

Figure 1: Estimated causes of premature deaths in America
(From *Healthy People: The Surgeon General's Report on Health Promotion and Disease Prevention*, 1980.)

LIFESTYLE LESSONS

We have no control over the genes we inherit or our luck, and only limited control over our environment and access to medical care. When it comes to lifestyle, however, we call all the shots, and our choices have a tremendous impact on how long and how well we live. Lifestyle choices are the key to good health that we all possess.

From the start of medical school, I was very interested in learning how to prevent disease and keep people well. To my dismay, I found that medical education was very disease-oriented, with little emphasis on prevention. Fortunately, one lecture bucked the trend and opened my eyes to the incredible power that simple lifestyle choices have on health. Based on life-insurance industry data, the speaker compared the average life expectancies of Americans with certain health habits. He found that people who practiced the following six simple habits lived *12 years* longer than those who did not:

1. Slept 7–9 hours a night
2. Ate breakfast
3. Exercised (even walking) three days a week for 20 minutes
4. Drank alcohol moderately (up to six drinks per week)
5. Didn't smoke
6. Wore a seatbelt

These "good" lifestyle choices were mostly common sense, not rocket science, yet they had a stunning impact on people's lives.

Though more than 20 years have passed since that lecture, the six good habits have stood the test of time. Individuals who adopt them are likely to live significantly longer, and feel much better day in and day out, than those who do not. Though many people don't realize it, making healthy lifestyle choices can do more for well-being and longevity than most modern medical interventions. Conversely, unhealthy habits cause as many premature deaths as environmental toxins, hereditary diseases, and lack of medical care combined.

You might find it surprising that lifestyle choices can so profoundly affect health. After years of caring for patients on the teaching service of the hospital where I work, however, I can assure you that lifestyle matters a great deal. I see a steady stream of smokers with emphysema complications, pneumonia, and lung cancers. Heavy alcohol drinkers come in with intestinal bleeding, cirrhosis of the liver, and injuries. Many seriously injured patients in the emergency room are those who chose to drive without a seatbelt, often after drinking. Overweight, sedentary individuals suffer from chronic illnesses and surgical complications more often that their normal weight, physically active peers. The list goes on, but the point is that the majority of serious health problems could be prevented if people made healthier lifestyle decisions.

> ✸ *Key point:* Over half of all deaths of Americans under age 65 are caused by unhealthy habits and are completely preventable.

GENETICS

When it comes to health, which has greater impact, the genes we are dealt at birth or the environment in which we live? This nature versus nurture debate has been going on in medical circles for as long as anyone can remember. Though there's still no simple answer to the question, research has shown that our genes play a powerful role in our health.

Studies of identical twins separated at birth and reared in different environments show that the genetic blueprint is a strong determinant of height, weight, and even blood pressure.[2] Genes also seem to be a key factor in how and when many of us will die. We've all heard of families in which everyone seems to live into their 90s or past 100. At the other extreme, I have patients whose parent, grandparent, and many other relatives on one side of the family have died of heart attacks in their 50s and 60s. I also have patients with several relatives who have died of cancer in middle age. Experts estimate that about 20 percent of premature deaths may be due to hereditary causes.[1]

So what about your own genetic make-up? Though you can't change the genes you've inherited (not yet anyway), I think it's still important to know as much as possible about them. Start by learning all you can about the health histories of your parents and grandparents.

If your genetic report card is excellent, rejoice and take comfort. Now the onus is on you to practice a healthy lifestyle to fulfill your genetic potential. If your genes are mixed or not so good—as is the case for most of us—do not despair. For you, practicing a healthy lifestyle is even more important, and knowledge is power. Learn and practice prevention strategies for health problems found in your family, such as heart disease, diabetes, high blood pressure, or certain types of cancer. In addition, find out when to have screening tests that identify problems early on.

Q *Health Tip:* Write down the medical history of your blood relatives, especially your parents and grandparents. Include major illnesses such as cancers (include the type), heart attacks, strokes, and diabetes. When a relative dies, record his or her age and the cause of death. Keep this record updated and have it available for your family physician and any new doctors you visit.

ENVIRONMENT

Many people believe that pollution and toxins pose the biggest threats to well-being. People who live near nuclear power plants, for example, list environmental contamination as their greatest health fear. This is despite the fact that illness from nuclear leaks is incredibly rare.

While the environment around us certainly has an impact on our health, it causes far fewer illnesses than unhealthy lifestyle choices. Thirty percent of all cancers are caused by smoking, for example, whereas fewer than 10 percent of cancers are thought to be caused by pollution, food additives, natural radiation, and workplace exposures combined.[3]

Environmental exposures that can hurt our health occur in three main settings—the workplace, the home, and outdoors.

Workplace safety has steadily improved since the 1800s, but occupational disease remains common. Though the Occupational Health and Safety Act (OSHA), passed in 1970, and related laws have helped reduce the risks, workers still must be vigilant about taking steps to protect themselves on the job. Excess noise, fumes, and particulates in the workplace, and jobs requiring repetitive motions account for most occupational health problems. To stay safe, workers should wear ear protection and masks or respirators if exposed to noise or fumes. They should also follow all recommended health and safety measures posted at the job site, and speak up if they feel their health is at risk.

Indoor pollution in the home has gotten a lot of press recently. Toxic molds and chemicals are blamed for a wide range of symptoms. Like the workplace, however, the home environment has improved a lot in recent decades due to public health measures, such as the banning of leaded paint in the 1960s and asbestos products in 1980. Still, concerns about chemicals, molds, and radon gas are real, and we do spend the biggest chunk of our time in our own homes. For more details on indoor pollution and ways to help you breathe easier, read the sidebar "Improving indoor air quality."

Outdoor air pollution, much of it caused by the burning of fossil fuels, clearly poses a health risk. In 1952, for example, 4,000 people died in London when a weather inversion kept the city enveloped for several days in cold, damp air full of pollution from burning coal. Most of the victims were older and already suffered from heart or lung problems. Today, many Americans have emphysema, bronchitis, and asthma that is triggered or worsened by air pollution. Day to day, there is not much you can do to limit exposure. On high pollution days in big cities, however, you should try to get your exercise indoors. Meanwhile, with help from the Clean Air Act, the country is striving for healthier air. Progress has been slow, but it's some comfort to know that air pollution and particulate levels have trended slightly downward over the past decade.

As for other environmental concerns, the water and food in America are generally cleaner and safer than at any time in history. Despite scares like E.Coli and mad cow disease, the risk of food-born illness is quite low. Reasonably clean air, water, and food are privileges Americans have come to expect, but that many people in the world only dream about. To keep our air, water, and food safe, we need to let lawmakers know that a healthy environment is a high priority, and that we are willing to pay for it.

Q *Health tip:* When renovating an older home, take precautions for removal of lead-containing paint and asbestos-containing tiles or materials. Any paint or building materials in an older home that are peeling or shedding should be repaired or sealed.

🖐 *Personal action plan:* Get a carbon-monoxide alarm if you use a fuel-burning stove, heater, or fireplace in your home. Find out whether radon gas is a problem in your area, and get your house tested if it is.

MEDICAL CARE

The United States has the most expensive medical-care system in the world. At its best, it includes check-ups that promote healthy lifestyles, immunizations that prevent infections, screening programs designed to find disease at an early, treatable stage, and medications that help control chronic diseases. Unfortunately, far too many Americans lack access to these preventive services. Forty million Americans have no health insurance and another 30 million are underinsured. These people are mostly the poor, minorities, young working adults, or elderly people on fixed incomes who can't afford medications needed to treat medical conditions.

Lack of access to medical care is believed to be responsible for up to 10 percent of premature deaths in the United States each year.[1] Typically, the uninsured and underinsured wait until they are seriously ill before visiting the emergency room, often their only health-care option, where doctors end up treating conditions that should have been treated earlier or could have been prevented entirely. Finding a solution to this problem of access for all is a daunting challenge and beyond the scope of *Wellness Prescriptions*.

Improving indoor air quality

There are four potential hazards in the air we breathe at home: irritant chemicals, allergy triggers, carbon monoxide, and radon gas. Formaldehyde is the most common of the irritant chemicals. It is released in the air in small amounts from new carpets, drapes, foam, and particle-board. Most formaldehyde is released during the first year after construction or installation. It can be an eye or skin irritant, but most people never have problems. Good ventilation and open windows during nice weather will remove most of these airborn irritants.

Dust, mold, animal dander, and insect parts are part of your indoor air, as well. Again, most people suffer no ill effects, but these allergy triggers may cause itchy eyes, sneezing, stuffy noses, or even breathing problems for people with allergies. Take the following steps to help clear allergens from your home's air:

- Get a vacuum cleaner made for allergy sufferers. These vacuums have filter bags with small pores that will trap small particles like pollens. Regular vacuums with large-pore bags do not effectively remove allergens from your home. In fact, they often suck up the allergens only to spew them back out in the vacuum's exhaust.
- Dust and mop with damp sponges and cloths, which pick up and remove allergens, instead of dry cloths or feather dusters, which only stir them around.
- Change filters on air conditioners and heaters every one to two months.
- If allergies persist, get a portable HEPA (high energy particulate arresting) filter. It can clean the air in a bedroom pretty effectively.

Carbon monoxide is the most deadly indoor pollutant, killing 1,500 Americans each year. Carbon-monoxide poisoning can occur in any home with a gas range, gas or kerosene heater, or wood- or coal-burning stove or fireplace. Carbon monoxide has no color or odor, so victims often die without warning. Inexpensive, plug-in carbon monoxide detectors sound a loud alarm if levels are going up inside the home. They can prevent most cases of carbon-monoxide poisoning.

Another potential danger in homes is radon gas. Radon is a radioactive gas that occurs naturally and can seep into homes from bedrock or soil. Most homes in the United States are just fine, but 5–10 percent may have radon gas levels that increase the occupants' risk of lung cancer. If high levels are present, ventilation of basements and crawl spaces and sealing foundation cracks often fixes the problem. Inexpensive home test kits for radon are available in regions where radon problems are common. For information on your area, check the following Web site: www.epa.gov/iaq/radon. ∎

If you're reading this book, you likely have health insurance or the means to pay for health care. Ideally, you should also have a relationship with a good primary-care physician, with whom you can schedule periodic check-ups to discuss ways to prevent illness and screen for problems based on your age and risk factors.

> ✻ *Key point:* In the United States, about 10 percent of premature deaths are due to lack of access to medical care and preventive services. Schedule a visit with your primary-care doctor to discuss prevention strategies and screening tests you might need.

RANDOM EVENTS (LUCK)

I was driving home through a sudden desert thunderstorm last year and heard that a man my age was killed when a freak gust of wind blew a light pole down on his car. This random tragedy left me wondering why him, why not me?

Unfortunately, such random events often receive sensational headlines and endless media analysis. This creates a great deal of anxiety, and makes people fear that their risk of a freak accident is far greater than it actually is. In reality, the chance that you will die prematurely due to a falling light pole, bolt of lightning, or some other unpredictable phenomenon is tiny. You are many times more likely to perish from a health problem or injury caused by unhealthy lifestyle choices.

In fact, most human illness and many accidents have causes that we can study, understand, and often prevent. Read on for practical advice on how to prevent health problems and stay well. We can all hope and pray that good fortune smiles upon us, give thanks when it does, but take an active role to keep the odds in our favor.

Key point: Though the media might lead us to believe otherwise, deaths and health problems caused by freak accidents and other random events are actually quite rare. We should quit worrying about these and focus more attention on lifestyle choices that can prevent common diseases.

Personal action plan: When world events are making you anxious, make a resolution to turn off all television news for three days. You will be amazed by how much better you feel.

THE KEYS TO A LONG HEALTHY LIFE

So what should you do to stay healthy? First, remember the six healthy habits that can add a dozen years to your life:

- Eat a healthy breakfast
- Exercise three days a week for 20 minutes (even a leisurely stroll will do)
- Get a good night's sleep
- Drink alcohol in moderation (or not at all)
- Don't smoke
- Wear your seatbelt (Riding in a vehicle is the single most dangerous thing most people do on any given day. Wearing a seatbelt makes it a far safer proposition for both driver and passengers.)

And second, be sure to read the rest of Part I on lifestyle. Following is a preview of chapters 2 through 6:

Diet

An old adage instructs us to "eat like a king in the morning, a prince at noon, and a pauper in the evening." What's so important about breakfast? Studies have shown that people who eat breakfast are less likely to be overweight, and more likely to eat a healthy diet.

Although breakfast is an important meal, healthy eating involves much more. What about fruits, vegetables, fiber, and fat? What about vitamins, calcium, anti-oxidants, and other supplements? Chapter 2 delves into diet and nutrition and presents a simple four-step plan for healthier eating.

Exercise

We have all heard about the health benefits of exercise. It can help reduce your risk of heart disease, high blood pressure, diabetes, and obesity. It can lower your stress level and improve your mental and emotional well-being. Unfortunately, though we all know that exercise is good for us, the majority of Americans don't do much or any. Chapter 3 explains that "No pain, no gain" is out and has been replaced by the philosophy "Every little bit helps." This chapter will help you jump-start your exercise program and keep it going. It's never too late to get active.

Stress

Why is sleeping on the list of healthy habits? Sleep is a time to rest, dream, and allow body and mind time to repair and recuperate. Too little sleep is often the result of a stressful lifestyle. Too much sleep can result from stress-induced exhaustion or depression. A healthy amount of sleep is a good indicator that you are successfully managing the stress in your life. Chapter 4 explores the health implications of stress, and gives some practical pointers on how to evaluate and manage stress constructively.

Alcohol

Alcohol has been part of human culture for thousands of years. Moderate drinking seems to have some health benefits, but excessive imbibing can exact a heavy toll. Chapter 5 reviews the health effects of alcohol, both good and bad.

Tobacco

Tobacco needs little introduction as public-health enemy No. 1. No other substance causes more preventable human disease. Chapter 6 avoids preaching but offers practical help for smokers who want to quit. Even committed nonsmokers will learn how to understand and possibly help their friends and family members who haven't yet kicked the habit.

> ❄❄ *Key point:* Regarding the keys to health—accept the genetic hand you've been dealt, hope or pray for "good luck" along the way, and seize every opportunity to make healthy lifestyle choices.

SUMMARY

Figure 1 shows the four primary causes of premature death in Americans and estimates how many of these deaths can be attributed to each cause. The random accidents and natural hazards that people worry so much about don't even show up on the pie chart. Lack of medical care is responsible for only about 10 percent of premature deaths; genetics and the environment are responsible for about 20 percent each; and lifestyle choices cause a whopping 50 percent of early deaths. There is little you can do to change your environmental or genetic risks of premature death. As for medical care, you can make an impact by seeking it out when you have symptoms or are due for check-ups or screening tests. By far the most important thing you can do to increase your longevity and improve your quality of life, however, is to adopt a few simple, healthy lifestyle habits.

CHAPTER TWO

Diet: A Four-Step Plan to Healthier Eating

"He is a heavy eater of beef. Me thinks it doth harm to his wit."
—Shakespeare in ***Twelfth Night***

EAT WELL, BE WELL

Do you eat a healthy diet?

Think about your diet. Is it healthy? With smoking, either you light up or you don't. With exercise, either you're doing some or you're not. With diet, the answer is more complex. You make food choices throughout each day. Some choices are healthier than others, and some days are better than others. Nutrition experts are still debating the make-up of the "ideal" human diet, but they overwhelmingly agree that the *typical* American diet is flat out unhealthy.

Junk foods such as donuts, hot dogs, chips, double cheeseburgers, fries, pizza, soda pop, and rich desserts have become staples of our typical diet. Loaded with fat, sugar, and salt, these foods are light on nutrition but heavy on the calories. Most of us eat too many harmful saturated fats, trans fats (see "Fat Primer" sidebar), and processed foods. Processing of grains removes most or all of the natural fiber content and destroys many of the vitamins. Processed meats—bacon, hot dogs, sausage, bologna, salami, and other cured meats—have been implicated as causes of both diabetes[1] and colon cancer.[2]

We are consuming junk foods, and healthier foods, too, in larger portions than ever before. Sadly, as our consumption of calories has increased, our level of physical activity has declined—a double-whammy that has fueled epidemics in obesity, diabetes, heart disease, and cancer.

Researchers studying the effects of diet on the development of chronic disease separate Americans roughly into two groups—those who eat a typical American or "Western" diet and those who eat a healthier or "prudent" diet.[1] A Western diet includes lots of red meat, processed meat, high-fat dairy products, French fries, refined grains, desserts, and sweets. A prudent diet emphasizes fruits, vegetables, whole grains, poultry, and fish.

If you already eat a prudent diet, this chapter should reassure you that you are doing a great deal to ensure good health. You will find some helpful pointers and the latest evidence concerning vitamin and mineral supplements. If you eat a typical American diet, I hope to convince you that there is a better way, and to suggest a simple four-step plan that will start you on the path to a longer, healthier life.

The four-step plan for healthier eating

John is a typical, frustrated dieter. He lost some weight on the Atkins diet, but gained it all back when he quit. He wants to eat healthier, but has no long-term plan to make it happen. He also hates to be told that he can't eat certain foods, or that he must limit his intake to a certain number or amount. I suggested a more positive approach, based on sound nutritional principles. It involves a conscious decision to *eat more*—of the healthier foods. Here is my four-step plan for healthier eating:

- Begin with breakfast
- Eat five fruits or vegetables each day
- Choose foods with more fiber
- Eat more of the good fats and less bad fats

Read on to learn why this approach will work and to get practical food ideas.

Begin with breakfast

Studies show that people who eat breakfast tend to eat less later on in the day and maintain a healthier weight than those who skip it. Breakfast gives you a handy energy supply for the day ahead. If you skip breakfast, your body has to mobilize energy stored in fat to get you through the day. This makes you hungrier and more likely to eat high-fat foods as the day goes on.

When I ask obese patients about their eating habits, most of them tell me they skip breakfast, and many say they skip lunch as well. When people go for long periods of time without eating, their metabolism slows down and fewer calories get burned. This explains why skipping breakfast really *does not* help people lose weight.

Breakfast is one meal you can add without much trouble. Healthy breakfast foods are easy to store, fast to prepare, and convenient to work into your lifestyle. By eating some low-fat, high-fiber foods in the morning, your entire diet will improve.

Some great breakfast choices include whole-grain cereals (look for fiber content of at least 3 grams), oatmeal, or whole-wheat toast. Whole-grain waffles or pancakes are fine, but in moderation. Go easy on the syrup and use soft margarine (ideally made with a monounsaturated fat like olive oil). Bagels are healthy and low-fat, but some are so big that one-half or one-quarter makes a nice serving. Balance the carbohydrates with some protein and healthy fats, which you can get from a serving of skim or 1 percent milk, low-fat cottage cheese, low-fat yogurt, an egg or egg substitute (i.e. Egg Beaters), or some peanut butter. Top off your breakfast with a piece of fruit—such as a banana, an apple, or half a grapefruit.

No offense to the French, but the croissant is packed with saturated fat and should not be a breakfast staple. Limit croissants, as well as traditional high-fat breakfast items like bacon, sausage, and hash browns, to special occasions. Be creative, there are a lot of healthier, lighter ways to start the day.

> ✋ *Personal action plan:* If you already eat a healthy breakfast, congratulate yourself and keep it up. If not, treat yourself to a healthy meal in the morning. It will make a difference.

Eat five fruits or vegetables each day

In 1991, the National Cancer Institute and the Produce for Better Health Foundation started a nationwide health campaign called "Five-a-day for better health." The message was simple, yet powerful: eat five or more servings of fruit or vegetables each day to achieve better health.

The original goal of the program was to prevent cancers. Researchers in the 1980s had concluded that up to 20 percent of all cancers could be prevented if people would simply add fruits and vegetables to their diet. The cancer-preventing punch comes from eating the right blend of vitamins, minerals, antioxidants, phytochemicals (plant chemicals), and fiber that come in these healthy foods. Unfortunately, researchers have never been able to show that people can achieve the same benefit by taking the vitamins and antioxidants as pills.

Increasingly, evidence suggests that a diet with more foods from plants than from animals offers benefits beyond potential cancer prevention. In addition to vitamins and minerals, plants contain hundreds of phytochemicals that protect them from too much sun, pollution, and disease. Researchers believe phytochemicals may have a similar protective effect on humans, boosting our immune systems, preventing diabetes, protecting our hearts, and slowing aging.

Eating more fruits and vegetables also results in more fiber and less harmful fat in our diet, which leads to less high blood pressure, lower cholesterol levels, less diabetes, and fewer heart attacks. A Harvard study in 2003 found that each extra serving of fruit or vegetables, especially green, leafy vegetables, lowered the risk of heart disease by 4 percent.[3]

"Five-a-day" really is a reachable goal for most people. One fruit or vegetable serving is described as follows:

Fruit One medium-size fresh fruit (an apple, pear, banana, etc.)
½ cup cut up
¼ cup dried
6 ounces of 100% fruit juice

Vegetable One cup raw, leafy vegetables
½ cup raw or cooked vegetables
½ cup dried, cooked or canned peas or beans
6 ounces of 100% vegetable juice

Make sure your breakfast contains some fruit. One salad during your day can provide a couple of vegetable servings and is a healthy choice at a fast-food restaurant. Sneak some vegetables, like carrots or celery, into your snacks. To make them tastier, dip them lightly in a low-calorie salad dressing. Be sure your dinner includes a vegetable serving, and how about some fruit for an after-dinner treat?

Remember that variety is the spice of life. A fun way to assure a healthy blend of vitamins, minerals, and phytochemicals is to choose fruits and vegetables from throughout the color spectrum—yellow, orange, red, green, blue, and purple. Do what your mama said: "Eat your vegetables."

 Personal action plan: Make a point to eat five or more servings of fruit or vegetables today and every day.

Choose foods with more fiber

The "fiber" sidebar reviews some of the many health benefits eating fiber-rich foods. But first, what is "fiber"? Simply stated, fiber is the part of the plants we eat that we don't digest or absorb. It passes through our digestive system and goes out in our stool.

Fiber's health benefits

Among rural Africans, whose diet is full of high-fiber foods, colon cancer, diverticulitis, and constipation are quite rare. When these people move to big cities or to America, they experience a dramatic increase in these gastrointestinal conditions. Researchers theorize that a lack of fiber, or roughage, in Western diets slows down passage of stool through the colon, allowing cancer-causing chemicals to spend more time there. This is believed to cause the growth of polyps, which eventually turn into colon cancers. A recent study at New York's Sloan-Kettering Cancer Center found that eating a couple of servings of high-fiber cereal each day made precancerous polyps shrink in both size and number over a six-month period.

The highly processed, low-fiber diets prevalent in America have resulted in an absolute epidemic of constipation. Look at the incredible array of stool softeners, laxatives, and fiber supplements available at the local pharmacy and you will realize that something is wrong. Harder stools require more pressure to expel and create pouches in the wall of the colon, a condition known medically as "diverticulosis." These pouches can get infected, causing "diverticulitis," often a serious or even life-threatening condition. Straining to have bowel movements also contributes to development of hemorrhoids.

In addition to lower incidences of colorectal diseases, countries where people eat high-fiber diets also have much lower rates of heart disease and diabetes than the United States. Eating more fiber can help Americans lower their risk of these diseases. In a Harvard study of 44,000 health professionals published in 1996, for example, men who ate the most fiber had one-third fewer heart attacks than men who ate the least amount of fiber. [4] ■

Fiber tends to hold on to water, so fiber-filled stools are bigger, but softer, than low-fiber stools. Pardon the analogy, but fiber-rich stools are banana-like, whereas fiber-poor stools struggle out looking like rabbit pellets.

Unfortunately, processing and refining food removes the fiber as well as many of the natural vitamins and nutrients. Foods with at least 2 grams of fiber per serving tend to have fewer processed ingredients and better nutritional value than foods with labels stating "dietary fiber less than 1 gram." Most Americans eat far less than the recommended 25–30 grams per day of fiber. You may be surprised when you check the fiber content of foods you purchase.

Whole-wheat flour is packed with fiber (3 grams per ounce), for example, while white pastry flour has almost none. Looking at crackers, Triscuits contain 4 grams of fiber per ounce, Wheat Thins have 1 gram per ounce, but Ritz crackers and Saltines have none.

Food labels sometimes mention insoluble and soluble fiber. Insoluble fiber, found in wheat bran and vegetables, doesn't dissolve in water as much as soluble fiber. Soluble fiber, found in oat bran and many fruits, is more jelly-like in the bowel and helps to lower cholesterol. Both kinds of fiber are healthy, and you should eat a mix of them.

For some good sources of fiber, see table 2.1. Fruits and vegetables contain fiber naturally. Each fruit or vegetable serving contains about 2–3 grams of fiber, maybe a little more if you eat the peel. Beans are another rich fiber source, with 4–8 grams per half-cup serving. If you achieve the five-fruits-and-vegetables-a-day goal, you'll be well on your way to a very healthy fiber intake.

Breakfast is a great time to get some fiber. Checking labels makes it easy to determine high-fiber choices. Cereals vary a lot, but tasty whole-grain cereals often have 4 or more grams of fiber per serving. Whole-wheat toast has 2–3 grams per slice. One-third cup of oatmeal contains 3 grams of fiber, while the same amount of 100% oat bran cereal packs 6 grams, half of it in the cholesterol-lowering soluble form. If you need more fiber, bran cereals supply 8–12 grams per serving, and prunes provide 1 gram each.

If you simply can't get enough fiber into your diet, fiber supplements taken with water are safe and helpful. Many people have trouble finding high-fiber foods while traveling, and take supplements along to help out. Each teaspoon of psyllium powder (Metamucil) contains 3 grams of fiber. Fiber supplements are also available over the counter as pills or capsules.

Personal action plan: Focus on fiber. Read labels and choose higher-fiber foods to try to consume 25–30 grams of fiber each day.

Table 2.1: Good sources of fiber

Food	Serving size	Grams of fiber
Cereal		
All-Bran 100%	½ cup (1 oz)	10
Oat Bran 100%	⅓ cup (1 oz)	6
Spoon-size Shredded Wheat	⅔ cup (1 oz)	4
Raisin Bran	½ cup (1 oz)	4
Cheerios	1 cup (1 oz)	3
Oatmeal	⅓ cup (1 oz)	3
Bread, pasta, grains		
Whole-wheat spaghetti	1 cup cooked	4
Whole-wheat bread	1 slice	3
Popcorn	1 cup	3
Bran muffin	1 regular	2.5
Rye Crisps	2 crackers	2
Fruits		
Apple with skin	1 medium	3.5
Apple without skin	1 medium	3
Prunes	3	3
Raisins	¼ cup	3
Strawberries	1 cup	3
Pear with skin	½ large	3
Pear without skin	½ large	2.5
Orange	1	2.5
Banana	1 medium	2.5
Vegetables, cooked		
Pumpkin pie filling	½ cup	5
Peas	½ cup	3.5
Corn, canned	½ cup	3
Potato with skin	1 medium	2.5
Broccoli	½ cup	2.5
Carrots	½ cup	2.5
Sweet potato	½ medium	2
Zucchini	½ cup	2

Beans, legumes, nuts

Baked beans	½ cup	6
Kidney beans	½ cup	6
Navy beans	½ cup	6
Black beans	½ cup	6
Lentils	½ cup	4
Almonds	1 oz	4

> ❈ *Key point:* If you are eating a high-fiber breakfast, and trying to eat five-a-day fruits and vegetables, you should be well on your way to a healthy amount of fiber in your diet.

Eat more good fats and less bad fats

This chapter's "Fat primer" sidebar describes both the harmful and healthy fats that we get in our diets. Unfortunately, Americans tend to eat way too much unhealthy saturated fat and trans fat. In excess, these harmful fats are a major cause of heart disease and contribute to cancers of the colon, breast, and prostate.

Try to eat more monounsaturated fats by using olive, canola, peanut, or safflower oils. Avocados, walnuts, almonds, and other nuts also contain healthier fats. Consume more fish oil, another source of good fats, by incorporating salmon, tuna, mackerel, tilapia, and other fish into your diet.

Read labels and try to limit foods with more than a couple of grams of saturated fat or trans fat per serving. By law, amounts of trans fats must appear on all food labels by 2006. This will make it easier to choose snack foods made with fewer trans fats. For now, limit foods containing hydrogenated and partially hydrogenated oils, and solid fats like lard, Crisco, butter, stick margarine, and palm and coconut oils. These include most candies, cookies, crackers and other baked goods. Also go light on marbled red meats, fried foods, and processed meats such as bacon, salami, bologna, hot dogs, and sausage.

Fat primer

We need some fat in our diet to supply energy and to help absorb the fat-soluble vitamins A, D, E, and K. Fats contain essential chemicals called "fatty acids" that are just as important as the amino-acid building blocks that come from protein. The problem is that most of us eat too much harmful fat.

Harmful fats

- *Saturated fat* wreaks havoc by raising the bad kind of cholesterol (LDL) that clogs arteries. As a rule, the more solid at room temperature, the more saturated the fat. Crisco and lard, for instance, have more saturated fat than liquid oils. Foods high in saturated fat include whole milk, butter, cream, hard cheeses, marbled meats, sausage, chicken skins, and palm and coconut oils.
- *Trans fats* (also known as "trans fatty acids") are especially nasty for your health because they raise cholesterol levels in your blood. Trans fats are made when liquid oils are "hydrogenated" or "partially hydrogenated," which makes them more solid. Commercially baked goods, fried foods, hard margarine, shortening, and many other processed foods are loaded with trans-fatty acids.
- *Cholesterol* itself is found only in animal-derived foods, especially egg yolks, liver, and dairy products. Although eating cholesterol can raise your cholesterol levels, it is much less of a problem than saturated fat because we simply do not eat as much. A typical American diet contains less than half a gram of cholesterol per day, compared with 20–40 grams of saturated fat.

Healthier Fats

- *Monounsaturated fats* are the healthiest fats and should be the fats of choice for cooking. They are found in olive, peanut, sunflower, and canola oils, as well as in avocados, walnuts, and almonds. Monounsaturated fats are often credited for the low heart disease rates in Mediterranean countries, where olive oil is popular.
- *Polyunsaturated fats* are found in most nuts as well as in vegetable oils derived from corn, soybeans, and cottonseeds. Polyunsaturated fats are fairly neutral from a health perspective, causing neither harm nor benefit.
- *Plant sterols/stanols* are plant compounds found in soybean oil and pine trees. They are contained in the margarines Benecol and Take Control and are being studied as cholesterol-lowering agents.
- *Fish oil* is loaded with unsaturated omega-3 fatty acids, which can help lower levels of triglycerides in the blood and may protect against heart disease. Tuna, mackerel, and salmon are excellent sources of fish oil. ■

✋ *Personal action plan:* For good nutrition, begin with a healthy breakfast, eat five fruits or vegetables each day, and try to add high-fiber foods and monounsaturated fats into your diet.

What should a healthy diet look like?

If you follow the four-step plan, you should be eating a pretty good diet. Still, many people find it helpful to have a visual image of a healthy diet. One approach that nicely complements the four-step plan is to envision the traditional Mediterranean diet still popular among many in Greece, Italy, and Crete (see figure 2.1). Ansel Keys' research in the 1960s found that people eating this diet had very low rates of heart disease and great longevity.

The diet is rich in fruits and vegetables, pasta made from fiber-filled whole grains, and lots of olive oil. Fish is a staple, but red meat is eaten only on occasion. Nuts and legumes like lentils and garbanzo beans add protein, and red wine is consumed in moderation. Imagine the kitchen of a cottage on the Mediterranean coast full of a colorful variety of the fresh foods described above, and you will have a nice image of what a healthy diet could look like.

DO YOU NEED VITAMIN SUPPLEMENTS?

Antioxidants

Recently, the health benefits of "antioxidants" have been promoted a great deal. In simplest terms, antioxidants are chemicals that block "oxidation." Oxidation refers to chemical reactions in which positive charges are increased. Examples we can see include rust forming on an iron pipe or a cut apple turning brown. Inside our bodies, charged atoms called "free radicals" promote oxidation. Like most things, we need a balanced amount of oxidation. Some oxidation is beneficial, making energy and helping to kill harmful bacteria. Too much oxidation, however, damages cells and causes inflammation that can contribute to heart disease or cancer.

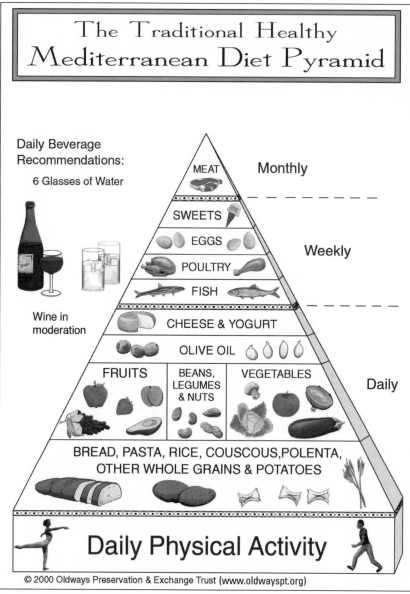

Figure 2.1: Mediterranean diet food pyramid

Among experts, there is a strong consensus that eating antioxidant-packed fruits and vegetables helps prevent both heart disease and cancer. Many also believe that eating fruits and vegetables might slow the development of Alzheimer's disease, macular degeneration, cataracts, and more. It is much less clear, however, whether *supplements* (pills) containing antioxidant vitamins offer any benefit at all. Below is a discussion of the commonly used antioxidants (folic acid, vitamin E, vitamin C, selenium, and beta carotene).

Folic acid

Folic acid (also known as "folate") is the only antioxidant definitely proven to have a health benefit when supplied as a supplement. This proof came in 1991 in the form of a randomized study of folic acid supplements in pregnant women.[5] Babies born to moms taking the supplement early in pregnancy had a marked reduction in "neural-tube defects," birth defects of the brain or spinal canal including spina bifida.

Scientists believe that folic acid supplements might help reduce the risk of heart attacks by lowering the level of homocysteine in the blood. Like elevated levels of LDL (bad) cholesterol, high homocysteine levels have been found to increase heart-attack risk. Taking in 400 micrograms per day of folic acid safely reduces homocysteine levels.

Evidence of a heart benefit from folic acid supplements is mixed. One study found less coronary artery blockage six months after angioplasty (use of a balloon to open a blocked artery) when people took 1,000 micrograms per day of folic acid compared with a placebo.[6] Another study, however, found no reduction in heart attacks when people with coronary heart disease took folic acid for two years.[7]

The potential benefits are significant enough that folic acid has been added to flour in the United States since 1998. As a result, you now get about 40 micrograms of folic acid per slice of bread. Other good dietary sources of folic acid include citrus fruits, green vegetables, and beans. Most people still get less than 400 micrograms a day in their diet. Since folic acid is very safe, a multivitamin that contains it is good insurance for a healthy heart.

Vitamin E

Vitamin E, also called "tocopherol," is found in nuts, wheat germ, fats, and oils. A healthy diet provides around 30 IU (international units) per day, while supplements containing up to 400 IU per day are generally thought to be safe. Early research raised hopes that vitamin E might prevent heart attacks by reducing plaque build-up and blood clots.

Unfortunately, a review of seven randomized trials involving 82,000 people found no reduction in death or heart attack rates among those taking vitamin E.[8] The Heart Outcomes Prevention Evaluation (HOPE) study of almost 10,000 Americans with diabetes or existing heart disease, published in 2000, likewise found no benefit from vitamin E after four years.[9] In fact, results on 4,000 HOPE participants who were followed for an additional three years actually raised concerns about the safety of vitamin E. Individuals in the group taking vitamin E were *more likely* to develop heart failure than those in the placebo group.

Due to vitamin E's blood-thinning effect, people taking it as a supplement should watch for excessive bleeding or bruising, especially if they take aspirin. Because of the disappointing studies and safety concerns, I no longer recommend vitamin E supplements.

Vitamin C

Vitamin C, also known as "ascorbic acid," is believed to reduce the risk of cataracts, heart disease, and cancer. However, with all due respect to Linus Pauling, there is no convincing evidence that taking supplements of vitamin C beyond normal daily requirements prevents any disease. Because vitamin C is water-soluble, excessive amounts taken as supplements are not absorbed, but merely passed out of the body in urine.

The healthiest way to assure adequate vitamin C intake is to eat fruits and vegetables that contain it. Unlike a vitamin C pill, they also contain hundreds of other phytochemicals, including limonene and carotenoids, that are thought to have health benefits. Fruits and vegetables are loaded with trace minerals and fiber, as well. While plant sources are best for vitamin C, a multivitamin will make sure you are getting enough.

Selenium

Selenium is an essential trace mineral found in many antioxidant enzymes inside the body. Selenium is needed for proper immune system and thyroid gland function. Though selenium may help to prevent cancers of the skin, prostate, colon, and lung, studies are not conclusive.

In some regions of China and Russia, where there are very low amounts of selenium in the soil, selenium deficiency is a health problem. Fortunately, soil in the American Midwest contains lots of selenium. The daily recommended amount of selenium is 55 micrograms. Most Americans get plenty by eating foods grown or raised in areas with selenium-rich soil.

If you're considering taking a supplement of this mineral, you should know that selenium has a narrow safety range. More than 400 micrograms per day can be toxic, causing upset stomach, hair loss, and nerve damage. At present, it's probably wise to avoid selenium supplements. Small amounts in multivitamins are generally safe.

Beta carotene

Beta carotene is turned into vitamin A inside the body. Rich sources include fruits and green and yellow vegetables. Dietary beta carotene is thought to reduce both heart disease and cancers. Unfortunately, supplements of beta carotene have been the most disappointing of the antioxidant supplements. In randomized clinical trials, beta carotene supplements actually *increased* the risk of heart disease and death.[8] One notable study to see whether beta carotene could prevent lung cancer among smokers was stopped because *more* lung cancers were being found in the group taking beta carotene than the placebo group. Because vitamin A is fat-soluble, the body has difficulty getting rid of excess amounts. Too much vitamin A can increase the risk of hip fractures and birth defects.

Iron: Too much can kill

Many people have never heard of the most common inherited genetic disease among Caucasians—hemochromatosis. This condition, in which the body stores too much iron, afflicts about one out of every 250 people. Iron overload can cause cirrhosis of the liver, joint pain, diabetes, heart failure, and impotency. When detected early, hemochromatosis is easily treated by an ancient medical remedy—blood-letting. People with hemochromatosis simply have a pint of iron-rich blood removed from their bodies on a regular basis. Their blood is drawn just as if they were donating it. Although women inherit the hemochromatosis gene as often as men, they are usually spared from damage because of monthly blood loss during menstruation.

An inexpensive test of your blood's iron level and iron-binding capacity can screen for hemochromatosis. Although not widely recommended, a one-time test for iron overload is a good idea for men between the ages of 20 and 60. Anyone with unexplained liver problems, joint pains, or diabetes should be tested as well. Meanwhile, since the body has trouble getting rid of extra iron, avoid iron pills or vitamins with iron unless you have been diagnosed with iron deficiency. ■

I strongly recommend against taking beta carotene or vitamin A as supplements. A multivitamin will provide a safe amount.

Other vitamins and minerals

Eating a good variety of healthy foods is the best way to be sure you are getting all the vitamins and minerals your body needs. However, diet surveys show that most Americans do not get enough calcium from their diets. Please read the calcium and vitamin D section in the osteoporosis chapter to see whether you need to take supplements of these nutrients to maintain strong bones.

Vitamin B-12 deficiency is a fairly common and overlooked problem for elderly people. It can cause fatigue, impaired memory, depression, or numb hands or feet. Fortunately, oral vitamin B-12 from supplements can prevent or correct these problems. People over age 65 should consider a vitamin B-12 supplement in addition to a once-a-day multivitamin.

Key point: Although certainly not a cure-all, a once-a-day multivitamin with folic acid will benefit most middle-aged and older people. Unless you have been told you have iron deficiency, pick a multivitamin without iron. People at risk for osteoporosis should take calcium supplements with vitamin D. Older people should consider a daily vitamin B-12 supplement.

SUMMARY

The typical American diet is not healthy. We live in a fast-paced, fast-food world, and many of us eat too much sugar and fat. High-fat, low-fiber foods in "super-sized" portions are causing the current epidemics of obesity and diabetes in this country. Fatty eating also contributes to our biggest killers: heart disease and cancer. There is no easy fix, but establishing a few good habits can help a great deal. Begin your day with a healthy breakfast. Try to eat five fruit or vegetable servings each day. For extra credit, focus on higher fiber foods and try to add monounsaturated fats to your diet. Finally, consider taking a multiple vitamin without iron to be sure you are getting the nutrients you need.

CHAPTER THREE

Exercise: Getting Active for Health and Happiness

"Eating alone will not keep a man well; he must also take exercise."
—Hippocrates, 400 BC

WHY AMERICA NEEDS TO GET OFF THE COUCH

Exercise: Is it worth the effort?

In a word, YES! Numerous studies over the past two decades have confirmed Hippocrates' belief. Fitness does matter. As part of the animal kingdom, we are meant to move—to walk, run, and climb—not to stay rooted in place. Without exercise, we get flabby and weak, and fall apart. Physically fit astronauts who are up in space weightless and without exercise for just a few weeks can hardly stand up, let alone walk, when they first return to Earth.

With regular physical activity, all body systems work better, including the heart, lungs, muscles, bones, gut, immune system, and even the brain.

Exercise helps prevent heart attacks, lower blood pressure, improve cholesterol levels, and lower the risk of colon and breast cancers. It also helps to control weight and can prevent the onset of diabetes. Weight-bearing exercise, basically any activity done outside of a swimming pool, strengthens bones and helps to prevent osteoporosis (bone thinning that can lead to fractures of the hips, spine, and wrists).

Physical activity provides impressive emotional and mental benefits, too. Exercise works as well as anti-depressant medications for depression, and helps to reduce stress and anxiety. People who are physically active have more energy during the day, concentrate better at work or school, and sleep better at night. With exercise, we live longer and better. As you will see, you don't have to run marathons or teach aerobics classes in order to benefit. In fact, people who currently do no exercise at all can improve their health by simply walking a few days a week.

Will exercise make you look better?

Yes, but it will take some time. Though an exercise program will rapidly improve your health and mood, it won't improve your appearance as quickly. Bodies do change as muscles are toned and fat is trimmed, but noticeable changes in appearance can take months. You'll be setting yourself up for disappointment if you expect to look like the "perfect" people you see on TV and in magazines after just a few weeks of exercising. In truth, most of us will never look like them. If you keep exercising regularly, however, you will begin to see a leaner, fitter, healthier you when you look in the mirror.

You're never too old to start

Middle-aged individuals who don't exercise often think it's too late to start. That's simply not true. It's never too late and you can't be too old to benefit from exercise. Sedentary middle-aged Harvard alumni who started a moderately intense exercise program, for example, had a 23 percent lower death rate after 11 years than similar men who did not exercise.[1] Without regular exercise, people lose about one-third of their muscular strength between age 50 and 70, and another third by age 80. Physical activity, especially in the form of strength training, can clearly reverse this decline.

In the 1990s, pioneering research by Dr. Maria Fiatarone Singh and her colleagues at Tufts University showed that even frail 80- and 90-year-olds in a nursing home benefited from a modest weight-lifting program. Within 10 weeks, the group that did strength training was stronger, walked faster, climbed stairs more easily, and socialized more than the group that was inactive.[2]

Exercise programs not only extend life expectancy, but also enhance quality of life. Unfortunately, older seniors who could benefit the most from an exercise program are the least likely to participate. Less than one in 50 seniors over the age of 75 currently engages in strength training. If you think you are too old to be active, think again. It's time to get off the couch. Age is no excuse.

> *Key point:* Modest amounts of exercise may not make you look like an Olympic athlete, but will do wonders for your physical and emotional health. You will have more energy, concentrate better, sleep more soundly, and feel better about life.

ASSESSING YOUR NEED FOR EXERCISE

National crisis of inactivity

It's ironic: In the past 20 years, as medical science has accumulated more and more evidence of the benefits of exercise, Americans have become less and less physically active. Back in the 1950s and '60s, when my baby-boom generation was growing up, all the kids went outside to play after school. We rode bikes around the neighborhood and played sports or games like kick the can, tag, and hide-and-go-seek. Today's children spend less of their time engaged in physical activity and much more time glued to the television, computer, or latest electronic game. Many of their parents feel too busy to work out.

Meanwhile, increasing automation and computers have reduced the amount of exercise people get at work. E-mail makes it easy to communicate without ever getting out of a chair. Similarly, remote

Does physical fitness really make you live longer?

For many years doctors assumed that physical fitness made people live longer, but it was hard to prove. In the 1980s, a study of healthy men and women at the Aerobics Research Center in Texas showed that fitness really does make a difference. More than 13,000 people had their fitness levels measured using a treadmill test. They then were observed over an eight-year period. The death rates among the fittest group were much, much lower than the death rates among the least fit group. Only one-fourth as many "fittest" people died as compared with "least fit" folks.[4] As expected, most of the deaths were from heart disease and cancer. Physical fitness was without doubt a predictor of good health.

Critics wondered whether genetic factors or undetected disease at the start of the study may have caused people to be less fit, eventually causing their demise. The Finnish Twin Cohort Study, which has followed 16,000 twins since 1975, has helped resolve the issue. Results published in 1998 confirmed that twins who reported more exercise outlived their twin siblings who were sedentary.[6] Experts now estimate that regular exercise adds about two years to lifespan. Another way to think about it is that *not* exercising shortens life about as much as having untreated high blood pressure or being 20 percent overweight. ∎

controls, garage-door openers, and other labor-saving devices have cut down on activity at home.

Though Americans could use some of their leisure time to exercise, most do not. According to a 2001 national health survey, almost 70 percent of American adults are sedentary, reporting little or no leisure-time physical activity.[3] In the dictionary, sedentary is defined as "accustomed to sitting, taking little exercise." Medically, this includes the 40 percent of adults who never exercise, and the 30 percent who are physically active less than one hour per week. Being sedentary is as much a health risk as having high blood pressure or high cholesterol. Unfortunately, as the Centers for Disease Control reports, "The United States remains predominantly a sedentary society."

Q *Health tip:* One hour of exercise per week provides a similar health benefit to taking medication that controls high blood pressure.

How active are *you?*

To assess your health risk, it's important to make an honest appraisal of your current exercise habits. Most people can place themselves in one of the following three groups:

I. *Sedentary:* You do no regular exercise. You might do leisure-time physical activity once in a while, but less than one hour per week. You drive around parking lots to find the "closest spot" and avoid breaking a sweat at all cost.

II. *Physically active:* You do regular, but not intense exercise totaling at least one hour per week. You walk, work in the yard, play some sports, jog, or do other moderate activities three or more times a week, and you don't mind breaking a sweat.

III. *Exercise nut:* You are a regular and intense exerciser. You run, bike, train at a health club, or do other intense, aerobic workouts three or more times per week. You love to break a sweat.

A little exercise goes a long way

If you are sedentary, you stand to benefit the most from starting even a modest exercise program. A fitness study at the Aerobics Research Center in Texas found that the greatest reduction in health risk occurred when people went from the lowest to second-lowest of five fitness categories.[4] This did not require a drastic change in lifestyle. A commitment of just one hour per week made the difference. For comfortably inactive folks who groan at the thought of a jog or a work-out class, the message is simple, "Walk, don't run!" Get a comfortable pair of walking shoes and take a 20-minute walk three days a week. That's all it takes to remove your name from the sedentary list and dramatically improve your health outlook.

Exercise for the overweight

If you are overweight you can reap many benefits from exercise, *even if you do not lose a pound.* Separate studies have found that getting more fit, even without losing weight, decreases blood pressure, improves cholesterol levels, and lowers the risk of diabetes. Other research has found that starting an exercise program, even with no change in diet, reduces the amount of harmful abdominal fat, improves aerobic fitness, and causes weight loss. Some of the benefit is thought to occur through a natural reduction of appetite after exercise, and may reflect an increased metabolic rate as the body responds to exertion by building muscle. Overall, it is probably healthier to be fit and overweight than trim but out of shape. ■

I hear lots of excuses why people can't do this, and I just don't buy them. Almost everyone can work one hour of exercise into their week. If you have no place to walk, get a treadmill machine and walk in your home. If you can't walk, get an exercise bike, turn the tension down, and pedal gently for 20 minutes. If you can't ride a bike, get a rowing machine or arm treadmill, or try swimming. If you think you don't have time, consider how much television you watch. Aren't you willing to watch one hour less per week to save your health? Can't you walk on a treadmill or ride an exercise bike while you watch television?

If you need motivation, consider this: Remaining sedentary has the same health risk as living with untreated high blood pressure. If you were told you had high blood pressure, would you choose to treat it? I hope so, just as I hope that you will choose to get moving one hour a week. Exercise is a human need as basic as eating and sleeping. As the Nike ads say, "Just do it."

Personal action plan: If you are sedentary, please allot just one hour out of the 168 hours in each week for some kind of physical activity.

Keep on trucking

If you already get regular exercise, even if it's not intense, congratulate yourself. You are reaping lots of health benefits and the challenge is to keep it fun, safe, and an integral part of your life. Read on to learn more about exercise, including some important tips on safety and injury prevention.

If you are among the minority of Americans who get regular vigorous or intense exercise, you have the right to feel a bit smug. Other people do envy you. You get to enjoy the endorphin rush, or "runners high," that comes with a good, hard workout. Based on the Harvard Alumni Health Study, you also get the biggest longevity benefit compared with people who do less-vigorous exercise.[5]

> ✎✎ *Key point:* Almost 70 percent of American adults do
> ➶✎ little or no physical activity on a regular basis. Their
> sedentary lifestyle is putting their health at high risk.
> If you are sedentary, you will benefit greatly by taking a
> 20-minute walk three days a week.

EXERCISING SAFELY

Sudden death

Many baby boomers remember Jim Fixx. In 1977, he helped inspire a whole generation of joggers with *The Complete Book of Running*. Then, in 1984, Fixx raised safety concerns among the same generation when he died while jogging. He was only 52 years old, but had smoked heavily for many years before he started running. He also had a strong family history of heart disease and may have ignored important warning symptoms. Jim Fixx's story teaches some important lessons.

First, do not ignore symptoms that could be caused by heart disease. The classic symptom, medically known as "angina," is pressure, tightness, or a squeezing sensation around the chest that comes on with exercise and goes away with rest. The pain can occur in the upper abdomen, behind the breast-bone, from the chest up into the jaw, or from the chest into the left arm. The important thing is to pay attention to your body and use common sense. If something doesn't seem right, stop your exercise and consult your doctor. This is a case where it's better to be safe than sorry.

Though it's true that there is some risk of dying suddenly of a heart attack while exercising, the risk is very small among regular exercisers. Exercise has such powerful health benefits that the overall risk of death is much lower among people who exercise than among those who are sedentary. The biggest risk of sudden death during exercise is among "weekend warriors," people who are usually sedentary but occasionally do some very strenuous activity. The lesson here is simple: If you rarely exercise, don't try to be a superstar at the company picnic. You need to walk before you should run.

Should you see your doctor before exercise?

People often wonder whether they should see their doctor, or maybe have a treadmill test, before starting an exercise program. A good way to find out is to take the Physical Activity Readiness Questionnaire (PAR-Q), which can help identify people at high risk for heart disease or other problems that require a supervised exercise program. Answer the following seven questions to see where you stand:

Yes   No

___   ___   1. Have you ever been told you have a "heart condition" and should only do physical activity recommended by a doctor?

___   ___   2. Do you feel pain in your chest when you do physical activity?

___   ___   3. In the past month, have you had chest pain when you were NOT doing physical activity?

___   ___   4. Do you lose balance because of dizziness or do you ever pass out?

___   ___   5. Do you have a bone or joint problem that could be made worse by a change in your physical activity?

___   ___   6. Is your doctor currently prescribing medications for your blood pressure or heart problem?

___   ___   7. Do you know of *any other reason* why you should not exercise or increase your physical activity?

If you answered "yes" to any of these questions, you should see your doctor prior to increasing your physical activity. If you can honestly answer "no" to all seven questions, you should be OK to gradually increase your exercise.

Do you need a stress test?

People with unexplained chest pain or dizziness during exercise need medical evaluation, but do individuals with no symptoms need a treadmill stress test before starting to exercise? Experts often debate this question. On the plus side, treadmill tests can identify most people who have significant blockage of their coronary arteries. Treadmills can also measure your fitness level before an exercise program, which provides motivation and allows measurement of improvements in fitness as physical activity increases. In addition, a treadmill test can help you learn what a safe level of exercise feels like.

Unfortunately, treadmill tests have drawbacks too. They are not foolproof. A "normal" treadmill test, while reassuring, is no guarantee that you are safe to exercise vigorously. At the same time, an "abnormal" test doesn't prove that you have a problem. As many as one in five healthy people will have an abnormal test even though their heart is fine. These false positive tests can cause a lot of worry and lead to further testing.

At present, there are no studies to prove that treadmill tests prior to starting an exercise program prevent deaths or heart attacks. Until more is known, I recommend treadmill tests primarily for sedentary people over 40 who want to start *vigorous* exercise programs. Treadmill tests are also reasonable prior to intense exercise for people of any age who have two or more risk factors for heart disease (such as smoking, diabetes, high cholesterol, high blood pressure, or family history). Healthy people who want to start walking or other mild-to-moderate exercises do not need treadmill tests. To avoid any problems, they should start gradually and slowly increase intensity over time.

Does exercise cause osteoarthritis?

Vigorous exercisers have long been concerned whether wear and tear from intense, weight-bearing activities such as running, hiking, tennis, and basketball will eventually cause osteoarthritis in their knees and hips. Although the actual cause of osteoarthritis is unknown, genetic tendency and obesity have been identified as the key risk factors. Currently, regular intense exercise does not appear to be a risk. In fact, several studies of long-distance runners have found no increase in osteoarthritis among runners compared with non-runners.

Patients of mine who *already* have osteoarthritis often worry that exercise could damage their joints further. Medical views on this topic have changed drastically in the past two decades. When I graduated from medical school in 1981, rest was the treatment of choice for osteoarthritis. Since then, studies of seniors with arthritis have found that walking and mild weight training actually *reduced* pain without worsening joint damage. Now medical experts recommend physical activity as a crucial part of managing arthritis. Stronger muscles are thought to protect joints, improve mobility, and lower the chance of injury. This does not mean that people with osteoarthritis should take up high-impact exercises like jogging, but they can benefit from adding low-impact activities such as walking, swimming, and housework to their daily routine.

Avoiding injuries

Injuries can happen during intense sports, recreation, or any kind of physical activity, but should fear of injury keep you from exercising? No, and here's why: Overall injury rates among people who do regular exercise are about the same as for people who are sedentary.

Predictably, most traumatic injuries (i.e., broken bones or torn ligaments) occur during competitive sports. "Weekend warriors," who participate in intense physical activity once in a while but don't exercise regularly, are especially susceptible to injury. People who exercise for health are more prone to overuse injuries, such as shin splints or tendinitis from doing too much too fast. You can reduce your risk of injuries by picking activities you're comfortable with and increasing the duration and intensity of your workouts gradually as your body strengthens.

Gentle stretching, which improves flexibility, might also help prevent injuries. Do some light exercises—such as 5 minutes of walking or slow jogging—to warm up, or wait until you have finished exercising before you stretch. Avoid lunging, bouncing, or jerking. Stretch gently to the point of slight discomfort only. Don't push it too far! Overstretching, particularly when muscles are cold, can actually cause injury.

Good shoes and appropriate safety equipment can help you avoid injury too. Invest in supportive footwear that is either designed for your favorite type of exercise or suitable for a variety of activities (i.e., "cross trainers"). If you're into wheel sports (biking, roller skating, inline skating), always wear a helmet to prevent head injuries. Though many teens and adults scoff at helmets, wearing one is preferable to risking brain damage or death.

> *Key point:* The health benefits of exercise greatly outweigh any risks associated with it. Answer the seven-question Physical Activity Readiness Questionnaire (PAR-Q) to see whether you should consult with your doctor prior to increasing your physical activity.

GETTING ACTIVE AND STAYING ACTIVE

Finding the right fit

When I was 13 years old, Dr. Kenneth H. Cooper's then-new book on aerobic exercise inspired me to start an exercise program as part of a school project. Charts in the book assigned points for many aerobic activities, based on duration and intensity. For 10 weeks, I carefully recorded the number of points I accumulated for each physical activity—including running, bicycling, and playing my favorite sports. Each week, I gradually increased my points, and at the end of the 10 weeks, I was in much better shape—and ran much farther in a 12-minute fitness test—than before the project. At the time, that program was the perfect fit to get me started on a life-long quest to stay in good physical condition.

What is the best exercise program for you? The right answer is unique to your life, and may require careful thought and some trial and error. Think of physical activity as a basic need that should be addressed as long as you live. Everybody is different, so I urge you to find the exercise program that best fits your lifestyle.

Here are some ideas for finding the right fit:
- Choose activities that you find both enjoyable and convenient.
- Purchase an inexpensive, simple-to-use step counter (pedometer) to measure your daily activity.
- Plot several safe, 10- to 30-minute walking routes in your neighborhood.
- Sign up for a fitness class at a local community college.
- Join a health club.
- Get an exercise bike, put it in front of a TV, and pedal while watching your favorite show.
- Set a goal that you have to train for. Make sure the goal is reasonable for your fitness level. It could be a charity walk or race, a scout hike, or just to make it around the block three times.
- After you have accomplished one goal, set another.

Focusing on aerobics

Aerobic activity—movement that gets your heart and lungs working—should be the foundation of any exercise program. Many experts recommend 30 minutes or more of moderate-intensity physical activity on most, if not all, days of the week. However, just 20 minutes a day, three days a week of aerobic activity will assure basic cardiovascular fitness. The activity need not be difficult or painful to be beneficial. Mowing the lawn, raking leaves, mopping and vacuuming inside the home, or walking nine holes of golf all count as aerobic activities. So does taking a walk.

For sedentary folks, walking is a great way to start getting active. It's safe, convenient, and something most people can do throughout life. Begin with a leisurely stroll a few days a week, then pick up your pace and distance gradually as desired. The faster you walk, the better the aerobic benefit. As you become a regular walker, consider purchasing supportive shoes specifically designed for walking.

For healthy people who are already active, jogging or running is the most time-efficient way to improve cardiovascular fitness. With new shoe technology, running is more comfortable than ever. To avoid injury, you should start out slowly and increase the speed and distance of your runs gradually. Oftentimes, novice runners start out by mixing walking and running until they feel fit enough to run throughout their workout. As you become more fit, you'll feel the "runner's high" brought on by mood-improving endorphins your body naturally releases during a high-intensity workout.

Despite its positives, running puts a lot of stress on the body and is not for everyone. Some people are genetically blessed and can jog or run their entire lives, but many of my friends and patients have given up running after many years because it bothered their knees, feet, or back. Fortunately, these active folks continue to walk, hike, and bike without problems.

The key to a sustainable exercise program is to pick aerobic activities that you *enjoy* and look forward to. In addition to walking and jogging, you might also consider bicycling, swimming, inline skating, rowing, stair climbing, elliptical training, spinning, dancing, kickboxing, pilates, yoga, or martial arts. You need not limit yourself to just one activity. Cross training (working a variety of activities into your exercise program) is an excellent strategy because it helps prevent overuse injuries and keeps you from burning out on the same old thing.

How hard should you push?

Improving fitness requires effort and commitment. Don't believe advertisements that try to convince you otherwise. In a recent ad for the "Ab-buster," a guy said with a straight face that he lost 40 pounds and 4 inches off his waist by merely wearing this electrical-stimulation device a few hours a day. If only it were that easy.

Though you will have to work at getting in shape, you should not have to experience pain. The old adage "No pain, no gain" fell by the wayside years ago. We now understand that pain is the body's way of protecting itself. It tells you that you have pushed too hard, and that you need to back off or change what you are doing to allow healing. So if something really hurts during exercise, stop!

This does not mean you will never have discomfort as you increase physical activity and improve fitness. Some muscle soreness is natural following exercise and lets you know you have done some good, honest work. Use common sense and the experience that you have gained over the years to find the balance between pushing hard enough, but not too hard.

Strength training

Weight, or strength, training can help you convert body fat to muscle and actually increase muscle mass, if desired. Weight workouts can also help prevent injuries and loss of muscle, especially in people over 50. Middle-aged individuals who already do aerobic exercise should consider adding some strength training. Working with weights for just 20–30 minutes, two days a week will reverse much of the loss of strength that will otherwise occur with aging.

Should you worry about your target heart rate?

Have you ever noticed someone else wearing a heart-rate monitor during exercise and wondered what your target heart rate should be? First, it's important to understand that you don't need a heart-rate monitor to exercise safely—as long as you increase the intensity of your workouts gradually and stop if you experience any dizziness, nausea, or chest pain. In general, if you can carry on a conversation while exercising, you're probably at a safe intensity level.

If you want to wear a monitor, here is a common method for determining target heart rate: Your *theoretical* maximum heart rate is 220 minus your current age. (Your *actual* maximum might be higher or lower than this number, but you do not want to push to maximum without supervision or monitoring.) A healthy training range to increase cardiovascular fitness is roughly 65 to 85 percent of predicted maximum and can be calculated as follows:

- *Beginner:* 65 percent of predicted maximum = (220-age) × 0.65 (Example for 50-year-old: 220 – 50 = 170; 170 x 0.65 = 111)
- *Intermediate*: 75 percent of predicted maximum = (220-age) × 0.75 (Example for 50-year-old: 170 × 0.75 = 128)
- *Experienced*: 85 percent of predicted maximum = (220-age) × 0.85 (Example for 50-year-old: 170 × 0.85 = 145). ∎

Whether you use free weights at home or do circuit training on machines at the gym, you should try to work a variety of muscle groups. Many health clubs provide a free orientation with a trainer, who will help you get started on an appropriately challenging circuit and/or free-weight program. Though body builders tend to prefer free weights, circuit training allows the rest of us to work several muscle groups in a shorter period of time. As with aerobic activities, you should start out easy and progress gradually.

A special note to women: Some women avoid weight training because they don't want the bulked-up muscles they've seen on body builders. They need not worry. Weight training for health a few days a week will tone and strengthen muscles and help prevent osteoporosis without making muscles too big.

> ✋ *Personal action plan:* Assess your current level of physical activity. If you already exercise regularly, keep it up. If not, commit to at least 20 minutes of aerobic activity three days per week. Make it enjoyable and convenient, and do more if you feel like it. Add some variety and consider strength training for even greater health benefits.

SUMMARY

Your body needs exercise to stay healthy. Even modest physical activity provides tremendous physical and emotional benefits. Unfortunately, over half of American adults accept a sedentary lifestyle and get less than 1 hour per week of physical activity. Sedentary folks who start walking as little as 20 minutes, three days per week have the most to gain. Anyone over 50 can also benefit a great deal by adding some weight-training to their activities. If you're over 40 and planning to start a vigorous exercise program, see your doctor first.

CHAPTER FOUR

Stress: Don't Sweat the Small Stuff

"Rule No. 1 is, don't sweat the small stuff. Rule No. 2 is, it's all small stuff. And if you can't fight and you can't flee, flow."

—Robert S. Eliot, M.D.
Professor of Cardiology
University of Nebraska

HOW STRESS HURTS YOUR HEALTH

A mother's lesson

A story about my own mother shows the powerful effect stress can have on well being. I got a call the other morning from Mom. She has a pacemaker that prevents her heart from beating too slowly, and she is a lifelong worrier. She wanted to know whether I could stop by on my way to work because she thought her pacemaker wasn't working right. She lives nearby, so I stopped in for an unofficial house call. Mom had a furrowed brow and a dry mouth. She was breathing fast, said she had nausea, and had been pacing around the house since early morning. She wasn't having any chest pain, but said her heart was beating fast and her blood pressure machine read much higher than usual.

Mom's pulse was fast, so I told her I thought her pacemaker was fine and sat to talk for a bit. It turned out Mom was also worried about a trip to see her new grandson and about her desert tortoise, which hadn't come out of hibernation yet. As we talked, I watched her breathing slow and her face relax as her whole body calmed down. After a few minutes, she re-checked her blood pressure and it was back to normal. Her heart rate soon slowed to a normal, steady rate that reassured me things were all right. As a precaution, I asked Mom to make an appointment with her doctor for a check-up. We were both struck by how terrible stress and anxiety can make a person feel, and by how much simple interventions, such as listening and providing reassurance, can help to ease the tension.

Fight or flight

What is stress anyway? We have all experienced it—when a deadline is looming and there's too much work to do; when we're running late for an important meeting and get stuck in traffic; when the house is a mess and the in-laws are on the way. Stress is that feeling of being under pressure or strain, in other words in *distress.*

When we feel stressed, our bodies respond by releasing adrenaline. Adrenaline makes the heart beat stronger and faster, increases the breathing rate, and causes muscles to tense and prepare for action. Chemicals are released in the blood to make it clot faster in case of an injury, and sugar is released into the blood for quick energy. This is a survival response to get a person ready to fight or to run for his or her life.

In modern times, we rarely have to actually fight or flee for survival, and the stresses that trigger an adrenaline rush usually are not life threatening. More likely, they are things like a fear of public speaking, frustration over the latest office memo, or getting stuck in the one line that is not moving. Though we might experience stress responses several times each day, they are rarely followed by a physical release that allows us to use our tensed-up muscles and burn the extra sugar in our bloodstream. Over time, stress can take a big toll on physical health.

Paying the price of unchecked stress

Too much stress can literally make you sick or even kill you. My wife's grandmother, Mabel, died from a sudden stress. Mabel had been married to Dale for 42 years when he dropped dead in the garden of a heart attack. Mabel found him and the shock caused her to have a massive stroke. She passed away quietly the next day. Fortunately, deaths from sudden stress are pretty rare. Far more commonly, however, chronic stress makes people sick.

An estimated 90 percent of all visits to primary-care doctors are for stress-related problems. Most often, stress impacts the nervous system, cardiovascular system, and gastrointestinal tract:

- *Nervous system*: Stress directly causes the most common kind of headache, aptly named a "tension headache." Stress and lack of sleep can also trigger migraine headaches. People facing a stressful event, such as giving a speech, often experience a tremor, or shaking, of the hands and voice. Unchecked stress can lead to anxiety, depression (see sidebar 4.1), and even panic attacks (see sidebar 4.2).
- *Cardiovascular system*: Stress clearly contributes to high blood pressure and is a major risk factor for coronary-artery disease and heart attacks. Interestingly, people have more heart attacks on Monday mornings than at any other time.[1] Stress can also cause or worsen palpitations, felt as the heart either skips beats or races.
- *Gastrointestinal tract*: Stress is a well-known contributor to indigestion, belly pain, and peptic-ulcer disease. Stress also triggers irritable-bowel syndrome, which causes lower abdominal cramping and loose stools during the day. Stress can make the mouth dry and the throat feel like there is a lump in it.

Unfortunately, many people react to stress with behaviors that hurt their health even more. These include smoking or chewing tobacco, drinking too much alcohol, and using drugs. Stressed out people also tend to overeat, especially junk food and sweets. And some people respond to stress with irritability or anger that harms their relationships. The toll stress exacts on our lives can indeed be high.

Depression

A major depression will affect one out of every seven Americans during their lifetime, causing a great deal of suffering. The main feature of a major depression is feeling sad, down, hopeless, or depressed for more than two weeks. If you're depressed, you might also experience the following:

- trouble falling asleep, waking up early in the morning, or sleeping too much
- fatigue or lack of energy
- loss of interest in activities
- trouble concentrating
- feelings of failure or of having let the family down
- appetite changes—either a decrease or an increase
- slowed speech and movement, or increased restlessness
- thoughts that you would be better off dead, or of hurting yourself

Fortunately, counseling, antidepressant medications, and exercise can all help a great deal. If you feel that you or a loved one may be experiencing a serious depression, please seek professional help. ■

Panic attacks

Some people under stress will develop sudden, intense feelings of terror or impending doom called "panic attacks." People experiencing panic attacks often feel shortness of breath, racing of the heart, chest pressure, upset stomach, and a smothering or choking sensation. Panic attacks usually begin to subside after about 10 minutes, but leave the affected person feeling drained and scared. People who have had panic attacks often live in fear because further attacks can occur without warning. Fortunately, even though stress and anxiety are very common, panic attacks are not. Current treatments for panic, including medications and behavioral modification, have been very successful. Please seek help if you or a loved one suffers from panic attacks. ■

ꕔꕔ *Key point:* Stress causes a huge amount of suffering
ꕔꕔ among human beings, ranging from everyday
headaches and upset stomachs, to anxiety and depression, to deadly heart attacks and strokes.

HOW TO MEASURE YOUR STRESS

Are you stressed out?

On surveys, most Americans say that they are under too much
stress. Knowing this, it might be nice to actually measure stress levels. Unlike blood pressure, weight or cholesterol, however, there is
no precise way to measure stress. Even though it is hard to quantify,
everyone knows what stress feels like.

To help evaluate the stress in your life, consider the following
questions:

1. Do you take time each day to relax?   Yes___ No___
2. Do you take minor hassles in stride?   Yes___ No___
3. Do you allow seven to nine hours each
    night for sleep?   Yes___ No___

If you answered "No" to one or more of these questions, chances
are pretty good that you are among the majority of Americans who
are facing too much stress.

To measure your personal stress, try doing a "stress check."
Think about your current stress level on a 1 to 10 scale. The number
1 represents the most calm and relaxed you have felt in many years,
while 10 represents the most anxious, agitated, and stressed out you
have ever been or can imagine. A quick stress check can help you
assess how stressed you are at any given time. Repeating the stress
check after trying a stress-reducing technique can help you gauge
the technique's effectiveness.

Major life events and stress

Change, both good and bad, creates stress. The following exercise
can help you measure the stress impact of recent events in your life.

In 1967, Thomas Holmes and Richard Rahe published a famous study that looked at the effect of major life changes on health.[2] They assigned points to the life events listed in table 4.1. For this exercise, mark any of the listed events that you have experienced during the past 12 months, and then add up the points from the events you marked.

Table 4.1: Major life events and illness

___ Death of spouse	100
___ Divorce	73
___ Marital separation	65
___ Jail term	63
___ Death of close family member	63
___ Personal illness or injury	53
___ Marriage	50
___ Retirement	45
___ Change in family member's health	44
___ Pregnancy	40
___ Sex difficulties	39
___ Addition to family	39
___ Business readjustment	39
___ Change in financial state	38
___ Death of close friend	37
___ Change to different line of work	36
___ More arguments with spouse	35
___ Mortgage or loan for major purchase	31
___ Foreclosure of mortgage or loan	30
___ Change in work responsibilities	29
___ Son or daughter leaving home	29
___ Trouble with in-laws	29
___ Outstanding personal achievement	28
___ Spouse begins or stops work	26
___ Starting or finishing school	26
___ Change in living conditions	25
___ Revision of personal habits	24

___ Trouble with boss	23
___ Change in work hours or conditions	20
___ Change in residence	20
___ Change in schools	20
___ Change in recreation habits	19
___ Change in church activities	19
___ Change in social activities	18
___ Mortgage for lesser purchase	17
___ Change in sleeping habits	16
___ Change in family get-togethers	15
___ Change in eating habits	15
___ Vacation	13
___ Christmas season	12
___ Minor violation of the law	11

From Holmes and Rahe, 1967

According to the study, if your points add up to 300 or more you have an 80 percent chance of suffering a significant illness in the near future. If your score is between 150 and 299, your chance of getting sick is 50 percent. With fewer than 150 points, your odds of becoming ill improve to less than 30 percent. This survey, still in wide use, shows how clusters of stressful events can negatively impact health and make people sick.

Granted, some of these events are beyond a person's control, and others are quite desirable. Still, it can be helpful to understand what kinds of life events are likely to cause stress and to recognize which ones you've had to deal with recently. This insight can help you plan events that *are* under your control, such as buying a new house or going back to school. Ideally, you'll be able to avoid stacking the stress deck too much in any given period of time, and to understand why you're stressed out when a series of difficult events occurs despite your best efforts.

Analyzing the causes of stress

Winston Churchill said, "It helps to write down half-a-dozen things which are worrying me. Two of them, say, disappear; about two of them nothing can be done, so it's no use worrying; and two perhaps can be settled." When *you* are feeling overwhelmed by stress, make some quiet time to sit down and think about all the things that are causing your stress (a.k.a. your "stressors"). Get a blank piece of paper and make two columns, "Stressors I can't control" and "Stressors I can change." Write down each stressor in either the "can't control" or the "can change" column. (This will only take about 15 minutes, so don't make excuses that you don't have time to do it.)

Next take a look at your two lists. For better or for worse, you have to accept that some of the stressors in your life are beyond your control. If you feel overwhelmed or hopeless because of the things on your "can't control" list, you should consider professional help. Fortunately, as Churchill noted, many stressors do ease or disappear with time. Sometimes it helps to simply identify the things that are stressing you out, even those you can't control.

Of course, it is most helpful to focus on the stress causers that you can change. Try to pick the simplest one as a starting point. Make a goal to resolve it and get it off your list within a few days or a week. If you can ease just one stressful situation per week, you will be amazed by the sense of control and relief you will gain.

> *Health tip:* To find out how much stress you are facing and to get on track to lighten your load, take the stress tests described above and write down your current list of stressors.

HOW TO MANAGE YOUR STRESS

No matter what you do, stress is not going to disappear completely from your life. Some stress is normal, and low or moderate amounts of stress actually improve performance. The key to managing stress is to recognize when it is harming your physical and emotional health, and to develop healthy strategies for controlling it. To get started, consider the following stress-reducing ideas:

Top 10 ways to de-stress:

1. Make time for 7–9 hours of sleep each night. Sleep is an important time for the body and mind to unwind, relax, and repair. Creative ideas and problem-solving are often inspired by a full night's sleep.[3] Lack of sleep is the biggest cause of fatigue and an important marker for stress. To free up time for sleep, you may have to simply do less. Cram fewer activities into each day, and spread out big commitments and projects.

2. Exercise. Lots of research confirms that physical activity is a powerful antidote for stress. Exercise releases relaxing endorphins into the bloodstream and increases alpha waves in the brain that are associated with a relaxed state of mind. Make time to walk the dog, ride a bike, or do any physical activity that you enjoy. If you can get outside for some fresh air, stress reduction may be enhanced.

3. Learn to say NO. For this to work, you need to consciously decide not to feel guilty. Focus on the good things you do, and don't waste energy and emotion by feeling guilty about what you can't do.

4. Take control. People are most stressed when they feel a lack of control over the people and events in their life—the unreasonable boss, the problem neighbor, the ill parent. As noted above (in "Analyzing causes of stress"), you'll feel better if you eliminate the stressors you can control one at a time, and let go of the stuff you can't control.

5. Practice self-relaxation. Buy a good self-relaxation tape, or follow the instructions in the "Self-relaxation technique" sidebar. Self-relaxation, or meditation, is easy to learn, takes only a few minutes, and can be done in the middle of a stressful day or situation. Take a few slow, deep, relaxing breaths anytime you feel tension building. Learn to slow down a little in order to enjoy life more. Take a little time each day to relax.

6. Schedule some personal time to do something you enjoy. When was your last relaxing vacation? Vacations have gotten shorter and more stressful in recent years, as people cram in more activities and stay in touch with the office by cell phone and pager. Plan a vacation during which you will have minimal hassles, no contact with work, and plenty of time to relax.

7. Laugh more. Groucho Marx said, "A clown is like aspirin, only he works twice as fast." Similar to exercise, a good laugh releases relaxing endorphins in the brain, lowers blood pressure, and relaxes muscles. Small children laugh 400 times a day, compared with about 15 times per day for adults. Try acting like a child once in a while. Play, have fun, smile, watch a comedy, spend time with friends, and try to laugh more.

8. Forgive and forget. Anger and hostility are destructive emotions that harm your health. People who silently stew and seethe are at greatest risk. Do yourself a favor and let go of your grudges. Holding onto a past conflict makes you relive the anger and stress each time you think about it. If you take a deep breath and let it go, you will lighten your stress load tremendously.

9. Have more human (or animal) contact. There is nothing like a good hug or back rub when you are feeling stressed. People often isolate themselves when under stress, but human contact and support is a great antidote for stress. When people let you down or aren't available, pets are a great substitute. Simply petting a cat or dog lowers blood pressure and helps you relax.

10. De-clutter your living space. Too much stuff cluttering up your life is a big source of stress. Everything you own has to be stored, cleaned, straightened out, and maintained. Get rid of anything that you do not use or really enjoy. Try to handle each piece of paper just one time. Trash the junk, and take action on items that require it. Arrange for automatic bill payments to reduce the items that need action each month. When charities call, get in the habit of giving them bags of your expendable stuff. You will feel good for helping others and less stressed in your less-cluttered space.

Self-relaxation technique

1. Sit quietly in a comfortable position. Gently close your eyes.
2. Breathe in slowly and deeply through your nose. As you breathe out, say the word ONE silently to yourself. Breathe IN…OUT, "ONE"; IN…OUT, "ONE"; etc. Become aware of your breathing. Breathe easily and naturally.
3. Concentrate on deeply relaxing your muscles, starting with your feet, and moving slowly up to your legs, abdomen, arms, and face.
4. Relax for 5–10 minutes. You may open your eyes to check the time, but do not set an alarm. When you finish, sit quietly for a couple of minutes with your eyes closed, then count backwards from 5 to 1 and open your eyes. You will feel refreshed, wide awake, and calm.
5. Don't worry about whether you are able to achieve a deep level of relaxation at first. Let relaxation occur at its own pace. The more you practice, the deeper your level of relaxation will be. If distracting thoughts occur, don't dwell on them. Return to repeating "ONE." With practice, the relaxation response will come easily. Practice self-relaxation once or twice a day, but not within two hours after a meal, since digestion can interfere with the relaxation process.
6. Imagery: You may find it enjoyable and helpful to imagine yourself in a place that is especially peaceful and relaxing. After thinking about your breathing for a minute or two, start to envision yourself in a calm and relaxing scene. Perhaps you are walking in the woods or lying on an empty beach. Notice the details of the scene—colors, peaceful sounds, a soft breeze, a relaxed feeling. Really be in that scene. Spend a few minutes enjoying it. ■

Although the self-help ideas above work well for many people, stress can be hard to manage. If tension, worry, anxiety, or feelings of depression intrude on daily activities, see your doctor or seek counseling. Professional help, sometimes combined with medication, can be quite helpful for anxiety disorders and depression.

Key point: Probably the most valuable message for managing stress is that "attitude is everything." Our minds have an incredible ability to respond to any situation in either a positive, relaxed fashion or a negative, stressful manner. Self-relaxation can be an enjoyable way to reduce stress and stay positive.

SUMMARY

Stress causes a great deal of human suffering and disease, ranging from headaches, stomach pain, and heart problems to anxiety, depression, and panic disorders. Much of the effect of stress on your health depends on your attitude, feelings, and thoughts. It is important to recognize when stress is causing problems in your life and to learn healthy ways to manage it. Practicing self-relaxation, exercising regularly, and getting a good night's sleep are lifestyle habits that can help reduce stress. Counseling or medication can help people with persistent anxiety or depression.

CHAPTER FIVE

Alcohol: Demon Spirits or Elixir of Life?

"Alcohol is the only nutrient anti-nutrient. It is a food that causes a very special kind of malnutrition. It is pleasurable to the majority who do not become addicted to it, but poison to those who do."
—Frank L. Iber, M.D.

HUMAN HISTORY OF ALCOHOL

An ancient art

The ancient Celts (Irish, Scots, and Welsh) distilled grains like rye and barley into whiskey at least as early as 800 B.C. The Celts thought the fiery brew was a gift from the gods that could restore health and even bring the dead back to life. Celtic whiskey was thus dubbed "uisge beatha"—the water or elixir of life.

Long before whiskey, wine was made in the warm Mediterranean countries where grapes were grown. The earliest record of wine-making was found on an Egyptian papyrus from 3,500 B.C. Wine remains a dietary staple in the Mediterranean region, where it may help to explain low rates of heart disease.

The most ancient form of alcohol imbibed by humans was beer, one of the earliest products made by civilized men. Anthropologists believe that Sumerians and Mesopotamians were brewing and enjoying beer as early as 10,000 B.C. The ancient Chinese, Egyptians, and pre-Columbus Native Americans all brewed beer as well. Alcohol, for better or for worse, has been part of human culture as long as civilization.

Alcohol in America

The United States has had a long love-hate relationship with alcohol. The Puritans stowed 14 tons of water for the long trip from England to America, but brought 42 tons of beer and 10,000 gallons of wine. Then, as now, some folks drank too much, lost their self-control, and misbehaved under the influence. Drunken misdeeds angered many law-abiding citizens, some of whom contended that drinking was immoral and should be outlawed. Nonetheless, people continued to drink toasts to good health and to use medicinal preparations and health tonics loaded with alcohol. Alcohol also became deeply entwined in religious ceremonies, holiday traditions, and social events.

By 1920, temperance advocates appeared to win out when the U.S. Constitution was amended to "forever" prohibit the use of alcohol. In reality, however, drinkers continued to drink as bootlegging thrived and production of wine for religious services skyrocketed. The failed experiment ended in 1933 with the repeal of Prohibition.

In the 21st century, the debate over the pros and cons of alcohol rages on, with ever-stiffer penalties for driving under the influence and more programs than ever to assist problem drinkers and their families.

Health potion or poison?

Though we humans are fond of our alcoholic beverages, we do not require ANY alcohol to live healthy lives. Too much alcohol is deadly, and can kill as a single overdose or by causing chronic disease. Yet low-to-moderate intake of alcohol appears to prevent heart attacks and strokes, and may help people live longer. The key message: If you can drink alcohol in moderation (1–2 drinks per day, or no more than 6 drinks per week), then go ahead. If you cannot drink moderately, then avoid alcohol altogether. Read on to learn more about the potential benefits and risks of drinking alcohol.

HEALTH BENEFITS OF ALCOHOL

How do you measure drinking?

Numerous medical studies have suggested that light-to-moderate alcohol drinking offers significant health benefits, including a longer life span, than either not drinking or drinking too much. But how much alcohol does a light or moderate drinker consume? In health studies and on charts of blood alcohol levels, one drink is defined as follows:

Beer	12 ounces
Wine	5 ounces
Liquor	1.25 ounces (one shot of 80 proof)

There are many ways to describe drinking habits, but most medical studies classify drinkers as follows:

Non-drinker:	Rarely or never drinks alcohol
Light:	Averages less than 1 drink per day (1–6 drinks each week)
Moderate:	1–2 drinks daily
Heavy:	More than 2 drinks per day *or* 5 or more on a frequent basis

Elixir of life?

Many studies have found that light-to-moderate drinkers have fewer heart attacks. Some of them suggest that red wine has a stronger protective effect on the heart than other types of alcohol. Red wine and dark beer contain *flavenoids* that are thought to slow the oxidation of LDL cholesterol (the "bad" kind). Oxidation, if unchecked, makes cholesterol much more likely to stick to the inside of arteries. *Polyphenols*, found in red grapes, appear to block the production of chemicals that narrow blood vessels and injure the lining of the arteries. Though the polyphenol effect also occurs with purple grape juice, it is much more potent with actual red wine. These properties help explain why the French, who commonly drink red table wine with meals, have low heart-disease rates despite a rich diet.

The health benefits of alcohol are not limited to red wine. The Physician's Health Study out of Harvard University collected information on 89,000 American doctors in 1982, and then followed their health outcomes for several years. The study's findings: Light-to-moderate drinkers of any kind of alcohol had fewer episodes of sudden heart-attack deaths, fewer strokes, and lower death rates than non-drinkers.[1] The stroke benefit occurred with as little as one drink per week. Of interest, men who were light-to-moderate drinkers were less likely to develop diabetes than those who did not imbibe.[2] Similarly, data from the Framingham Heart Study, published in 2002, found that men who drank moderate amounts (8–14 drinks per week) were half as likely to develop congestive heart failure compared with the non-drinkers.[3]

Alcohol may also help to prevent memory loss. The Rotterdam Study observed 8,000 Dutch people over age 55 for an average of six years. It found that people who drank 1–3 alcoholic drinks of any kind each day were less likely to develop Alzheimer's disease, and much less likely to develop memory loss due to small strokes.[4]

Finally, for the beer-drinking crowd, a study of 17,249 Canadians found that people who drank one or more beers per day had significantly fewer illnesses (25 percent) than non-drinkers.[5] Wine and hard-liquor drinkers had slightly fewer than the expected number of illnesses (2 percent fewer and 1 percent fewer respectively), but moderate beer drinkers definitely fared best.

> ❋ *Key point:* A great deal of medical evidence suggests that light-to-moderate alcohol consumption can improve health. The greatest benefit is a reduction in heart disease and stroke. Potential benefits include less memory loss, a lower risk of diabetes, and a longer life.

If you drink, do you need vitamins?

Malnutrition is a serious concern among heavy drinkers.

Alcohol, actually ethanol, contains lots of calories, but they are "empty" calories without the vitamins, minerals, and other nutrients contained in foods. One average drink of alcohol contains about 100 calories, but has almost no nutritional value. The more alcohol calories people consume the less healthy food they tend to eat. This is why heavy drinkers are so prone to vitamin deficiencies, especially of folic acid, B vitamins, and vitamin A. Moderate drinkers generally will not have problems, but a daily multivitamin pill with folic acid is an inexpensive and safe way to assure optimal nutrition.

> *Health tip:* If you drink alcohol on a regular basis, take a one-a-day multivitamin just to be on the safe side.

Alcohol and aging

No one approaching the "Golden Years" will want to hear this, but as you get older, your tolerance for alcohol decreases. Older folks simply have less body water to dilute alcohol compared with younger folks. Thus the same drink at age 70 will increase blood-alcohol levels more and result in more impairment and a higher risk of injury than the same drink at age 30. Even without alcohol on board, the risk of falling and traffic accidents increases with aging. In addition, many medications interact with alcohol, and older individuals are more likely to be on chronic medications. For all these reasons, the U.S. Department of Health recommends that people over age 65 limit alcohol use to one drink per day.

> Q *Health tip:* People over age 65 should limit their alcohol intake to one drink per day.

If you don't drink, should you start?

Considering the benefits of light or moderate drinking, many teeto-talers wonder whether they should start to take an occasional drink for their health. Limited medical evidence suggests that there is not enough benefit to make that recommendation. The British Regional Heart Study has followed a group of 7,700 middle-aged and older men for over two decades. Data from 2002 showed that men who took up regular drinking *during* the study had no improvement in death rates compared with men who did not drink.[6] In other words, taking up drinking in middle age did not seem to protect health.

HEALTH TOLL OF ALCOHOL

Demon spirits?

Though alcohol offers some legitimate health benefits, it also causes devastation in many peoples' lives. At least 20 million Americans suffer from alcoholism. One in four Americans report that drinking has caused trouble in their family; more than half have a relative who is or was alcoholic.[7] Alcohol abuse exacts a tremendous toll on families, the legal system, and, of course, on health. Hospitals across the country are burdened with patients suffering from alcohol-related problems like acute intoxication, alcohol withdrawal or delirium tremens (DTs), traumatic injuries, internal bleeding from the stomach or esophagus, pancreas inflammation, and liver failure.

Around 4 percent of all deaths in the United States are caused by alcohol use.[8] These include half of all fatal accidents, many suicides and murders, and most cases of cirrhosis of the liver. Many of the deaths are due to heart disease from heart failure and alcohol-induced high blood pressure. Others are from cancers, especially of the head, neck, esophagus, liver, and even breast. Alcoholics have overall rates of cancer 10 times as high as everyone else.

For every person who dies of alcohol-related problems, many family members, friends, co-workers, and innocent accident victims suffer. Unborn babies suffer when their mothers drink too much. Binge drinking among teens and young adults cause countless tragedies. All in all, alcohol abuse takes a heavy toll on human lives.

> ✎✎ *Key point:* Abuse of alcohol exacts a huge toll on
> ✎✎ American society, causing illness, preventable
> deaths, emotional pain, and family turmoil.

How much is too much?

I learned some important lessons about alcohol from a patient I'll call Dale. Dale is a successful corporate vice president and fitness enthusiast. We met when Dale scheduled a routine physical. He was in great shape except for high blood pressure. As with all patients, I asked about alcohol use. Dale said he enjoyed two drinks every evening and had done so for years. I asked no more, proclaimed him fit, and prescribed medication for his high blood pressure.

For the next couple of years, Dale's blood pressure didn't seem to respond to medication and was never as low as I hoped. I was embarrassed one visit when Dale said, "Doctor, you never asked me how much was in those drinks." He told me that while he only had two drinks, each drink was mixed with *five shots of liquor*. He started this habit to relax in the evening and help him sleep. Dale knew all along it was affecting his health, but brought it up only when he was ready to make a change. He quit drinking completely, on his own, and his blood pressure returned to normal. He also found that he slept better than ever without his "two" drinks and had more energy during the day.

Women and alcohol

My first week of medical school included a visit to the anatomy lab and a look at the cadaver that my team would work on all semester. I was surprised and a bit disturbed to find the corpse of a rather young woman, about 40, with nicely painted fingernails. She looked fairly normal except for a swollen abdomen from the cirrhosis of the liver that led to her death.

Years later I learned that it is not uncommon for alcoholic women to develop problems like cirrhosis earlier than their male counterparts. Although there are fewer female than male alcoholics, women are more susceptible to alcohol-related problems. Women become addicted faster and develop complications over shorter time periods and after less alcohol intake than male drinkers.

Indeed, female drinkers are more likely to die of cirrhosis of the liver than male drinkers. My wife and editor read this and said she now understands why a female colleague died so unexpectedly of cirrhosis of the liver at age 44 several years ago. The woman was a talented employee whose coworkers did not learn until her final illness that she suffered from alcoholism. Like many female alcoholics, she had a well-hidden drinking habit.

Common sense tells us that a small woman will end up with higher alcohol levels in her blood than a larger man if the two drink identical amounts of booze. Even when weight is equal, however, women have less body water than men and, therefore, will have higher concentrations of alcohol in their bloodstream after drinking. Because of these gender differences, women should limit alcohol intake to one drink per day and society should become more aware of problem drinking among women. ∎

So how much alcohol is too much? When your alcohol consumption is causing health, legal, or relationship problems, then you're drinking too much. Though Dale never increased the amount he drank and functioned quite well, it is clear in retrospect that he was drinking too much because it worsened a health problem. I learned the hard way how people can downplay or hide the amount they drink, and that alcohol abuse does not fit any stereotype.

Key point: Although people often deny it, they know they are drinking too much when their drinking causes health, legal, or relationship problems.

Alcoholism

The classic stereotype of an alcoholic is the town drunk, who can't hold a job and ends up in a gutter on skid row. The reality is far more complex. Alcoholics come in all shapes and sizes. They hold jobs in all fields—from blue collar, to the military, to top executives. They include both men and women, come from all racial backgrounds, and range in age from preteen to elderly.

It has been hard to actually define alcoholism. A panel of 23 experts from the National Council on Alcoholism and Drug Dependence took two years to come up with this profound definition in 1992:[9]

"Alcoholism is a primary, chronic disease with genetic, psychosocial, and environmental factors influencing its development and manifestations. The disease is often progressive and fatal. It is characterized by impaired control over drinking, preoccupation with the drug alcohol, use of alcohol despite adverse consequences, and distortions in thinking, most notably denial. Each of these symptoms may be continuous or periodic."

This definition is important in many respects. For one thing, it recognizes that alcoholism is a disease, not a moral weakness. For another, it admits that alcoholism has many contributing factors. While studies of twins and adopted children have shown that there is a genetic tendency toward alcoholism, for instance, they've also found that other factors come into play. Thus an identical twin of an alcoholic is more likely to be alcoholic, but may not end up so.

It's hard to know why some people become alcoholic while most do not. In the baby-boomer generation, for example, the age of taking a first drink and the amount of partying or binge drinking during the late teens and early 20s was no different between those who went on to become alcoholic and those who didn't. By the mid-to-late 20s, however, most baby boomers moderated their drinking habits, while those with alcoholism began to drink more. Were they drinking to escape depression? Did they become alcoholic because their parents were alcoholic? Did they simply become too fond of alcohol? Whatever the reasons, these heavy drinkers likely went on to experience a major life problem due to alcohol between their late 20s and early 40s.

Contrary to old stereotypes, alcoholics do not inevitably spiral downward to a bleak end. More typically, they have a series of bad drinking spells followed by remissions during which they drink less or stop. Although many alcoholics worsen and die of the disease, some do manage to quit drinking. At least one out of five gets sober and stays sober permanently, either on their own or with the help of a group like Alcoholics Anonymous (AA).

Are you or a loved one alcoholic?

Not all heavy drinkers are alcoholic. Alcoholism is not defined by how much or how often you drink, but by the problems alcohol causes in your life. If your drinking has caused *any* trouble with family, friends, jobs, money, the law, emotions, or health, its probably out of control. You can be sure you're an alcoholic if drinking has destroyed your marriage, gotten you fired from a job, led to a night in jail after driving under the influence, or caused a serious health problem.

Several screening tools can help drinkers and those who care about them recognize that there's a problem. The best known is the C.A.G.E. questionnaire:

If you drink, ask yourself honestly if you have ever:
1. Felt the need to Cut down on your drinking?
2. Felt Annoyed by criticism of your drinking?
3. Felt Guilty about your drinking?
4. Had a drink first thing in the morning (Eye-opener) to steady your nerves or get rid of a hangover?

A "yes" answer to any one of the questions means you could have a problem with alcohol, while two or more "yes" answers means you probably do.

Drinking and driving: Is it ever safe?

How much alcohol can you drink before becoming too impaired to drive safely? Is there a safe limit? These questions have generated much debate. Blood-alcohol levels are affected not only by how much you drink, but also by your body weight, gender, age, medications, and the amount of food you've eaten. Unfortunately, impairment in reaction time, coordination, and judgment start to occur at very low blood-alcohol levels. After just one drink, you will not drive as well as if you were completely sober.

As a rule, people who are smaller, older, and female will be impaired more by the same amount of alcohol than those who are larger, younger, and male. Impairment increases dramatically as blood-alcohol levels go above 0.08 percent, the level most states have set to define drunk driving. Alcohol impairment charts show blood-alcohol levels of average men (see table 5.1) and women (see table 5.2) based on body weight and number of drinks consumed. It is important to realize that a small woman can be legally drunk after just two quick glasses of wine, while an average-sized man who has one beer during a two-hour meal probably has little to worry about. For safety's sake, remember that impairment begins with the first drink. The safest policy is to simply never drink and drive. ■

Here's another question to help screen for problem drinking: If you're a man, when was the last time you had six or more drinks during a 24-hour period? If you're a woman, when was the last time you had five or more drinks during a 24-hour period. If it was within the past couple of months, there's a high chance that you have a drinking problem.

Finally, ask yourself whether you've ever had a health, legal, or personal problem as a result of drinking alcohol. Of course, denial and evasiveness are very common when it comes to admitting alcohol abuse, so you may not be willing to answer honestly. Keep in mind that recognizing and acknowledging the problem is an important first step toward recovery.

For alcoholics who want to quit drinking, help is available from treatment programs and support groups throughout the country. If someone you care about has an alcohol problem, let them know you are concerned, encourage them to seek treatment, and share your concerns with their doctor. People cannot be forced into treatment, however. To succeed in breaking their addiction, alcoholics must be active, engaged participants in their treatment and recovery.

🖐 *Personal action plan:* If you have a problem with alcohol, help is available. Talk to your doctor, minister, spouse, good friend, or local AA chapter and get your life back on track.

SUMMARY

Beer, wine, and liquor have been part of human culture for countless centuries. Light or moderate alcohol use does offer health benefits, mostly by lowering the risk of heart disease and stroke. Excessive alcohol use, however, is a national tragedy that harms millions and kills thousands of Americans each year. Alcoholics should seek treatment, and those in recovery should be congratulated and encouraged to stay sober one day at a time. People who do not drink should not start for health reasons, and those who do drink should practice moderation. Up to one drink a day for women, and one to two daily for men can enhance health and relaxation. Moderate and heavy drinkers should take a multivitamin pill to help assure good nutrition, and people over age 65 should limit alcohol use to one drink per day.

Table 5.1: Alcohol impairment chart for men

	APPROXIMATE BLOOD ALCOHOL PERCENTAGE								
Drinks	**Body Weight in Pounds**								
	100	120	140	160	180	200	220	240	
0	.00	.00	.00	.00	.00	.00	.00	.00	**ONLY SAFE DRIVING LIMIT**
1	.04	.03	.03	.02	.02	.02	.02	.02	**Impairment Begins**
2	.08	.06	.05	.05	.04	.04	.03	.03	
3	.11	.09	.08	.07	.06	.06	.05	.05	**Driving Skills Affected**
4	.15	.12	.11	.09	.08	.08	.07	.06	**Possible Criminal Penalties**
5	.19	.16	.13	.12	.11	.09	.09	.08	
6	.23	.19	.16	.14	.13	.11	.10	.09	**Legally Intoxicated**
7	.26	.22	.19	.16	.15	.13	.12	.11	
8	.30	.25	.21	.19	.17	.15	.14	.13	**— Criminal Penalties**
9	.34	.28	.24	.21	.19	.17	.15	.14	
10	.38	.31	.27	.23	.21	.19	.17	.16	

Your body can get rid of one drink per hour.
Each 1½ oz. of 80 proof liquor, 12 oz. of beer or 5 oz. of table wine = 1 drink.

Table 5.2: Alcohol impairment chart for women

	APPROXIMATE BLOOD ALCOHOL PERCENTAGE									
Drinks	**Body Weight in Pounds**									
	90	100	120	140	160	180	200	220	240	
0	.00	.00	.00	.00	.00	.00	.00	.00	.00	**ONLY SAFE DRIVING LIMIT**
1	.05	.05	.04	.03	.03	.03	.02	.02	.02	**Impairment Begins**
2	.10	.09	.08	.07	.06	.05	.05	.04	.04	**Driving Skills Affected**
3	.15	.14	.11	.10	.09	.08	.07	.06	.06	**Possible Criminal Penalties**
4	.20	.18	.15	.13	.11	.10	.09	.08	.08	
5	.25	.23	.19	.16	.14	.13	.11	.10	.09	
6	.30	.27	.23	.19	.17	.15	.14	.12	.11	**Legally Intoxicated**
7	.35	.32	.27	.23	.20	.18	.16	.14	.13	
8	.40	.36	.30	.26	.23	.20	.18	.17	.15	**— Criminal Penalties**
9	.45	.41	.34	.29	.26	.23	.20	.19	.17	
10	.51	.45	.38	.32	.28	.25	.23	.21	.19	

Your body can get rid of one drink per hour.
Each 1½ oz. of 80 proof liquor, 12 oz. of beer or 5 oz. of table wine = 1 drink.

Source: Pennsylvania Liquor Control Board

CHAPTER SIX

Smoking: Why to Quit, How to Quit

"Cigarettes cause more deaths *each year* in the United States than the combined American fatalities in WWI, WWII, Korea, and Vietnam."

—Charles LeMaistrie, M.D.
    President, American Cancer Society

THE TRAGEDY OF TOBACCO

I was stunned when I first read Dr. LeMaistrie's statement. The number of cigarette-caused deaths is so large that it's hard to grasp. More than 400,000 American lives are lost to tobacco each year, one out of every five U.S. deaths.[1] That is the equivalent of *four* fully loaded 747 jumbo jets crashing every single day. These smoking-induced deaths come in the form of heart attacks, cancers, and emphysema; and smokers are not the only ones affected. Some of the deaths involve smokers' family members and friends, nonsmokers made ill by years of regular exposure to second-hand smoke.

Heart attacks

Most people know that smoking causes lung cancer. They might not realize that more smoking deaths are due to heart attacks (180,000 per year) than cancers.[2] The nicotine in cigarettes squeezes arteries shut, raises blood pressure, and contributes to hardening of the arteries. Carbon monoxide in the smoke replaces oxygen in the blood. This adds insult to injury because vital oxygen can't get to areas that are already hurting from lack of circulation. Throw in smokers' increased tendency for blood clots, and you have a heart attack waiting to happen.

Cancer

In 1964, when baby boomers were growing up, a landmark surgeon-general's report broke the news that cigarettes cause lung cancer. Knowing that smokers and tobacco companies would try to refute this claim, the surgeon general made sure researchers had irrefutable evidence to back it up. One way scientists study cause and effect is to look for rates of diseases in people who do something compared with those who don't. Recently, for example, researchers found that people who never exercise are twice as likely to have a heart attack as people who exercise regularly. If a health problem is one-and-a-half or two times as likely to occur among people who behave in a certain way, as compared with those who don't, it is pretty good evidence of cause and effect. In the 1960s, scientists found that smokers were *18 times* as likely as nonsmokers to develop lung cancer.

It turns out that tar (think of hot asphalt) is highly cancer causing or "carcinogenic." So are many other of the hundreds of chemicals found in cigarette smoke, including arsenic, benzene, and cadmium. Not surprisingly, smoking can cause cancer wherever these chemicals go in the body—especially in the lungs, mouth, voice box, and esophagus. Smoking-related cancers also appear in the kidneys and bladder (carcinogenic chemicals are cleared from the blood by the kidneys and pass through the bladder), as well as in the pancreas and cervix. In all, lighting up is responsible for 150,000 cancer deaths a year.[3]

Emphysema

The final whammy from cigarettes is emphysema. Years of smoking wear out the elastic, rubber band-like elements of the lung that let the air out after you take a breath. Gradually, little air sacks within the lungs die off, leaving empty spaces that can't absorb oxygen. The lungs' little sweepers, called "cilia," get damaged and can't sweep out the tar and mucous from smoking, so they build up. Eventually, you just can't breathe. Emphysema has become the fourth-leading cause of death in America, killing 85,000 smokers per year.[2]

I can tell you from personal experience that death is not the only consequence of emphysema. Death comes only after years of suffering and struggling to breathe. My father was a heavy smoker and died of emphysema at age 75. The last five years of his life, he needed an oxygen tank while he slept. Growing up, I never went for a hike or played sports with my dad because he couldn't breathe well enough. We could always tell when dad was around because you could hear his loud, wheezy breathing and hacking cough.

> *Key point:* The single most effective way to prevent heart-attack deaths in America is to get people to stop smoking.

SECOND-HAND SMOKE

Unfortunately, it's not just smokers who get cancer. When I was in high school, a good buddy's mother was diagnosed with lung cancer. She wasted away and died six months later, leaving behind four children. No one understood why she had gotten lung cancer, and it didn't seem fair. She had never smoked, while her husband had puffed away with a three-pack-a-day habit. Much too late for my friend's family, researchers learned that smoke from a cigarette burning nearby—called "second-hand smoke"—poses a serious health risk. Long-term exposure more than doubles the risk of lung cancer in people who have never smoked.[3]

A hidden threat

Today, the dangers of second-hand smoke are well understood. When a cigarette burns, most of the smoke goes unfiltered directly into the air. This is known as "sidestream smoke," and it differs significantly from the "mainstream smoke" that is pulled through a filter into a smoker's lungs. A smoker actively inhales mainstream smoke for about a half-minute per cigarette. The rest of the time the cigarette is burning, about 12 minutes, its sidestream smoke is polluting the air.

Can you guess which type of smoke is dirtier? Sidestream smoke actually has twice as much tar and nicotine, five times as much carbon monoxide, and 50 times as much ammonia as mainstream smoke. No wonder it is so irritating to our eyes and noses. After half an hour in a smoke-filled room, nonsmokers have higher blood pressure, faster heart rates, and higher levels of carbon monoxide in their blood than they did while breathing normal air.

If you're a parent and a smoker, your children's health is perhaps the best reason not to smoke at home. Kids exposed to second-hand smoke are more likely to develop asthma and have more asthma attacks than kids whose homes are smoke free. In addition, young children whose parents smoke at home have twice as many respiratory illnesses, such as bronchitis and pneumonia.[4]

Polluting your air

Recently, there was an air-pollution advisory in the Phoenix area. Due to an air inversion brought on by winter weather, the carbon-monoxide level went above the Federal Air Quality standard for clean outside air of 9 parts per million (ppm). The air looked brown, and people with chronic heart and lung problems were told to stay indoors. I can only hope they didn't stay inside with anyone who smokes, however, because the carbon-monoxide level from second-hand smoke is far higher than 9 ppm.

Safer tobacco? I don't think so!

The tobacco industry has tried to convince Americans that there are "safer" tobacco alternatives to cigarettes, such as chewing tobacco or "light" (low tar and nicotine) cigarettes. Don't be fooled. While chewing tobacco probably is less damaging to the lungs than smoking, the nicotine levels in chewing tobacco are just as high as in cigarettes and can do just as much damage to the heart and blood vessels. In addition, tobacco chewers have a much higher incidence of cancers of the mouth, gums, and tongue than smokers due to the direct exposure to cancer-causing tobacco juices in the mouth. Chewers who don't get cancer have more gingivitis, gum recession, and early loss of teeth. As for light cigarettes, they are no safer than regular ones. A National Cancer Institute report in 2001 concluded that smokers of light cigarettes are exposed to the same amounts of tar and nicotine as smokers of regular cigarettes.[9] As the tobacco industry has known for years, this is because people smoke light cigarettes differently to get the same dose of nicotine. They take deeper drags, more frequent puffs, and smoke more cigarettes per day as part of their addiction. There is simply no such thing as safe tobacco. ■

In fact, smoking, even in a well-ventilated room, increases the carbon-monoxide reading to 20 ppm. If you're sitting right next to the smoker, it goes up to 90 ppm. Levels of 90 ppm have also been recorded in cars in which a half-pack of cigarettes had just been smoked. (In a scary footnote to the car study, drivers breathing 90 ppm of carbon monoxide had a slower reaction time after seeing brake lights than drivers in a control group.) The bottom line is that a smoke-filled room or car has worse air than you are likely to breathe outdoors on the most polluted day of the year.

> Q *Health tip:* When you feel threatened by second-hand smoke, don't hesitate to invoke the Non-smoker's Bill of Rights. In short, it says:
> - Your right to breathe clean air supersedes the right to smoke.
> - You have a right to politely object when smokers light up nearby.
> - You have the right to act to keep public places free of smoke.

TOBACCO HISTORY AND TRENDS

America's dubious gift

Long before Europeans visited America, Native Americans grew tobacco and smoked it as medicine and in ceremonies. Christopher Columbus brought tobacco back to Europe, where its use slowly spread. The first commercial tobacco crop was harvested in Virginia in 1612. Tobacco soon became the colony's biggest export, and increasing production over the next two centuries created much of America's demand for slave labor.

Early on, tobacco was smoked in pipes, chewed, or used as snuff. Cigars became popular in the 1800s. The smoking habit didn't really catch fire, however, until cigarette-rolling machines and safety matches made cigarettes widely available around 1900. The tobacco industry fanned the flames of the smoking epidemic with mass-market advertising and by systematically increasing the addictive chemicals in cigarettes. Yearly cigarette consumption in America increased 80-fold from 1900 to its peak in 1973; it has been gradually decreasing for the past 30 years.

Anti-smoking accomplishments

In the United States, the number of adults who smoke has decreased from over 50 percent to about 25 percent during the past 50 years. I am proud to say that doctors have led the way in kicking the habit. Many quit when health risks became apparent, and fewer than 10 percent of doctors now smoke. Doctors may have led the way in giving up smoking, but millions of other Americans deserve credit for following their example. Our country now boasts more than 40 million ex-smokers enjoying healthier lives.

The health benefits for those who quit are very real. A study of 10,000 California doctors found that death rates from lung cancer dropped drastically among them as their smoking rates declined from 1950 through 1979.[5] Death rates from heart disease have decreased by 25 percent over the past few decades, largely due to the downward trend in smoking. Nonsmokers now enjoy clean air in airplanes and in the many public places where smoking has been banned.

Stamping out teen smoking

Despite all this progress, 3,000 American teenagers start smoking every day. Among today's group, 30 will eventually die in car accidents, 20 will be murdered, but 750 will be killed by their tobacco habit.[6] We need more research into why teens start smoking and what kinds of programs will keep them from doing so. We have learned that programs designed to educate teens about smoking and instill fear of tobacco don't work very well. They can backfire by glorifying smoking among youths who are risk-takers already. Peer-led programs promoting a tobacco-free lifestyle and focusing on short-term effects of smoking like "dragon breath" and yellow teeth may be more effective. One thing we know for sure: Though high cigarette prices don't get many established smokers to quit, they can prevent teens from starting to smoke.

Perhaps more important than the message teens receive about smoking at school and from peers is the message they receive at home. Parents should not underestimate the value of setting a good example and giving a clear message that they do not want their children to smoke. Parental smoking remains a strong predictor of teen smoking. A recent study of Vermont schoolchildren found that parents' attitudes do matter. Students who thought their parents would be upset and tell them to quit if they smoked were much less likely to smoke three years later.[7]

❧❧ *Key points:* Congratulate the 40 million Americans who have quit smoking. Keep talking to your children and teenagers about why they should never smoke.

HOW TO "KICK BUTT"

The rest of this chapter is a practical guide designed to help smokers kick the habit. Reading this material can also help nonsmokers support, understand, and assist a loved one or friend who is trying to quit smoking.

Why is it so hard to quit?

Pam, a patient of mine and an ex-smoker, admits that she was terribly addicted to cigarettes. She had quit twice, but each time restarted and smoked even more. Ten years ago, she was up to two-and-a-half packs per day when she got a nasty chest cold. Too sick to smoke, she quit cold turkey. Pam had intense physical cravings for the first three weeks, but she persevered. She bought a stop-smoking kit that had some great tips and a funny video to help her through the tough times. She wrote a list of her reasons for quitting and looked at it when she was tempted. She wanted to smoke every day for the first year, but the urge gradually faded after two or three years. Pam says quitting was the hardest thing she's ever done—and one of her proudest accomplishments. Her message to current smokers: Quitting isn't easy, but you can do it.

Both physically and psychologically addictive, smoking is indeed a hard habit to break. Nine out of 10 Americans who smoke today started before they were 21, most of them by age 14. They started lighting up to fit in, feel grown up, or for other reasons, and they quickly became hooked on the nicotine. Nicotine is a stimulant drug that makes people feel more alert and can help them concentrate. As smokers quickly learn, nicotine is also incredibly addictive—as much so as cocaine or heroin.

Those who stop smoking experience intense cravings for cigarettes. The physical addiction lasts only a few weeks after quitting, but the psychological addiction can last for years. Habits such as lighting up with a cup of coffee or a glass of wine, or during moments of stress often are as hard to give up as the nicotine itself. Despite the difficulties, millions of smokers have successfully quit. Ask them how they did it, and you will hear personal stories of triumph like Pam's.

Are you ready?

Based on careful studies, psychologist James Prochaska theorized that individuals go through five "stages of change" when trying to break an addiction such as smoking:

1. *Precontemplation* (Smoker has no intention of quitting.)
2. *Contemplation* (Smoker is thinking of quitting, but is not fully committed to the idea.)
3. *Preparation* (Smoker has committed to quitting in the next month, is making plans, and has already begun small changes.)
4. *Action* (Smoker follows a plan and quits smoking.)
5. *Maintenance* (Ex-smoker has quit and is working to prevent a relapse.)

Not all smokers go through Prochaska's stages of change, but I've found that most smokers relate very well to them. A few years ago, I agreed to speak about health issues to a group of workers near my office. Because the company blamed a lot of worker sick days on health problems related to smoking, the group's manager asked me to address the dangers of smoking and how to quit. The workers were required to attend my talk. It was kind of tense at first, and the smokers were very defensive. Then I described Prochaska's stages of change. Soon we were having an open and honest discussion about readiness to quit, barriers, and successes. Workers were raising their hands and introducing themselves: "My name is Joe. I'm a contemplator, and I think..."

Ever since that day, I've believed that all smokers could benefit from determining where they are among Prochaska's stages. Knowing how close to (or far away from) quitting they are can help guide smokers' actions and expectations, as well as those of their families and medical caregivers.

Precontemplators—not quite ready

Smokers in the precontemplation stage tell me they are simply not ready or willing to quit. They may be under stress at work or at home, and the time is not right. That doesn't mean the time will never be right. For loved ones eager for the smoker to quit, recognizing that the smoker is still "precontemplation" helps prevent discouragement, frustration, and giving up.

Doctors or loved ones of a precontemplative smoker can try to help the person move to the next stage by gently pointing out the benefits of quitting and the dangers of smoking. They can also offer to help any obstacles that are keeping the smoker from quitting. I try not to push, but I let my smoking patients know that I will be asking about their readiness to quit at a future visit.

Of course, life is full of surprises. On occasion, one of my smoking patients who, last I heard, had absolutely no intention of quitting will suddenly get the motivation to skip to the action phase: Developing angina didn't convince Joe to quit, but his emergency bypass surgery changed his mind in a hurry. George kept smoking despite a smoker's cough, but reconsidered once he developed a spot on his lung. The spot turned out to be benign, but the realization that it could have been cancer got him to quit cold turkey. Sue hadn't been giving it much thought, but decided to quit when her daughter came home from school after a health class and said, "Mom, I love you and want you to be around when I grow up."

More commonly, however, smokers start to mull over the notion of quitting long before they act.

> **Personal action plan:** Make a list of the reasons you feel unable to quit smoking at this time. Post the list and commit to eliminating at least one item on it.

Contemplators—thinking about it

Contemplative smokers are thinking about quitting but haven't made a definite commitment. Friends and loved ones can help them by being supportive, but not pushing too hard. Bringing up all the benefits of quitting is a natural strategy for convincing contemplators to commit.

Fortunately, there are many great benefits to quitting smoking. In the long term, ex-smokers have a lower risk of developing heart disease, cancer, strokes, and emphysema and, therefore, are likely to live longer than smokers. In addition, ex-smokers' families and friends are no longer exposed to dangerous second-hand smoke, and their children and grandchildren are less likely to begin smoking.

Short term, ex-smokers have a better sense of taste and smell, more energy, and better wind while walking or climbing a set of stairs than smokers. They also have whiter teeth, healthier gums, fresher breath, and cleaner air inside their homes. In addition, ex-smokers save money. I recommend they keep track of how much they've saved not buying cigarettes, and then treat themselves to a dream trip or something else they might not have been able to afford if they were still smoking.

For contemplators who need more incentive to commit, the Arizona Smokers' Helpline offers the following time line of what happens to a smoker's health after kicking the habit:

Within:	This is what happens:
20 minutes	Blood pressure, pulse rate, and body temperature return to normal.
8 hours	The body starts to heal itself, the carbon monoxide level in the bloodstream drops to normal, and the oxygen level increases to normal.
24 hours	The chance of heart attack decreases.
48 hours	Nerve endings start re-growing and the ability to smell and taste things is enhanced.
72 hours	Bronchial tubes relax, lung capacity increases, and breathing becomes easier.
2–12 weeks	Circulation improves, walking becomes easier, and lung function increases up to 30 percent.
1–9 months	Cilia re-grow in the lungs, increasing their ability to handle mucous, clean the lungs, and reduce infection. Coughing, sinus congestion, fatigue, and shortness of breath decrease; and the body's overall energy level increases.
1 year	Risk of heart attack drops to half that of a smoker.
5 years	Lung cancer death rate for the ex-smoker decreases almost 50 percent from that of the average smoker.
10 years	Lung cancer death rate for the ex-smoker drops almost to the rate for nonsmokers.

I think contemplators should also make a list of all the reasons they want to quit smoking. The list might look something like this:

1. To help Jenny's asthma get better.
2. To get in good enough shape to go on Nick's scout hike into the Grand Canyon.
3. To save $1,200 per year to take a Mediterranean cruise three summers from now.

If you are a smoker, post the list where you will see it every day, and get motivated.

The next step is to make a firm commitment to quit. This is a good time to think about whether you would do better with an intervention program or on your own. Find out what smoking cessation programs are available in your area (see "Preparing to quit" section, below) and what's worked for friends or coworkers. For more advice, see your doctor.

Personal action plan: Make a list of reasons to quit smoking. Post the list where you will see it every day. Make a commitment to quit.

Preparing to quit

The preparation-stage smoker has committed to quitting within one month. This person has a plan for quitting, is mentally prepared to quit, and is already making some behavioral changes. Most smokers have personal experience with trying to quit. If you smoke, you know best what will or won't work. In this struggle, you are the expert. There is no right or wrong approach. Learn from your past efforts and get ideas from friends who have successfully quit.

You'll need to make a couple of basic decisions: Are you going to quit on your own, or do you want to work with a group in a formal program? Are you going to quit cold turkey, or are you going to cut down gradually? Do you want to try medication or nicotine-replacement therapy (patches or gum) to help with the physical dependence?

The majority of smokers opt to quit on their own. Many take advantage of self-help materials that target smoking cessation. If you're in the planning phase, find out whether your employer or a local organization provides smoking-cessation classes, support groups, or materials that will meet your needs. Here are some places to start: The American Lung Association offers "Freedom from Smoking" clinics in most cities, as well as self-help tapes and videos. The American Cancer Society sponsors a "Fresh Start" group program and a "Smart Move" self-help program. The American Heart Association provides a free "Calling It Quits" program.

Some smokers have used hypnosis and acupuncture to help them kick the habit. Though both methods are considered safe, skeptics have questioned their effectiveness. Hypnosis works best when smokers are highly motivated and interested in a behavior-altering approach. Though scientists debate whether acupuncture can really help people quit smoking, some ex-smokers swear it worked for them.

Some smokers quit "cold turkey", while others taper down the number of cigarettes smoked each day until they reach a final "quit day." Either way, it can help to keep a smoking diary a few weeks before the quit day. Write down the time, place, and what you are doing when you smoke each cigarette. This will help you understand your smoking habit and plan for alternatives when your urge to smoke is the strongest (i.e., chewing sugarless gum, going for a walk, drawing to keep your hands busy). Cutting down gradually for two weeks prior to a quit date does have some advantages: It confirms your commitment to quit and locks in the actual quit date, lets you practice your alternative-to-smoking strategies a few times a day as you get ready, and it helps reduce your body's dependence on nicotine.

Nicotine replacement, anyone?

Getting nicotine through a patch, gum, nose spray, inhaler, or lozenge helps nicotine-addicted smokers give up cigarettes. Numerous medical studies have shown that nicotine replacement is most effective for people who smoke a pack or more each day. These moderate-to-heavy smokers are almost twice as likely to be nonsmokers after six months if they use nicotine replacement as if they don't.[8]

Nicotine replacement makes quitting easier by reducing the craving for nicotine while the smoker breaks the habit of lighting up. Nicotine gum and patches are available over the counter without a prescription. The cost of nicotine replacement is about the same as that of smoking.

Although either one can work, I usually recommend the patch instead of the gum. The gum is very sticky and needs to be chewed, and then parked between the cheek and gum to release nicotine. To avoid craving, a piece has to be chewed every 1–2 hours for a couple of months. Several of my patients became hooked on the gum and continue to chew instead of smoke.

For most smokers, I recommend a full-strength patch (15–22 mg of nicotine) starting on the morning of their quit day. Patches worn only while awake work just as well as those worn 24 hours a day. Experience shows that using a nicotine patch for eight weeks works as well as longer courses, and that stopping the patch abruptly works as well as tapering to a lower strength. It is, of course, very important not to smoke while using a patch.

In addition to nicotine gum and patches, the prescription antidepressant drug bupropion (marketed as Zyban) also has been shown to improve smoking cessation rates in clinical studies.[8] Smokers should begin taking bupropion one week prior to their quit date, and the drug should be used in conjunction with a support program and/or nicotine-replacement therapy. Bupropion often causes insomnia and there is some risk of seizures. Because of the seizure risk, bupropion should not be used by epileptics, diabetics taking insulin, and even heavy drinkers. Because of cost and side effects, bupropion is not for everyone, but should be considered when a smoker has been unable to quit using other methods.

> *Key point:* Smokers who burn through a pack or more of cigarettes per day benefit most from nicotine-replacement patches. Heavy smokers who use patches have more success in kicking the habit than those who don't.

> ✋ *Personal action plan:* Set a quit date. Write down your personal plan of action or enroll in a smoking-cessation group. Consider a nicotine-replacement patch and see your doctor if you have any questions.

Action time!

When quit day finally arrives, make the most of it. You are embarking on one of the biggest challenges of your life, and your life literally depends on it. First-day strategies include cleaning up, keeping busy, and celebrating. Clean your personal space by throwing away all ashtrays and lighters. Wash the cigarette smell out of your clothes. Clean your house and car. It's a great day to have your teeth cleaned. Do something you enjoy that you don't associate with smoking, such as a bike ride or a movie. Do something special for yourself—go out to dinner or buy yourself a present. Throw a non-smoking party for your support group.

The first three weeks without cigarettes will probably be the hardest. Use your alternative-to-smoking strategies (i.e., sugarless gum, doodling, or whatever you come up with) when you do things you used to associate with smoking. Expect to be more irritable, hungry, and tired. Warn friends and family to give you some slack. Reward yourself for each milestone you reach. Put your cigarette money aside for a treat. Try to spend more time in places where you can't smoke, like stores, museums, and libraries. Look often at your list of reasons to quit smoking. Be aware of your improving health as your senses of taste and smell return, your cough decreases, and your energy increases. Especially when the desire to smoke is strong, mark your success one minute, hour or day at a time.

> ✋ *Personal action plan:* When quit day arrives, get rid of all your ashtrays and lighters, keep busy, and celebrate your success one day at a time.

Maintaining success (and a healthy weight)

Think of quitting smoking as a journey. The bad news is that over half of people who quit relapse, most during the first three months. The good news is that millions of ex-smokers, despite faltering along the way, have ultimately been successful. If you do light up, don't be too hard on yourself. It doesn't mean you've failed. It does mean you need to recommit to quitting and get back on the wagon. A support group, an exercise program, and looking at the reasons you quit smoking can all help in the maintenance phase.

It's no myth that people who quit smoking gain weight. However, the problem is not as bad as you might think, and it is certainly not inevitable. In the year following their quit date, ex-smokers have an average weight gain of only about 6 pounds, and most eventually return to their normal weight.

To help prevent unwanted weight gain, try some of the following tricks: To satisfy oral cravings, carry sugar-free candy or gum. Keep each piece in your mouth as long as possible. Keep your hands busy with something fun, such as a craft, video game, crossword puzzle, musical instrument, or gardening. Pick snack foods that keep your hands busy, like sunflower seeds in the shell or nuts that have to be cracked, and are relatively low in calories, such as raw carrots, celery, rye crackers, or low-fat popcorn. Do not seek comfort in high-fat, high-calorie "junk" snacks—i.e., potato chips, cookies, candy bars, or soda pop (unless it's sugar-free). Try to exercise several times a week, and remember that you are still far, far better off without cigarettes even if you do gain a few pounds.

SUMMARY

Despite declining smoking rates, smoking remains the biggest cause of preventable death and disease in our country. If you have never smoked, or if you are one of the millions of Americans who have quit, take a deep, healthy breath and give yourself a hearty congratulation. You have made the single most important lifestyle choice for good health. Insist on your right to breathe clean, smoke-free air. Remember that most people who smoke want to quit. Be patient with and supportive of your friends and family who smoke, especially when they are trying to kick the habit. If you do smoke, understand that quitting is the single, most powerful action you can take to preserve your health. Think about where you are as far as readiness to change and try not to be annoyed by people who constantly bug you about your smoking. Finally, don't give up on yourself. With determination, you can join the growing ranks of ex-smokers.

PART II

Heart Health

CHAPTER SEVEN

·····················

Heart Disease: Protecting the Pump

"As the arteries grow hard, the heart grows soft."
—H. L. Mencken

GREAT STRIDES IN THE FIGHT AGAINST HEART DISEASE

Good news, bad news

Although I wouldn't wish it on anyone, there has never been a better time to have a heart attack. The past few decades have brought tremendous progress in both the prevention and treatment of heart disease. Since the 1950s, death rates from heart attacks at any given age have dropped by more than one-third. Balloons, stents, and clot-busting drugs have greatly improved outcomes for heart-attack victims.

Despite these advances, however, heart disease remains the No. 1 cause of death in the United States. This year alone, Americans will suffer 1.5 million heart attacks and 700,00 deaths from heart disease.[1] For two-thirds of men who develop coronary heart disease, a heart attack or dropping dead is the first indication of a problem. A 50-year-old woman who is terrified of breast cancer actually is three times as likely to die from coronary heart disease.

The toll heart disease takes in this country need not be nearly so high. In fact, if you're willing to follow certain preventive strategies, you can lower your heart-attack risk dramatically.

What is heart disease?

Broadly speaking, heart disease includes any condition that damages the heart. The heart is a strong muscle that pumps blood throughout the body. The heart gets its energy supply via the coronary arteries (think of pipes, or fuel lines supplying fuel to an engine). The heart has valves that let blood go forward as the heart pumps, but not backward as it refills. The heart also has an electrical system that controls how fast it beats.

Any of these systems can go awry. Heart valves can leak too much or become too narrow. This is known as "valvular heart disease" and can often be fixed through valve repair or replacement. The electrical system can go haywire, causing the heart to beat too slowly or too fast. Slow heart rates are sometimes fixed with a pacemaker, while fast heart rates are often controlled with medication or electrical shocks.

By far the most common type of heart disease, however, is "coronary artery disease" (CAD), also called "coronary heart disease" (CHD). This is when the coronary arteries become blocked, either slowly or all of a sudden, keeping the heart muscle from getting enough oxygen. If the blockage is partial, people often experience chest pain known as "angina." A heart attack occurs when the blockage is complete, causing part of the heart muscle to lose its blood supply and die. This is known medically as a "myocardial infarction."

"Heart failure" occurs when a person's heart is damaged so much that its pumping action is too weak to allow the person to carry out normal physical activities. The damage can be due to a valve problem, an electrical problem, long-term high blood pressure, or, most often, from loss of heart muscle due to heart attack. With heart failure, the heart has trouble pumping all of the blood out of the lungs and lower extremities. Fluid builds up in the lungs, and feet and legs often become swollen. People complain about shortness of breath on exertion, needing more pillows to sleep, and having to sit up at night to catch their breath.

When medical people (myself included) talk about heart disease without mentioning a specific type, they generally mean coronary artery disease.

What is arteriosclerosis?

In general, "arteriosclerosis" is a process that causes hardening, thickening, and loss of elastic stretch in the walls of arteries, the high-pressure pipes that carry blood throughout the body. "*Athero*-sclerosis" is a type of *arterio*sclerosis that leads to the build-up of fatty, yellow deposits and plaques full of cholesterol on the inside of an artery. Atherosclerosis is the main process that causes coronary artery disease. In fact, another term for coronary disease is "athero-sclerotic cardiovascular disease (ASCVD).

Autopsy studies on Americans have found that yellow, fatty streaks start to appear in coronary arteries as early as the late teens and early 20s. New theories on coronary artery disease contend that fatty plaques build slowly, especially after the lining of the arteries have been damaged by cigarette smoking or high blood pressure. Most heart attacks are thought to occur in arteries that are only par-tially blocked, when a fatty plaque ruptures and spills debris into the artery. A blood clot forms at the site of the rupture, blocking the artery completely and triggering the heart attack.

> *Key point:* Rates of coronary heart disease in America have dropped during the past 50 years, but heart disease still takes an enormous toll. We now know a great deal about why fat deposits build up in arteries, as well as ways to prevent and treat the heart problems caused by this "atherosclerosis."

WHAT PUTS YOU AT RISK?

Cardiac risk factors

A number of things influence whether or not you will develop coronary artery disease. Some of the following risk factors cannot be changed, but many can be reduced or eliminated through healthy lifestyle choices.

Risk factors beyond your control:

- *Being male.* Men are more prone to heart disease than women.
- *Getting older.* Heart disease risk increases with age. Men over age 45 and women over age 55 generally are considered to be at higher risk than younger individuals.
- *Family history of heart disease.* Your risk is highest if your father or brother had coronary artery disease before age 55, or if your mother or sister was diagnosed before age 65.

Risk factors within your control:

- *Smoking.* This is the single biggest preventable risk factor for coronary disease (see Chapter 6). If all smokers in the United States quit smoking, 180,000 heart attacks per year would be prevented.[2]
- *Inactive lifestyle.* Being sedentary is another major contributor to heart disease. This risk can be greatly reduced just by modest increases in physical activity (see Chapter 3).
- *High-fat American diet.* Experts believe rates of coronary disease in this country could be cut in half if Americans would trim the fat in their diet (see Chapter 2) and exercise regularly.
- *Stress.* Stress is believed to be a significant contributor to coronary disease. One indicator of stress is a lack of sleep. Interestingly, a recent study found that women who sleep eight hours a night have lower rates of heart disease than those who chronically sleep six or fewer hours.[3] Stress can be reduced via self-awareness, relaxation techniques, and making time for a good night's sleep (see Chapter 4).

Medical conditions that increase risk:

- *Obesity*. After smoking, obesity is the most common preventable cause of heart disease in the United States (see Chapter 8).
- *High blood pressure*. Inadequately controlled high blood pressure is a leading cause of heart failure in America (see Chapter 9).
- *High cholesterol*. Reducing levels of harmful cholesterol is a potent way to prevent heart disease (see Chapter 10).
- *Diabetes*. Diabetics have a greatly increased risk of heart attack, as high in fact as that of non-diabetics who have *already* survived one (see Chapter 11).

Recognizing and treating each of these medical conditions can reduce the risk of coronary disease, save lives, and improve quality of life.

> ✻ *Key point:* When it comes to cardiac risk factors, you can't do much about your family history, age, or gender. You have lots of control, however, over smoking, physical activity, what you eat, and how you respond to stress. If you have high blood pressure, obesity, high cholesterol, or diabetes, good lifestyle choices and medical treatment are the key to preventing heart disease.

Measuring your risk

Several tools can help you estimate your chances of developing coronary artery disease. One of them, "Calculating 10-Year Risk" (see table 7.1), uses a risk-scoring system from the Framingham Heart Study to assign points to CAD risk factors. To calculate your likelihood of developing serious coronary artery disease (i.e., heart attack or sudden death) in the next 10 years, you simply add up the points from your risk factors. Your point total corresponds to a percentage that represents your risk (5 percent or less is low; 10 percent or higher is cause for concern). Similar tools are available on the Internet. Try *www.med-decisions.com* or search for "cardiac risk calculator" or "heart risk calculator."

Table 7.1 Cardiac Risk Assessment Table for Men

Age	Points
20-34	-9
35-39	-4
40-44	0
45-49	3
50-54	6
55-59	8
60-64	10
65-69	11
70-74	12
75-79	13

Total Cholesterol	Points				
	Age 20-39	Age 40-49	Age 50-59	Age 60-69	Age 70-79
<160	0	0	0	0	0
160-199	4	3	2	1	0
200-239	7	5	3	1	0
240-279	9	6	4	2	1
≥280	11	8	5	3	1

	Points				
	Age 20-39	Age 40-49	Age 50-59	Age 60-69	Age 70-79
Nonsmoker	0	0	0	0	0
Smoker	8	5	3	1	1

HDL (mg/dL)	Points
≥60	-1
50-59	0
40-49	1
<40	2

Systolic BP (mmHg)	If Untreated	If Treated
<120	0	0
120-129	0	1
130-139	1	2
140-159	1	2
≥160	2	3

Point Total	10-Year Risk %
<0	< 1
0	1
1	1
2	1
3	1
4	1
5	2
6	2
7	3
8	4
9	5
10	6
11	8
12	10
13	12
14	16
15	20
16	25
≥17	≥ 30

Table 7.1 Cardiac Risk Assessment Table for Women

Age	Points
20-34	-7
35-39	-3
40-44	0
45-49	3
50-54	6
55-59	8
60-64	10
65-69	12
70-74	14
75-79	16

Total Cholesterol	Points				
	Age 20-39	Age 40-49	Age 50-59	Age 60-69	Age 70-79
<160	0	0	0	0	0
160-199	4	3	2	1	1
200-239	8	6	4	2	1
240-279	11	8	5	3	2
≥280	13	10	7	4	2

	Points				
	Age 20-39	Age 40-49	Age 50-59	Age 60-69	Age 70-79
Nonsmoker	0	0	0	0	0
Smoker	9	7	4	2	1

HDL (mg/dL)	Points
≥60	-1
50-59	0
40-49	1
<40	2

Systolic BP (mmHg)	If Untreated	If Treated
<120	0	0
120-129	1	3
130-139	2	4
140-159	3	5
≥160	4	6

Point Total	10-Year Risk %
<9	< 1
9	1
10	1
11	1
12	1
13	2
14	2
15	3
16	4
17	5
18	6
19	8
20	11
21	14
22	17
23	22
24	27
≥25	≥ 30

Estimating your CAD risk is a good idea for several reasons: It can help you decide whether to try risk-reducing measures like taking an aspirin a day (see below) or medication to lower cholesterol. It can reassure you if you are at low risk but were worried you might have a problem. And it can spur lifestyle changes and medical interventions if you are, indeed, at high risk.

> ✋ *Personal action plan:* Use table 7.1 to calculate your risk of having a heart attack or coronary death in the next 10 years. If your risk is 5 percent or less, you don't have much to worry about. If your risk is more than 5 percent, read on to learn how to lessen your risk.

HOW CAN YOU HELP YOUR HEART?

Lifestyle

As emphasized earlier, a healthy lifestyle is the foundation for a healthy heart. In a nutshell, here's what you should be doing:

- If you smoke, quit. This should be your top priority.
- Improve your diet. Start the day with a healthy breakfast and try to eat five fruit or vegetable servings each day. Eat more high-fiber foods, more fish, and less fatty red meat. Minimize high-fat foods like French fries and rich desserts. When cooking, use more monounsaturated oils such as olive oil.
- Get physically active. At the very least, go for a walk three days a week.
- Drink 1–2 alcoholic drinks per day if you enjoy it and are not prone to drinking in excess.
- Make time in your life for a good night's sleep (7–9 hours).
- If there's too much stress in your life, take steps to manage it.
- If you heed most of this advice, you will feel better and greatly reduce your chance of having a heart problem.

Aspirin

Heart attacks occur when small blood clots stick to fatty plaques inside coronary arteries, blocking the flow of blood and oxygen to the heart. Low doses of aspirin act as a blood-thinner and help prevent blood clots from forming in arteries. That's why chewing on an aspirin is the first treatment for people having a heart attack in the emergency room, and why most heart attack survivors are told to continue taking an aspirin each day.

Should you take aspirin to prevent a heart attack? The answer is a bit complicated. Several good randomized, controlled clinical trials have found that aspirin can reduce the risk of a heart attack in high-risk people (most of those studied were men) by about one-third.[4] This sounds great, but there can be side effects from thinning the blood. The most worrisome, though rare, effects of aspirin are bleeding strokes and stomach bleeding.

The benefit of aspirin depends on your individual risk of having a heart attack—the higher your risk, the greater the benefit. In the aspirin trials, people with a 10 percent or greater risk over the next 10 years had the most benefit. For each person who had serious bleeding, roughly 2–4 heart attacks were prevented.

For a low-risk person, the benefit was much less clear. If 10-year cardiac risk was only 2 percent, the number of heart attacks prevented by aspirin roughly equaled the number of serious bleeding episodes. Does this limited cardiac benefit outweigh the risk of bleeding? Low-risk people will have to decide for themselves, but the U.S. Preventive Services Task Force has provided some guidance. In 2002, the agency concluded that aspirin does prevent coronary heart disease, and that the benefit-versus-risk is most favorable in people with a 10-year heart-attack risk greater than 5 percent.[5]

For prevention, the dose of aspirin most commonly prescribed is 81 mg— one "baby aspirin"—per day. Diabetics, smokers, and people who have already had a heart attack will benefit most and should definitely ask their doctor about aspirin.

> ✋ *Personal action plan:* If you are a man over age 40 or a woman past menopause, calculate your 10-year risk of developing coronary heart disease (see table 7.1) and carefully read the section about aspirin. Discuss with your doctor the pros and cons of using aspirin for heart-attack prevention. If you've already been diagnosed with coronary heart disease, take a "baby aspirin" per day unless you have a good reason not to.

Homocysteine and folic acid

Similar to high cholesterol, high levels of homocysteine in the blood increase rates of coronary heart disease.[6] An amino acid, homocysteine is very toxic to the smooth cells that make up the lining of our arteries. When these endothelial cells are damaged, fatty deposits and plaques start to occur. Homocysteine also makes blood more likely to clot and trigger a heart attack.

Folic acid, an antioxidant vitamin that reduces homocysteine levels in the blood, has emerged as a powerful weapon in the fight against heart disease. Also called folate, folic acid is cheap, safe, and very reliable in controlling harmful homocysteine. Because folic acid is water soluble, it is non-toxic and merely passes in your urine if you take too much.

Since 1998, folic acid has been added to flour in the United States. Folic acid is also found in green vegetables, citrus fruit, and beans. Unfortunately, even a healthy diet supplies a less than optimal amount of folic acid to protect the heart.

If a blood test determines that you have high homocysteine levels, or if you are at risk for coronary artery disease, you should take 400 micrograms of folic acid either in a multivitamin (without iron) or as a plain supplement. For people with known coronary disease, some experts recommend as much as 800–1000 micrograms of folic acid daily.

Q *Health tip:* For some extra insurance against heart disease, take a 400 microgram supplement of the antioxidant folic acid each day.

Fish oil and omega-3 fatty acids

Do you eat fish? If not, you might want to start. Groups of people who eat lots of fish—including Japanese fisherman, Alaskan Natives, and Greenland Eskimos—have very low rates of coronary heart disease. In addition, several studies have shown that people who eat fish have lower death rates from coronary disease than people who don't.

Even fish-oil supplements can be beneficial. An exciting study from Italy found that heart-attack survivors who took 1 gram per day of fish oil as a supplement were much less likely to die during the next few years than those who didn't.[7] This protective effect was at least as strong as that of commonly prescribed "statin" drugs to lower cholesterol.

Fish oil is believed to prevent many sudden cardiac deaths, though experts aren't sure why. One theory holds that fish oil lowers levels of harmful trans fats in the blood. Trans fats are the "hydrogenated" (hardened) or "partially hydrogenated" oils found in lots of fried, processed, and commercially baked foods. High levels of trans fats have been found in the blood of many sudden-death victims. Fish oil is a healthy replacement for harmful fats, and appears to have an anti-inflammatory effect on arteries as well.

Fish oil consists mostly of two different omega-3 fatty acids, abbreviated EPA and DHA. These omega-3 fatty acids are most plentiful in the oil of fish like salmon, albacore tuna, sardines, mackerel, lake trout, and herring. Based on current knowledge, you would be wise to eat more of these fish and less of fatty and fried meats. The American Heart Association recommends eating fish twice a week. You should also cut down on hydrogenated and partially hydrogenated oils by eating more fresh foods and fewer processed foods.

Due to concerns over the purity of fish-oil supplements (in capsule form) and the limited number of studies showing their benefit, the American Heart Association does not yet recommended them for heart-disease prevention. However, if you already have established coronary heart disease and won't eat fish, a daily 1 gram supplement of fish oil is a good idea.

> ❯❮ *Key point:* Fish consumption appears to reduce the
> ⤢⤡ risk of dying from heart disease. People should try
> to eat fish twice a week to help prevent coronary disease.

Cholesterol

High levels of low-density lipoprotein (LDL) cholesterol are a major risk factor for coronary heart disease. Although technically just a risk factor, high cholesterol has taken on a life of its own and is treated as a distinct medical condition or disease. In fact, cholesterol testing and treatment has become so complicated that I have devoted an entire chapter to demystifying and explaining its intricacies. Please refer to Chapter 10 for everything you need to know about cholesterol and lipids for the prevention of heart disease.

C-Reactive protein and inflammation

C-reactive protein is a substance that increases in the bloodstream when inflammation occurs in the body. Originally, measures of this protein were used to track the degree of inflammation in arthritis sufferers. Recently, however, researchers have noticed that people with higher levels of C-reactive protein seem more prone to developing heart disease.[8] These findings have triggered a great deal of research into whether and how much inflammation, the body's immune response, and even infections might be contributing to coronary disease.

At this time, we still don't know much about how to reduce C-reactive protein levels or whether such interventions can help prevent heart disease. In 2003, however, an interesting possibility emerged from the Arthritis, Diet, and Activity Promotion Trial (ADAPT), which studied overweight people with arthritis. During the trial, C-reactive protein levels fell significantly in the group that followed a low-fat, low-calorie diet and participated in an exercise program; levels did not change in the control group.[9]

Though the study was not designed to look at heart disease, its findings suggest that people worried about C-reactive protein should adopt healthy diet and exercise habits. I do not recommend routine testing for C-reactive protein, but the test can be helpful for people who are trying to decide whether to take aspirin or cholesterol-lowering drugs. In those situations, an elevated C-reactive protein could shift the balance in favor of trying the preventive medications.

> *Key point:* A healthy lifestyle, a baby aspirin each day, a daily 400 microgram dose of folic acid, and eating fish a few times per week can greatly reduce your risk of having a heart attack.

HOW TO HANDLE A HEART ATTACK

Don't ignore warning symptoms

Jack is a healthy, vigorous patient who did all the right things to prevent a heart attack. At age 68, he took a baby aspirin each day, took a statin drug to help control high cholesterol, ate a healthy diet, and walked and played tennis to stay fit. One warm summer day he was digging in his back yard when he felt heavy, tight pressure across his chest and into his left arm. He sat down for a couple of minutes, but when the pain failed to disappear he found his wife and asked her to call 911.

Jack was soon in our hospital, where tests confirmed that he was having a heart attack. He promptly had an angiogram, which showed a narrowed area in one of the main coronary arteries on the left side of the heart. Fortunately, the rest of his arteries looked great. A cardiologist skillfully opened the blockage with a balloon, and placed a straw-like stent through the area to keep it open. Jack went home two days later and has done very well.

Jack's story teaches some great lessons. First and most important, as surprised as he was by unexpected chest pain, Jack did not ignore it. Tragically, many people *do* ignore classic heart-attack symptoms and end up dying as a result. It is vital to recognize the following symptoms and seek immediate medical help if they occur:

- Chest pain, often behind the breastbone (a squeezing sensation; heavy, band-like pressure; or like an elephant is sitting on your chest)
- Pain that radiates from the chest to the neck, jaw, left shoulder or arm
- Persistent indigestion or upper abdominal pain
- Unexplained sweating, shortness of breath, nausea, or a light-headed feeling

Second, Jack's story shows how far we have come in the treatment of heart attacks. Balloons, stents, and clot-dissolving drugs have revolutionized treatment by quickly opening clogged coronary arteries before the heart muscle becomes permanently damaged. Consequently, hospital stays are shorter, long-term outcomes are better, and people lead more normal lives following heart attacks now than in the past.

Health tip: Be aware of heart-attack warning symptoms and seek medical help immediately if they occur.

Preventing a second heart attack

If you've survived a first heart attack, you know for certain that you have coronary disease and that you are at high risk of having another heart attack. Your survival has provided you the opportunity to begin intensive efforts to improve your odds. Fortunately, some simple steps are very successful in preventing further heart attacks, heart failure, and sudden death:

- Quit smoking. People with heart disease who continue to smoke have five times the death rates of those who quit.
- Exercise. Begin light-to-moderate physical activity. Getting active dramatically improves long-term survival rates.
- Take 81–325 mg of aspirin a day. Aspirin reduces your chances of further heart attacks and sudden death.[10]
- Ask your doctor whether you need cholesterol-lowering statin drugs. Statins can reduce your chances of future heart attacks and sudden death by 30 percent.[11]
- Ask your doctor about ACE inhibitors. These medications save lives by preventing heart failure.
- Ask your doctor whether you need a beta-blocker medication. Beta-blockers help prevent deaths from arrhythmias after heart attacks.

Personal action plan: If you have had a heart attack, bypass surgery, or a diagnosis of coronary artery disease, review the interventions to prevent further heart disease. If you are not trying something on the list, ask your doctor whether it might benefit you.

SUMMARY

Recent decades have brought great advances in both the prevention and treatment of coronary heart disease in America. Despite this progress, smoking, inactivity, high-fat diets, and stress continue to promote the atherosclerosis (clogging of the arteries) that leads to heart attacks. In addition, Americans increasingly suffer from obesity, high blood pressure, high cholesterol, and diabetes—all conditions that cause heart disease. Healthier lifestyles, aspirin, folic acid, and fish in the diet can all help to prevent coronary disease. In the 21st century, having a heart attack is not the end of the world. Prompt access to care and early treatment with balloons, stents, and clot-busters have all improved outcomes. After a heart attack, aggressive *secondary* prevention efforts are very successful in prolonging life and preventing progression to heart failure.

CHAPTER EIGHT

Overweight: The Fight Against Fat

"While we have made dramatic progress over the last few decades in achieving so many of our health goals, the statistics on overweight and obesity have steadily headed in the wrong direction. If this situation is not reversed, it could wipe out the gains we have made."

—David Satcher, M.D., Ph.D.
Surgeon General's Report, 2001

AMERICA'S WEIGHT PROBLEM

Health crisis for the 21st century

In 1964, a famous Surgeon General's Report alerted the nation that smoking causes lung cancer. The report kicked off a long-term campaign that has reduced smoking rates significantly and saved countless lives. In December 2001, a less-publicized Surgeon General's Report, David Satcher's "Call to Action to Prevent Overweight and Obesity," urged Americans to reign in their expanding waistlines or face an epidemic of weight-related health problems. Time will tell whether Satcher's warning will have the dramatic impact of the report linking smoking and lung cancer, but it should. Today in America, we may be winning the war against tobacco, but we are losing the fight against fat.

Since I graduated from medical school in 1981, obesity has doubled among American adults, while overweight among teens has tripled. Indeed, all segments of our society have been affected, with almost 100 million Americans now considered overweight—including 55 percent of those over age 20.[1]

No one knows for sure why this has happened, but our fast-paced, fast-food, convenience lifestyles certainly have played a role. Many people don't make time for breakfast, but eat bigger dinners and snack more at night. More than ever, Americans are getting their meals at restaurants, where plates are bigger and portions are larger than 20 years ago. At burger joints, a lot of us are tempted by grease-bomb breakfast sandwiches, triple-patty bacon cheeseburgers, and super-sized drinks and fries.

Weight gain also correlates with hours of television watched—the more you watch, the more you tend to weigh.[2] When I was growing up, we only had four TV channels and personal computers were still science fiction. Today, we have hundreds of cable channels, computer games, and the Internet to keep us rooted in place as we put on the pounds.

✶ Key point: During the past two decades, more and more American adults and teens have become overweight. Currently, the majority of adults are overweight.

Health risks of obesity

So Americans are getting heavier. Is that really a cause for concern? Unfortunately, the answer is a resounding yes. Obesity kills. Data from the Framingham Heart Study published in 2003 found that obese men and women died an average of seven years earlier than their normal-weight peers.[3] Obesity now rivals smoking as the most common preventable cause of early death in the United

States. The combination is especially deadly: Obese smokers die almost 14 years earlier than non-smokers with normal body weight.[3]

Most obesity-related deaths are due to *heart disease*. People who are obese have more heart attacks, heart failure, and sudden deaths than their non-obese counterparts. Blood clots in the legs (phlebitis) and lungs (pulmonary embolism) also are more common among the obese. Being even moderately overweight makes you twice as likely to have high blood pressure and three times as likely to develop diabetes, both of which lead to heart disease.

Alarming new studies have discovered an increased number of *cancer deaths* among overweight adults, as well. One of them, the 16-year Cancer Prevention Study II, published in 2003, followed 900,000 Americans. It found that extremely obese men and women were 52 percent and 62 percent more likely to die of cancer, respectively, compared with their normal-weight peers.[4] Researchers attributed the higher cancer-death rate to three things: The obese patients had an increased incidence of cancers; their cancers were diagnosed at more advanced stages (because excess weight can make tumors harder to detect); and they had worse outcomes with treatment than their normal-weight counterparts. Deaths from cancers of the colon, breast, pancreas, prostate, and uterus were all more common as weight increased. Another study found that a woman who gains 20 pounds from age 18 to midlife doubles her risk of breast cancer.[5]

Being overweight also contributes to less dangerous, but often painful conditions such as hemorrhoids, varicose veins, gallstones, and osteoarthritis (the wear-and-tear type of arthritis that commonly affects knees, hips, and the low back).

Interestingly, researchers have learned that the location of excess fat on your body has a lot to do with how dangerous it is to your health. "Apple-shaped" people who store fat around the belly, for example, release more fat into the blood than "pear-shaped" people who store fat on the hips and thighs. Consequently, apple-shaped people tend to develop heart disease more quickly and suffer more heart attacks than their pear-shaped peers. Unfortunately, *where* your fat will be stored is determined largely by your genes and beyond your control. Your best bet, especially if you carry extra weight around your midsection, is to take steps to control *how much* fat you store.

> ❧❧ *Key point:* Excess body fat, especially located at the waistline, is bad for health and contributes to 300,000 preventable deaths per year in America.

Measuring up

Do you have a weight problem? Two key measurements—your Body Mass Index (BMI) and waist size—remove the guesswork and let you know right where you stand.

BMI is a single number calculated from your height and weight. To find your current BMI, use the BMI Table (see table 8.1). Find your height in the column on the left, look to the right along the row until you reach the number closest to your current weight in pounds, then move down that column to find your BMI. (If your height and weight are not in the table, or you want to calculate your BMI more exactly, use the formula at the bottom of the table.) Here is what your BMI means:

18 or less	Underweight
19–24	Normal
25–29	Overweight
30–39	Obese
40 or more	Extreme obesity

If you are a highly trained athlete, or built like Arnold Schwarzenegger in his prime, your BMI will unfairly overestimate your body fat. For the rest of us, it is a pretty good gauge. An average-sized American woman, for example, is 5'4" tall and weighs 140 pounds. This gives her a BMI of 24, and although she may think she is too heavy, she is actually in the normal range.

Eating disorders

Anorexia nervosa is a potentially deadly condition in which a person loses weight to the point of becoming underweight, yet remains convinced that he or she is still overweight. People with anorexia have an intense fear of gaining weight even when they are severely underweight. Bulimia is a related eating disorder in which people overeat ("binge"), then purge by inducing vomiting or using laxatives. Both conditions are most common among young women. Eating disorders can cause osteoporosis, weakness from low potassium levels in the blood, dizziness, dry skin, irregular heartbeat, and even death. If you or someone you care about might have an eating disorder, please seek professional help. ■

Your next job is to measure your waist at the level of your iliac crest. This is the top of your pelvis and can be found by running your hands down your sides from your rib cage to the top of your hip bones. Do the measurement standing up, with the tape parallel to the floor. The tape should be snug, but not tight. Worrisome or high-risk measurements are:

> Men: greater than 40 inches.
> Women: greater than 35 inches.

Personal action plan: To help determine whether you have a weight problem, calculate your Body Mass Index (BMI) and measure your waist.

WHERE DO YOU STAND, WEIGHT-WISE?

Underweight (BMI 18 or less)

If you are underweight, you are in a distinct minority in this country. You are probably quite healthy, but read Chapter 2 on nutrition and vitamins to make sure you are eating enough healthy foods. Be sure to read the sidebar on eating disorders to see whether you should be concerned. If you have had *unexplained* weight loss, see your doctor for an evaluation.

Table 8.1 Body Mass Index (BMI) Table

BMI	19	20	21	22	23	24	25	26	27	28	29	30	31	32	33	34	35
Height (inches)								Body Weight (pounds)									
58	91	96	100	105	110	115	119	124	129	134	138	143	148	153	158	162	167
59	94	99	104	109	114	119	124	128	133	138	143	148	153	158	163	168	173
60	97	102	107	112	118	123	128	133	138	143	148	153	158	163	168	174	179
61	100	106	111	116	122	127	132	137	143	148	153	158	164	169	174	180	185
62	104	109	115	120	126	131	136	142	147	153	158	164	169	175	180	186	191
63	107	113	118	124	130	135	141	146	152	158	163	169	175	180	186	191	197
64	110	116	122	128	134	140	145	151	157	163	169	174	180	186	192	197	204
65	114	120	126	132	138	144	150	156	162	168	174	180	186	192	198	204	210
66	118	124	130	136	142	148	155	161	167	173	179	186	192	198	204	210	216
67	121	127	134	140	146	153	159	166	172	178	185	191	198	204	211	217	223
68	125	131	138	144	151	158	164	171	177	184	190	197	203	210	216	223	230
69	128	135	142	149	155	162	169	176	182	189	196	203	209	216	223	230	236
70	132	139	146	153	160	167	174	181	188	195	202	209	216	222	229	236	243
71	136	143	150	157	165	172	179	186	193	200	208	215	222	229	236	243	250
72	140	147	154	162	169	177	184	191	199	206	213	221	228	235	242	250	258
73	144	151	159	166	174	182	189	197	204	212	219	227	235	242	250	257	265
74	148	155	163	171	179	186	194	202	210	218	225	233	241	249	256	264	272
75	152	160	168	176	184	192	200	208	216	224	232	240	248	256	264	272	279
76	156	164	172	180	189	197	205	213	221	230	238	246	254	263	271	279	287

Table 8.1 Body Mass Index (BMI) Table (continued)

BMI	36	37	38	39	40	41	42	43	44	45	46	47	48	49	50	51	52	53	54
58	172	177	181	186	191	196	201	205	210	215	220	224	229	234	239	244	248	253	258
59	178	183	188	193	198	203	208	212	217	222	227	232	237	242	247	252	257	262	267
60	184	189	194	199	204	209	215	220	225	230	235	240	245	250	255	261	266	271	276
61	190	195	201	206	211	217	222	227	232	238	243	248	254	259	264	269	275	280	285
62	196	202	207	213	218	224	229	235	240	246	251	256	262	267	273	278	284	289	295
63	203	208	214	220	225	231	237	242	248	254	259	265	270	278	282	287	293	299	304
64	209	215	221	227	232	238	244	250	256	262	267	273	279	285	291	296	302	308	314
65	216	222	228	234	240	246	252	258	264	270	276	282	288	294	300	306	312	318	324
66	223	229	235	241	247	253	260	266	272	278	284	291	297	303	309	315	322	328	334
67	230	236	242	249	255	261	268	274	280	287	293	299	306	312	319	325	331	338	344
68	236	243	249	256	262	269	276	282	289	295	302	308	315	322	328	335	341	348	354
69	243	250	257	263	270	277	284	291	297	304	311	318	324	331	338	345	351	358	365
70	250	257	264	271	278	285	292	299	306	313	320	327	334	341	348	355	362	369	376
71	257	265	272	279	286	293	301	308	315	322	329	338	343	351	358	365	372	379	386
72	265	272	279	287	294	302	309	316	324	331	338	346	353	361	368	375	383	390	397
73	272	280	288	295	302	310	318	325	333	340	348	355	363	371	378	386	393	401	408
74	280	287	295	303	311	319	326	334	342	350	358	365	373	381	389	396	404	412	420
75	287	295	303	311	319	327	335	343	351	359	367	375	383	391	399	407	415	423	431
76	295	304	312	320	328	336	344	353	361	369	377	385	394	402	410	418	426	435	443

Source: U.S. Department of Health and Human Services NIH Publication No. 00-4084
Public Health Service October 2000
National Institutes of Health
National Heart, Lung, and Blood Institute

$$BMI = \frac{(wt. \text{ in pounds})(703)}{(ht. \text{ in inches})(ht. \text{ in inches})}$$

People who are not underweight should realize that thin individuals often are just as self-conscious about their weight as those who are heavy. I was a skinny kid, and I can tell you that jokes or thoughtless comments about being underweight are just as hurtful and inappropriate as those directed to the overweight.

Normal weight (BMI 19–24)

If your weight is in the normal range and has been fairly stable, congratulate yourself. Your unique combination of genes, diet, and exercise is obviously working. You can improve your odds of staying well by making healthy food choices, so please review Chapter 2 on nutrition and vitamins. If you're not happy with your body's shape, exercising to tone up is generally a better solution than dieting to lose weight.

Overweight (BMI 25–29)

If you are overweight, don't despair. You have lots of company, and you can certainly take steps to reduce your health risk. First, though, you should consider your waist measurement. If you carry too much weight around your belly (40 inches or more for men, greater than 35 inches for women), your health risk increases. You need some extra help and should follow recommendations for the obese group.

For those in the overweight group, losing weight is in theory the best way to lower health risk. Shedding pounds is easier for some than for others, however. If your weight gain has been recent, during the past year or so, you stand a good chance of getting the weight off and keeping it off. This is especially true for people who gain weight when they quit smoking, but also applies to those who find themselves overweight after a pregnancy or stressful event like a move or job change.

If this is your situation, set a goal to get back to what you weighed one year ago. Look at the weight-loss strategies that appear later in this chapter, review the nutrition information in Chapter 2, seek a support group like Weight Watchers, and go for it.

If your weight gain has been gradual over the years, medical evidence suggests you are not likely to lose a lot of weight and keep it off. Some experts attribute this bad news to the "fat-cell theory," which postulates that we are born with a set number of fat cells that get bigger when we store fat. If we store too much fat for too long, the cells divide and create more cells to store fat. Unfortunately, even with dieting, the new cells do not disappear. They get smaller, but retain their ability and tendency to store fat when we let them, and we usually do let them.

If you have become overweight gradually, but are not obese, focus on *stabilizing* rather than reducing your weight. Prevent more fat cells and future weight gain through a lifelong commitment to healthy lifestyle choices (see chapters 1 through 6). This strategy is much better for your body than going through multiple cycles of dieting to lose weight and then gaining it back. You should be screened for high blood pressure, high cholesterol, and diabetes on a regular basis, but remember that good medical treatment is available for each of those conditions.

Obese (BMI 30 or more)

Twenty-eight percent of men and 33 percent of women in America are obese.[1] In the past, a lot of effort was spent trying to "cure" obese people. Today, the medical community understands that obesity is a chronic condition that needs lifelong management and is rarely cured. As stated earlier, obesity is a serious risk to your health. On the plus side, however, obese people can greatly reduce their likelihood of health problems through a combination of good lifestyle choices and medical care.

For the obese, heart disease is the biggest health concern. The No. 1 priority, even at the risk of further weight gain, is to absolutely avoid smoking. Smoking combined with obesity is almost guaranteed to hasten coronary artery disease, which often leads to deadly heart attacks. High blood pressure, high cholesterol, and diabetes—which also contribute to heart disease—are very common with obesity, but quite treatable.

If you are obese, you should be checked for high blood pressure once a year. Your cholesterol and blood sugar should be checked every few years. In addition, you should follow screening recommendations for colon, breast, and prostate cancer.

I strongly recommend that you also establish a relationship with a good primary-care doctor (family physician or internist) and schedule a preventive visit at least once a year. Find someone who understands how difficult it is to lose weight and who will work with you to optimize your well-being. Read on for some helpful dos and don'ts if you struggle with weight. The "Getting Real With Weight Management" section is especially important for you.

Health tip: If you are obese based on your BMI—or overweight with a generous waistband (exceeding 40 inches for men or 35 inches for women)—please seek medical care to screen for potential health problems and discuss weight-control options.

THE TRUTH ABOUT TRIMMING DOWN

Fad diets and devices

When you hear about the latest miracle diet or quick-and-easy weight-loss device, remember the adage, "If it sounds too good to be true, it probably is." To lose weight, you have to burn more calories than you eat. There is no way around this core principle. You must eat less, exercise more, or some combination of the two if you want to lose weight.

Aspiring entrepreneurs have promoted an amazing array of weight-loss products over the years, including fat-burning wraps and creams, special suits designed to sweat away the pounds, electrical-stimulation devices, and appetite-suppressing glasses. If any of them worked as promised, we would not have a problem with weight in America.

Most health experts believe that weight-loss diets, if attempted, should contain a balanced mix of carbohydrates, proteins, and fats. Many fad diets promise they will "burn fat" faster by changing the mix or balance of these calorie sources. Some diets promise that you can eat as much as you want and still lose weight. Time for a reality check—such promises are simply not true.

Low carbohydrate diets

The very-low-carbohydrate Atkins Diet has become quite popular in recent years. On the Atkins Diet, the body enters a starvation state called "ketosis," in which it tries to burn fat for energy. A lot of the initial weight loss is due to water lost as the body gets rid of fat-breakdown products in the urine. Unfortunately, it is easier for the body to burn muscle than fat. Severely restricting carbohydrates thus forces the body to break down muscles and vital organs for its basic energy supply.

Another problem is the high amount of saturated fat in the Atkins Diet. Several of my patients had alarming increases in harmful LDL cholesterol levels after starting the Atkins Diet. In my experience, the majority of people who lose weight on Atkins or any rapid-weight-loss diet regain all of it over the next year.

More promising may be the South Beach Diet developed by cardiologist Arthur Agatston. It starts with a strict two-week low-carbohydrate phase, but promotes foods containing healthy fats rather than harmful saturated fats and trans fats. It gradually adds carbohydrate foods back in, but encourages healthier whole-grain, high-fiber, and low-glycemic index choices (see glycemic index sidebar 11.2 in the diabetes chapter). Early results from studies of people following South Beach have been encouraging: People lose weight on the diet, and it appears to have a healthy effect on their blood cholesterol levels. As we wait for further research, I believe the South Beach Diet is a reasonable option for overweight or obese people who want to try a "diet."

Sensible diet tips

Try modifying your diet by cutting down on "junk" foods that are low in nutrition but high in calories, i.e., non-diet soft drinks, chips, cookies, candy, etc. When you want a snack, reach for a piece of fruit, a small plate of vegetables dipped in low-calorie salad dressing, a small handful of whole-grain crackers, or a half-cup of low-fat cottage cheese with tomatoes or fruit added.

At mealtime, strive for a balance of protein (from lean meats, soy products or beans), fruit and vegetables (fresh or frozen are best), and whole grains (such as a serving of cous-cous or a slice of whole-wheat bread). Keep portions moderate, avoid rich sauces and fatty dressings, and use minimal amounts of oils (olive is best), margarine, and butter. A baked potato with a small amount of margarine is lower in calories and higher in fiber than a serving of buttery mashed potatoes. Baked or broiled meats are healthier than fried. If you're dying for seconds, focus on the low-calorie, low-fat vegetables.

Healthier fast-food choices are also available. Consider a tasty salad at Wendy's; a low-fat sandwich at the sub shop or deli; lean chicken or salmon and vegetables over rice or an Asian salad at a quick-Japanese restaurant. For additional advice on healthy eating, see Chapter 2. ■

Q *Health tip:* There is no free lunch. Fad diets and devices that sound too good to be true simply will not lead to permanent weight loss. The South Beach Diet, on the other hand, may be worth a try.

Magic Pills

Modern medicine has a long tradition of trying to cure afflictions with medications. As yet, however, there is no wonder drug for obesity. In fact, drug treatments intended to assist weight loss have been disappointing, to say the least. Stimulant medications, touted for their appetite-suppressing effect, are a fine example. For years, various types of stimulants have been prescribed or sold over-the-counter to obese people. Though stimulants can suppress appetite somewhat, weight loss with their use is generally modest and temporary. Even more discouraging, stimulants tend to be addictive and can have dangerous side effects, including high blood pressure or worse.

In the 1990s, the stimulants fenfluramine and phentermine, dubbed "fen-phen," were wildly popular in weight-loss programs. The FDA banned fen-phen from the market in 1997, after many users were diagnosed with damaged and leaky heart valves. Users of the stimulant dexfenfluramine (Redux) developed the same problems, and it also was removed from the market.

In 2000, the Food and Drug Administration ordered the stimulant phenylpropanolamine pulled from store shelves after reports that it caused bleeding strokes in women. Phenylpropanolamine was the active ingredient in many over-the-counter decongestants and appetite suppressants, such as Dexatrim.

Today, sibutramine is the only weight-loss stimulant still being sold. Available by prescription only, sibutramine can increase blood pressure but has few other side effects. Like the other stimulants, this one offers only modest results. In randomized trials, those who took sibutramine for one year lost an average of 9 pounds more than people who took a placebo.[6]

A different type of weight-loss drug, Orlistat, has problems of its own. Taken with meals, it prevents the absorption of about one-third of the fat in foods consumed. That might sound good, until you learn that the unabsorbed fat comes out the other end in the form of a rather soft, oily stool. In fact, the manufacturer warns of "anal leakage" as a possible side effect. Orlistat also has the potential to prevent fat-soluble vitamins from being absorbed in adequate amounts. In randomized trials, those taking Orlistat for one year lost an average of 6 pounds more than study participants who took a placebo.[6]

Looking at the evidence, it's clear there are no magic weight-loss pills. Medications that assist weight loss may have a role in treating select, high-risk, very obese people in medically supervised weight-loss programs. Otherwise, though, I feel they don't do much good, and I don't recommend them.

> ❄ *Key point:* Medications have been disappointing in the treatment of obesity. Many have been taken off the market due to safety concerns, and none has been proven to have long-term benefit.

Surgery

Liposuction is *not* a treatment for overweight and obesity. It can remove small amounts of overall body fat to improve body contours and self-image, but it is not a means to achieve weight loss. In the medical field, weight-loss surgery refers to operations that make stomach capacity smaller, commonly known as "stomach stapling" or "gastric bypass surgery." Sometimes the surgery bypasses part of the digestive track, as well.

Improved surgical techniques and care have made weight-loss surgery a reasonable option for select individuals with extreme obesity (BMI greater than 40) and obesity-related medical problems. This type of surgery has gained a lot of attention in recent years, following successful procedures on TV personality Al Roker and singer Carnie Wilson. But make no mistake, weight-loss surgery is not for everyone, and it is not risk-free: 1–4 percent of patients die of complications. After surgery, lifelong medical monitoring and vitamin supplementation is required. When successful, however, the surgery can result in significant long-term weight loss. It can also improve weight-related medical conditions such as diabetes and high blood pressure.

> ❄ *Key point:* Weight-loss surgery may be an option for extremely obese people with obesity-related medical problems who have been unable to lose weight through conventional weight-loss programs.

GETTING REAL WITH WEIGHT MANAGEMENT

Reasonable goals and expectations

If you are obese or significantly overweight as an adult, your chances of reducing to a "normal" weight and staying there are very slim. Anyone who tells you otherwise is either misinformed or dishonest. This is not cause for despair. Though you may never be slim, you can do a great deal to improve your overall health and fitness, and to decrease the possibility of serious illness. A positive life plan starts with a commitment to being the best you can be and to setting reasonable goals and expectations.

I have witnessed the tremendous health benefits of this approach in my own practice. My patient Lynn is a great example. When we first met, Lynn was 35 years old and 5'6" tall. She had been heavy since high school and weighed 242 pounds (BMI: 39). When Lynn had several infections that were slow to improve, I ordered a blood-sugar test and diagnosed Type 2 (adult onset) diabetes. Lynn also had high blood pressure, but she really wanted to avoid medication.

I told Lynn that moderate weight loss could make a difference. She met with a dietician and decided to make some changes she could live with. She cut down on junk foods and joined a gym. She committed to exercising five days a week. After six months, Lynn's weight had dropped to 220 pounds. She felt much stronger, had better energy, and was thrilled that her blood pressure and sugar levels had returned to normal. Over the years, Lynn has found 220 to be a healthy weight. The few times she has strayed from her diet and exercise regimen, her weight, blood sugar, and blood pressure have crept up and motivated her to get back on track.

Lynn's story teaches some important lessons. When obese individuals suffer from medical complications, 10–20 pounds of weight loss can greatly impact their health. Each person is different, of course, but setting modest and achievable goals encourages success. The evidence shows that drastic diets don't work; they merely cause weight to go down and up like a yo-yo. By contrast, a common-sense plan for healthier living can stabilize weight and improve health.

People often ask me what their "ideal" weight should be. The best and simplest definition I've heard comes from the staff of Canyon Ranch Health Resort near Tucson, Arizona: "Your ideal weight is your weight after a period of time when you eat as well as you can reasonably eat, and exercise as much as you can reasonably exercise."

Live a healthy lifestyle

If you are overweight or obese, please take to heart the advice on nutrition and exercise provided in chapters 2 and 3. Here are some simple steps that will put you on the right track:

- Eat a healthy breakfast (i.e., a bowl of oatmeal or other high-fiber, low-fat cereal with nonfat or low-fat milk).
- Eat five servings of fruit and vegetables each day.
- Focus on higher fiber foods (i.e., whole-wheat bread instead of white; cous-cous instead of rice; more beans, less meat; an apple in place of a candy bar).
- If you enjoy soft drinks, switch from regular (150 calories per 12 oz. serving, mostly sugar) to diet (0–1 calories per 12 oz., sugar-free). If all else stayed the same, but you eliminated one can of regular soda per day from your diet, you would lose 15 pounds over a one-year period.
- When it comes to alcohol, limit yourself to one or two drinks per day.
- Get some kind of exercise five days a week, even if it's just a stroll with the dog.
- If it will help motivate you to exercise, join a health club.
- Take stock of your stress level and find ways to reduce stress (i.e., deep breathing, meditation, exercising, a relaxing hobby). Lowering stress will make you feel better and help curb anxious eating.

- Schedule regular checkups with your family doctor, and don't ignore new symptoms that could signal a health problem.
- Take Canyon Ranch's advice: Eat as well as you can reasonably eat, and exercise as much as you can reasonably exercise for several months, then see where you're at and how you feel. You may be pleasantly surprised.

Key Point: If you are overweight or obese, healthy lifestyle choices regarding tobacco, nutrition, exercise, alcohol, and stress are especially crucial for your well-being.

Diet strategies that work

To achieve lasting weight loss, you must make a commitment to lifelong dietary and lifestyle changes. Here are some proven strategies:

- Set realistic goals. If you are obese and determined to embark on a weight-loss program, a good rule of thumb is to strive for a 10 percent weight loss. Evidence suggests that many people can lose 10 percent of their body weight in three to 12 months with programs that include calorie reduction, exercise, and behavioral support.[7]
- Don't starve yourself. The only way to lose weight is to burn more calories than you take in, and 3,500 calories equals 1 pound. Therefore, if you cut 500 calories per day from your current diet—a modest reduction for most people—you will lose 1 pound per week or about 25 pounds in six months. Losing weight at a faster rate *does not* yield a better long-term result.[7]
- Increase physical activity. Eating fewer calories combined with increasing physical activity works better for weight loss

than either calorie reduction or exercise alone.[7] The combination also works better for reducing dangerous abdominal fat. Review Chapter 3 to plan an effective and sustainable exercise program. Simply walking 20 minutes, three days a week is a great way to start.

- Write down what you eat each day. Researchers have found that dieters who keep the most careful food records lose the most weight.[8] Pam is a patient who prefers a computer program that combines a food record with a calorie count. The program includes charts that tell her how many calories are in various foods and how many calories she'll burn doing various activities based on her current weight. Pam lost 20 pounds many years ago, and attributes her success in staying trim to her religious dietary record keeping.

- Weigh yourself regularly. Regular weigh-ins provide strong motivation and instant feedback, both keys to losing weight and then maintaining. Pam weighs in first thing in the morning, at least once a week, and keeps a weight record.

- Join a weight-loss support group, such as Weight Watchers, that is founded on sound nutritional principles rather than the latest dieting fads. Both behavioral therapy and group support help with weight loss and maintenance of a healthier weight. Most communities offer weight-loss programs. Ask your doctor or a registered dietician for a recommendation in your area.

Key point: If you do decide to diet, setting achievable goals and keeping a written record of everything you eat will greatly increase your chances of success.

Changing community habits and perceptions

In 2001, Surgeon General David Satcher, M.D., Ph.D., pointed out that obesity in America is no longer strictly a personal matter; it has become a major public-health problem. School and community efforts are needed to help change the way Americans eat and exercise. Schools should offer physical education on a daily basis so children learn that exercising their bodies is as important as exercising their minds. School cafeterias should offer lower fat, healthier foods. Parental input and involvement can help make these things happen.

Communities can assist in the fight against fat by providing safe places for people to walk, skate, jog, or bike. Employees can request healthier food choices in workplace cafeterias, and employers can offer more on-site exercise programs or discounts to local health clubs. Employers should provide incentives that encourage employees to take advantage of such opportunities. After all, healthier employees are more productive and cheaper to insure.

Some people blame America's overweight epidemic on the fast-food and restaurant industries, but blame doesn't help. The truth is we don't have to buy their unhealthy food. And if we would demand and choose healthier items, it would lead to change. To some degree, we can already see that happening, as healthy-sandwich purveyor Subway soars in popularity and McDonald's retools its menu to offer healthier items.

Finally, the perception of obesity in American society needs to change so that the main concern is wellness, not thinness. Some of us are genetically predisposed to carry some excess weight and will never be thin. Such individuals, and our society as a whole, should accept this. Though the mass media might imply otherwise, you don't have to be thin to be an attractive member of society. You also don't have to be thin to be healthy. In fact, moderately overweight people who are physically active, eat sensibly, and avoid smoking can live long, healthy lives.

SUMMARY

America has experienced an alarming epidemic of obesity and diabetes over the past two decades. Excess fat, especially when it is concentrated around the waist, is bad for the heart and plays a role in as many as 300,000 preventable deaths each year. A simple calculation of your Body Mass Index (BMI) and your waist measurement will let you know where you stand from a health perspective. Unfortunately, dieting and medications have not been very successful in the treatment of overweight and obesity. Surgery is a viable treatment only for extremely obese people. Overweight and obese people should set realistic goals to stabilize or reduce their weight and control weight-related medical problems such as diabetes, high blood pressure, and high cholesterol. As a society, we need to recognize that obesity is a chronic medical condition. However, a healthier diet, an increase in physical activity, and even modest weight loss can greatly reduce health risks.

CHAPTER NINE

High Blood Pressure: Don't Blow a Gasket

"One in four U.S. adults has high blood pressure, but because there are no symptoms, nearly one-third of these people don't know they have it."
—American Heart Association

BABY BOOMERS BEWARE!

Should you worry?

My 48-year-old friend Rob is a little overweight, but he is very active and feels fine. Rob's only health problem is high blood pressure, and he asked me whether he really needs to take medication to lower it. Like most people with high blood pressure, or "hypertension," Rob has no symptoms whatsoever and no indication that the disease is doing any damage. Unfortunately, it probably is. I told Rob that if he lives with untreated high blood pressure over several years, he is much more likely to suffer a stroke, heart attack, arterial disease such as abdominal aneurism, or kidney damage. The higher the blood pressure, the greater the chance it will eventually cause serious problems.

Currently, 50 million Americans have high blood pressure, and many of them eventually will die or become disabled from complications of the disease. Though baby boomers have yet to hit their peak blood pressure years, hypertension already is their most common reason for visits to primary-care doctors. Should Rob consider medication and other measures to control his hypertension? Absolutely. Much can be done to prevent high blood pressure, and to treat it when it does occur.

....
Q *Health tip:* Get your blood pressure checked at least once a year, and read on to learn healthy ways to keep it down.
....

What is high blood pressure?

High blood pressure, medically known as hypertension, is a common condition diagnosed when blood pressure readings are too high over an extended period of time. "Blood pressure" refers to the pressure in the arteries as the heart pumps or pushes blood into them. For many years, a blood pressure reading of 120/80 (measured in millimeters of mercury) was considered normal. The 120, or upper number, is the *systolic* blood pressure. It reflects the highest pressure in the arteries, which occurs when the heart is forcefully contracting. The 80, or lower number, is the *diastolic* blood pressure. It represents the lowest pressure in the arteries, which occurs when the heart relaxes between beats to refill with blood.

High blood pressure is defined as systolic pressures *consistently* greater than 140, and/or diastolic pressures *consistently* greater than 90. Hypertension is usually diagnosed after high readings are recorded on at least three different occasions. Hypertension is also classified based on its severity (see table 9.1).

In 2003, a panel of experts coined the term "prehypertension" for people with a systolic blood pressure between 120 and 139, or a diastolic pressure between 80 and 89.[1] Prehypertension indicates that the blood pressure is higher than ideal, but not high enough to require medication. This new classification recognizes that a person with a systolic blood pressure between 120 and 139 has a slightly higher risk of heart disease and stroke than a person with a systolic blood pressure below 120. If you have prehypertension, be sure to follow the advice in the section on "preventing high blood pressure".

Table 9.1: High blood pressure classifications for adults

Category	Systolic	Diastolic
Normal:	< 120	< 80
Prehypertension:	120–139	80–89
Stage 1 hypertension	140–159	90–99
Stage 2 hypertension	≥160	≥100

Note: Classification is based on readings when people are not taking blood pressure medications. If the systolic and diastolic pressures fall into different categories, the more severe category applies (i.e. 170/90 is stage 2 high blood pressure).

Bane for baby boomers

An eye-opening report in 2002 estimated that *90 percent* of middle-aged and older Americans eventually will develop high blood pressure.[2] This research, part of the ongoing Framingham Heart Study, reported on 1,300 people who had normal blood pressure and were between ages 55 and 65 at the start of the study. After 20 years, fully 90 percent had developed hypertension.

This storm cloud did, however, have a silver lining. Most cases of high blood pressure in this Framingham group were mild (stage 1), making them easier to treat and less harmful than severe cases. The lifetime risk of developing stage 2 high blood pressure actually was lower among the Framingham participants than among people in earlier studies. Current efforts to treat high blood pressure apparently have been successful in preventing more severe cases. Nonetheless high blood pressure will clearly be a huge issue for aging baby boomers.

> ❧❧ *Key point:* High blood pressure is likely to affect 90
> ❧❧ percent of all baby boomers at some time during
> their life.

Systolic hypertension

In recent years, research findings have brought about an important shift in the way physicians view different types of high blood pressure. Not long ago, doctors were most concerned about *diastolic* pressure, the lower number. As it turns out, mild elevations of the lower number (up to 90 or so) are not as harmful as once believed. *Systolic* pressure, the upper number, appears much more important for health, especially for people over the age of 50. A long-term study of French men found that those with a systolic pressure above 160 had twice the death rates from heart disease as those with systolic pressures less than 140. High diastolic readings did not increase risk at all in the study group.[3]

For decades, doctors did not worry much when only the upper number was elevated, a condition known as "isolated systolic hypertension." We now know that high systolic pressure is a significant risk factor for strokes and heart attacks, and that there is benefit to treating it.[4] As people age, isolated elevation of systolic blood pressure is by far the most common type of high blood pressure. This is because arteries in the body stiffen as they get older. With less give, pressure in the arteries is higher when the heart pumps (the systolic pressure), but drops promptly to normal when the heart relaxes (diastolic pressure).

> ❧❧ *Key point:* For most people, the upper or systolic
> ❧❧ blood pressure is the one to watch. Levels less than
> 130 are fine, while levels consistently above 140 should be
> treated with medication.

PREVENTING HIGH BLOOD PRESSURE

What puts people at risk for high blood pressure?

As with most medical conditions, genetic risk factors for high blood pressure cannot be changed. Hypertension runs in some families, and is especially common among African-Americans. Many other risk factors, however, are lifestyle related and can be modified. These include:

- Overweight and obesity
- Lack of physical activity
- Eating too much salt (for people who are salt sensitive)
- Lack of calcium or potassium in the diet
- Excess alcohol consumption
- Too much stress
- Smoking (which also greatly increases the risk of heart disease among people who have hypertension)

Healthy lifestyle choices are the first line of prevention against high blood pressure.

> ✴ *Key point:* Lack of exercise, overweight, stress, and excess alcohol are the controllable risk factors that contribute most to high blood pressure.

Diet

What do fruit and vegetables have to do with blood pressure? Quite a lot, it turns out. Recently, researchers at Oxford University in England randomly assigned 700 adults to either their usual diets, or to a diet that included at least five servings of fruit and vegetables each day. During the six-month trial, blood levels of antioxidants like vitamin C and beta-carotene were higher in the fruit and veggie group, and their systolic blood pressure fell by an average of four points (mm Hg).[5] While four points may not sound impressive, powerful drugs approved for treating hypertension lower systolic blood pressure an average of only five to 10 points in clinical trials.

Dietary approaches to stop hypertension (DASH)

The "DASH" diet has been promoted by the National Heart, Lung, and Blood Institute as the best way to eat to prevent or help treat high blood pressure. DASH recommends:

- 4–5 servings of fruit *and* 4–5 servings of vegetables each day. (A serving equals a medium-sized peach or apple; ½ cup of cooked vegetables; or ½ cup of fresh or canned fruit.)
- 6–8 grain servings per day. (A serving equals 1 piece of bread, 1 oz. dry cereal, or ½ cup cooked rice or pasta)
- 2–3 dairy servings per day. (A serving equals 8 oz. of milk, 1 cup of yogurt, or 1½ oz. of cheese)
- No more than two, 3 oz. servings (about the size of a deck of cards) of meat, poultry, or fish per day.
- No more than three servings per day of fats and oils. (A serving equals 1 tsp. margarine, 1 Tbsp. mayonnaise, or 2 Tbsp. dressing)
- No more than 4–5 servings per week of nuts, beans, and seeds. (A serving equals ½ cup cooked dry beans, ⅓ cup nuts, or 2 Tbsp. seeds)
- No more than five servings of sweets each week. (A serving equals 1 Tbsp. sugar or jam, or ½ oz. candy)

People who limit their salt use and follow the DASH diet are almost certain to achieve lower blood pressure. The DASH diet is not for everyone, however. High in carbohydrates, it is not suitable for diabetics. ∎

Researchers believe the potassium contained in fruits and vegetables has a blood pressure-lowering effect because it counteracts the blood pressure-raising tendency of salt (sodium). Foods full of potassium include bananas, oranges, cantaloupe, melons, tomatoes, potatoes, avocados, and beans.

Calcium and magnesium also help prevent high blood pressure. Dairy products are the richest sources of calcium. Lots of magnesium can be found in whole grains, nuts, tofu, spinach, wild rice, and brown rice.

> ❧❧ *Key point:* To prevent or help treat high blood pressure, eat foods low in salt and fat, and high in potassium, calcium, and magnesium.

Q *Health tip:* Eating five servings of fruit or vegetables per day has been promoted for cancer prevention, but will also help to lower blood pressure.

Exercise

Whether you are overweight, normal weight, mildly hypertensive, or moderately hypertensive, regular, moderate exercise is one of the best ways to lower blood pressure. Exercise can eliminate the need for medication in people with mild high blood pressure; it can also help medication work more effectively in those who do need it.

Interestingly, systolic blood pressure actually increases during vigorous exercise. In an exercise treadmill test, for example, systolic pressure is expected to rise—often as high as 160, 180, or above. With rest, though, the pressure should quickly return to normal. As fitness improves, average blood pressure readings drop. Several studies have found that systolic pressure drops by an average of four points (mm Hg) when sedentary people start a regular, moderate exercise program.[6]

Q *Health tip:* Regular, moderate physical activity is a great way to lower blood pressure.

Alcohol

Although light-to-moderate alcohol consumption is healthy for the heart, heavy intake is harmful. One way in which heavy drinking hurts health is by raising blood pressure. People who consume three or more drinks per day have average increases in systolic pressure of six to 10 points (mm Hg); the more they drink, the higher their blood pressure climbs. Heavy drinking also makes blood pressure-lowering medications less effective. The medications simply don't work as well when the body is awash in alcohol. On the plus side, any blood pressure elevation caused by alcohol goes away within a few weeks of abstaining.

Remember Dale from Chapter 5? His story is a great example of how alcohol can impact blood pressure. Dale is the executive whose high blood pressure seemed impossible to control with medication. Unbeknownst to me, he was having a couple of stiff drinks every night before bed. When Dale quit drinking, his blood pressure returned to normal.

> ⚡⚡ *Key point:* Limit alcohol to one or two drinks per
> ⚡⚡ day to help maintain a healthy blood pressure.

Stress

Stress is often overlooked as a cause of high blood pressure. I learned this lesson from my medical school buddy, Bob. Bob had always had very low blood pressure, and was surprised when his readings went up during his internship. They remained mildly high for the whole year, a stressful stint at a busy county hospital. When Bob settled into a less stressful residency program at a community hospital, his blood pressure quickly returned to normal.

Bob's story shows how outside stress can trigger high blood pressure. It also teaches that blood pressure is dynamic and changing for each individual. By using self-relaxation techniques, people often are able to lower their blood pressure. Reducing stress can be an important step in managing high blood pressure.

> ○ *Health tip:* If your blood pressure readings have
> gone up, review Chapter 4 on stress and try some of
> the stress-reduction techniques.

> ⋀⋀ *Personal action plan:* To prevent high blood pres-
> sure or to help control it, eat plenty of fruit and veg-
> etables, be physically active, drink in moderation, and
> don't let stress get the best of you.

TREATMENT OF HIGH BLOOD PRESSURE

When do you need treatment?

The higher your blood pressure, the more urgently it needs to be treated to prevent problems. People with very severe hypertension (greater than 210/120)—which is quite rare—need to be treated immediately in the hospital to prevent complications or even death. Those with severe hypertension (greater than 180/110) need medication urgently, but can usually be treated as outpatients with close monitoring.

Fortunately, the great majority of people with high blood pressure fall into the mild or moderate categories. They have much more time to try lifestyle modifications and to measure blood pressure over several weeks or months to see what it's doing. When to start medication and which one(s) to try are complex decisions that should be sorted out with a good personal physician. Following are some pointers that can help in the determination process:

- Blood pressure should be measured on at least three different occasions, a couple of days apart, to evaluate mild to moderate hypertension.
- Medication is usually recommended when blood pressure remains elevated on three different occasions despite lifestyle efforts to lower it.
- The old rule, "once on medication always on medication," no longer applies. With careful monitoring, people on medication for hypertension often can be taken off medication when lifestyle changes aimed at lowering blood pressure have been successful.
- A home blood pressure cuff is a great tool for helping decide whether treatment is needed, and for monitoring how medication is working (see sidebar on home cuffs).

Number needed to treat (NNT)

If you have hypertension or any medical condition, it's nice to know how much benefit a proposed treatment will provide. For many years, medical studies have reported benefit in terms of "reduced risk." For example, your risk of a stroke might be reduced by 25 percent if you take a blood pressure medicine for the next five years. Unfortunately, it's hard to understand what that actually means. How likely are you to have a stroke if you don't take the medicine? What if your risk is only four in a thousand? Would you take medicine to lower your risk to three in a thousand?

A newer and more useful tool is the "number needed to treat" (NNT). NNT is a statistical way to help make sense out of treatment decisions. It tells how many people need to be treated over a period of time to prevent complications related to a medical condition. Treatment of hypertension provides a good example: If you have severe or very severe hypertension, the NNT is 3 to prevent death, stroke, or a heart attack over a five-year period. In other words, *for every three people who are treated, one really bad complication is prevented.*

In medicine, that is about as good as it gets, and is a very strong reason to treat severe hypertension. In contrast, the NNT for people with mild hypertension, but no other risk factors, is 128. In other words, *for every 128 people treated, one really bad complication is prevented.* Treatment is still beneficial for people with mild high blood pressure, but nowhere near as beneficial as for people with severe hypertension. ■

"White-coat" hypertension

Many people have high blood pressure readings while in the doctor's office, but normal readings while relaxing at home. This so-called "white-coat" hypertension is a dilemma for both doctors and their affected patients. Should people with white-coat hypertension be treated as though they truly have high blood pressure or reassured that they are all right? The answer that has emerged in recent years is somewhere in between.

People with white-coat hypertension seem to react to stressful situations with bigger increases in blood pressure than most folks. They are more likely in the long run to develop true hypertension, but it is unclear whether medication is helpful in reducing their

Home blood pressure cuffs

When Daniel Bernoulli discovered blood pressure in the 1700s, the only way to measure it was to stick a sharp glass tube directly into an artery. We've come a long way baby! Accurate, inexpensive, automatic blood pressure cuffs are now widely available to the public. Like computers, they have gotten better and less expensive over time.

Unfortunately, blood pressure monitors that attach to a finger or wrist do not give reliable readings. Arm cuffs work best. The easiest to use are electronic models with a cuff that wraps snugly around the upper arm. Then all you have to do is push a single button to automatically inflate the cuff and measure the blood pressure.

Omron makes high-quality electronic cuffs sold both as Omron and as store brands for stores like Target. Priced at $50–$90, a home cuff is a great investment for anybody with borderline or high blood pressure. For accurate readings, the cuff must be the right size and positioned properly. I recommend bringing a new cuff to your doctor's office to be sure you are using it correctly. ■

overall risk of strokes and heart problems. Until more is known, people with white-coat hypertension should adopt healthy lifestyle patterns, check their blood pressure periodically both at home and in the doctor's office, and discuss treatment options with their doctor.

What medication is right for you?

Though there are dozens of blood pressure medications on the market, they all come from only a few distinct *classes* of drugs: diuretics, beta blockers, ACE inhibitors, ARBs, calcium channel blockers, and alpha blockers. For the most part, the medications in each drug class have similar side effects and similar benefits (or lack of benefits). The best medications not only lower blood pressure, but also help prevent deadly complications like strokes and heart attacks. Most people with high blood pressure feel just fine, so the ideal drugs are those proven to prevent bad outcomes without causing too many side effects.

If you need blood pressure medication, it may take some trial and error to determine which drug class or combination of drug classes is right for you. Chances are good that it will take two or more different drugs to control your blood pressure. Read on to learn some of the pros and cons of the different classes.

Preferred drug classes

These drugs have the best evidence of improving outcomes in people with high blood pressure:

Diuretics, old-fashioned water pills, are very effective drugs for hypertension, and they make all the other drugs work better when used in combination. Diuretics help flush sodium (salt) out of the circulatory system so that there is less fluid (pressure) and the arteries are more relaxed. Diuretics consistently have been shown to prevent strokes among patients with high blood pressure. They are also the preferred drug class for older people with isolated systolic (upper number) hypertension. Very inexpensive generic diuretics are widely available and have few side effects when used in low doses.

Over the years, we have learned that low doses work well to lower blood pressure, while causing much less urination and loss of potassium than older, higher-dose regimens. When I started practicing medicine in the 1980s, for example, hydrochlorothiazide (HCTZ) was commonly prescribed at 50 to 100 mg per day. We now prescribe 12.5 to 25 mg per day with great results. Other diuretics used for blood pressure control include chlorothiazide, chlorthalidone, and indapamide.

Beta blockers slow the heart and make it beat less forcefully. This drops blood pressure and eases strain on the heart. Like diuretics, beta blockers have been proven to prevent deadly complications in people with high blood pressure. In those who have already had a heart attack, beta blockers can prevent new heart attacks and deaths. Beta blockers also help to prevent migraine headaches and control shaky hands in people with performance anxiety or tremors. These drugs can cause fatigue, especially among vigorous exercisers, and are not recommended for people with severe asthma or emphysema. Inexpensive generic forms are available. Beta blockers include atenolol, metoprolol, propranolol, nadolol, and other drugs that end in "...lol".

ACE inhibitors, technically called angiotensin-converting enzyme inhibitors, work through the kidneys to prevent a substance called angiotensin from forming. This relaxes blood vessels and makes pressure go down. ACE inhibitors are the first-choice blood pressure drugs for people with diabetes because they help prevent kidney damage. They also help prevent heart failure in individuals with coronary-artery disease. Users of ACE inhibitors often complain of a nagging cough, an annoying but not serious side effect. Availability of generic ACE inhibitors has dropped the cost of this class of drugs into the moderate price range (less than $1 a day). ACE inhibitors include captopril, enalapril, lisinopril, moexipril, quinapril, ramipril, and other medications that end in "...pril".

ARBs (angiotensin receptor blockers) are newer generation drugs similar to ACE inhibitors. Rather than blocking the formation of angiotensin, ARBs prevent it from working on blood vessels. The result is the same: relaxed vessels and lower blood pressure. But ARBs have one big advantage over ACE inhibitors: they don't stimulate a nagging cough. ARBs are relatively new and have yet to be studied as thoroughly as older drug classes, but so far they appear to have benefits similar to those of ACE inhibitors for diabetics and people with coronary artery disease. One study even suggested ARBs might provide greater stroke reduction and diabetes prevention than beta blockers.[7] As yet, there are no generic ARBs and prices remain moderately expensive ($1–$2 per day). ARBs include losartan, irbesartan, valsartan, and other drugs that end in "...sartan".

Alternative choices

These drugs have less evidence of improved outcomes for people with high blood pressure:

Calcium channel blockers prevent calcium from getting into muscle cells of the heart and blood vessels, causing the arteries to relax and blood pressure to go down. Different calcium channel blockers have different side-effect profiles. Verapamil and diltiazem tend to slow things down—particularly the heart (which can help with some rapid heartbeat conditions) and the bowels (which can lead to constipation). Nifedipine, amlodipine, felodipine, and the others that end in "…dipine" are stronger dilators of blood vessels. They may help with poor circulation and some types of angina, but are more likely to cause swollen feet from dilated leg vessels. Calcium channel blockers are quite effective at lowering blood pressure, especially isolated systolic hypertension. Unfortunately, some evidence suggests that heart attack rates may be higher among users of calcium channel blockers than among those who use diuretics, beta blockers, or ACE inhibitors. Calcium channel blockers are useful second-line drugs for high blood pressure.

Alpha blockers act through the nervous system to relax blood vessels and reduce blood pressure. They also relax the urinary-tract sphincter, which is a great help for men who have trouble urinating due to an enlarged prostate gland. The most worrisome side effect is a tendency toward fainting, especially after the first dose. Alpha blockers include prazosin, terazosin, and doxazosin. Unfortunately, there is not much evidence that they reduce the serious complications of high blood pressure. Alpha blockers are probably best used in men with prostate symptoms.

> *Key point:* Diuretics, beta blockers, and ACE inhibitors have a great track record and solid scientific evidence to support their use as first-line drugs for the treatment of high blood pressure.

SUMMARY

High blood pressure currently affects 50 million Americans and is the most common reason for visits to primary-care doctors. Up to 90 percent of all baby boomers, who have yet to reach their peak blood pressure years, will face the disease at some time during their life. Fortunately, most will have only mild hypertension, and lifestyle choices such as regular physical activity, moderation of alcohol use, and a diet loaded with fruit and vegetables can help to control it. We now know that high systolic (upper) pressure is more of a concern than high diastolic (lower) pressure, especially for people over age 50. Home blood pressure monitoring will play an ever-increasing role in the treatment of high blood pressure. When medication is needed, the diuretics, beta blockers, and ACE inhibitors have the best track record for preventing complications from strokes and heart disease.

CHAPTER TEN

Cholesterol: Friend or Foe?

"Life expectancy would grow by leaps and bounds if green vegetables smelled as good as bacon."
—Doug Larson

CHOLESTEROL CONFUSION

June is 74 years old and quite healthy, but she tells me she's worried that her cholesterol is too high. When checked, her total cholesterol is 242 mg/dL, but her LDL cholesterol is 128 mg/dL, HDL cholesterol is 86 mg/dL, and triglycerides are 140 mg/dL. I tell June that she has nothing at all to worry about; she will probably live as long as her 98-year-old mother.

Joe, on the other hand, always thought his cholesterol was good and can't understand why he had a heart attack at age 57. When checked, his total cholesterol is 190 mg/dL, but his LDL cholesterol is 140 mg/dL, HDL cholesterol is 25 mg/dL, and triglycerides are 125 mg/dL. I tell Joe that he needs cholesterol-lowering medication right away.

Sound confusing? How come some people with "high" cholesterol like June's are okay, while others with "normal" cholesterol like Joe's need treatment? It's a little complicated, but if you read on, you will learn about the types of cholesterol and how to make sense of your own cholesterol numbers in light of your risk factors for heart disease.

Cholesterol in context

Implicated as a main cause of heart disease, cholesterol has gotten a tremendous amount of attention over the past couple of decades. Huge efforts have been mounted to increase cholesterol screening and improve treatment. To keep things in perspective, however, it's important to remember that high cholesterol is not a disease. Rather, it is one of many risk factors for developing heart disease, like smoking, high blood pressure, obesity, or an inactive lifestyle. When and how to treat abnormal cholesterol levels is greatly affected by a person's other risk factors. New treatment guidelines take this into account in helping doctor's determine which patients need to worry about their cholesterol, and which ones don't.

What is cholesterol anyway?

Cholesterol is a fatty chemical that plays a vital role in the human body. Cholesterol's main job is to carry fat through the bloodstream to help supply and store fuel for energy. A small amount of the body's cholesterol comes from eating high-cholesterol foods like eggs, but the majority is actually made by the liver. Genetics determine the level and types of cholesterol in a person's blood to some degree, but diet and exercise play significant roles as well. When you eat a lot of saturated, hydrogenated, and partially hydrogenated fats, for example, your body has to transport and store that fat, and prompts your liver to make more fat-moving cholesterol units. Conversely, when you increase your exercise and burn more fat, your liver makes less cholesterol.

Fats in your blood: the bad, the good, and the ugly

Most people have heard of "bad" cholesterol and "good" cholesterol, but there really are three distinct types of fats, or "lipids," that can be measured in your blood.

LDL cholesterol, the so-called bad cholesterol, is low-density lipoprotein. LDL cholesterol can be thought of as fat-moving units that take fat around the body to storage areas like the hips, thighs, and belly. Unfortunately, some of this fat sticks to the walls of arteries that LDL-rich blood flows through. The higher the LDL, the more fat builds up in the arteries. Called "atherosclerosis," this build up of fatty, cholesterol-filled deposits is like sludge in a pipe and can eventually restrict or block blood flow. Atherosclerosis can lead to heart attacks, strokes, and poor circulation to the legs.

HDL cholesterol, also known as good cholesterol, is high-density lipoprotein. Whereas LDL *deposits* surplus fat around the body, HDL *removes* fat from storage areas so that it can be used by the body as energy. Like catfish cleaning the bottom of a pond, HDL cholesterol units also help remove the fatty streaks from the walls of arteries. In fact, healthy amounts of HDL cholesterol largely neutralize the harmful effects of LDL cholesterol. The more HDL in your bloodstream, the better off you are.

Triglycerides are the third type of fat commonly measured in a "lipid profile" blood test. Although not as dangerous as high LDL levels, high triglyceride levels do increase a person's risk of heart disease. Very high levels can trigger an inflammation of the pancreas known as "pancreatitis." Triglycerides can be high due to genetic tendency, but are also elevated with diabetes, heavy alcohol drinking, fatty diets, and a lack of exercise.

> *Health tip:* All adults should have a fasting lipid profile to screen for high-risk cholesterol levels. If the results are good, the test should be repeated in five years.

Apolipoproteins

In the bloodstream, LDL and HDL cholesterol and the other fats (or lipids) are actually transported in larger, more complicated units known as apolipoproteins. Apolipoproteins are units of fat combined with special proteins. There are several classes of apolipoproteins—Apo A, Apo B, Apo C, and Apo E—and different subtypes in each class. Currently, researchers are studying the health effects of different levels and types of these apolipoproteins. Most healthy HDL cholesterol in the blood is contained in Apo A-1, and most harmful LDL cholesterol is found in Apo B. Apo E-2 is healthy, but Apo E-4 may be harmful. In the future, as we learn more about apolipoproteins, we may measure them instead of lipids to gain a more complete understanding of fats in the blood. For now, however, the traditional lipid profile is still our best tool for measuring fats in the blood. ∎

The lipid profile

A lipid profile is a blood test that measures certain fats, or "lipids," in your blood. The test should be done after 12 hours of fasting. You can drink water or black coffee and take your usual medications during fasting without affecting test results. In a typical lipid profile, four numbers are reported:

- Total cholesterol
- LDL cholesterol
- HDL cholesterol
- Triglycerides

If triglyceride levels are very high (greater than 400 mg/dL), it interferes with the calculation of the LDL cholesterol level, so no LDL level will be reported.

> ↘↙ *Key point:* Cholesterol is a fatty chemical that helps
> ↗↖ store and supply energy to the body. Most cholesterol is made in the liver. Low-density lipoprotein, or LDL cholesterol, contributes to fatty buildup in the arteries (atherosclerosis). High-density lipoprotein, or HDL cholesterol, helps clean the fat out of the arteries.

WHAT DO THE NUMBERS MEAN?

Forget about total cholesterol

Remember June and Joe? June was advised not to worry despite total cholesterol of 242, while Joe was told he needs medication with total cholesterol of 190. This is puzzling until you understand that total cholesterol doesn't tell the whole story. Total cholesterol is made up of both harmful LDL cholesterol and healthy HDL cholesterol. *It is your levels of HDL and LDL, and not your total cholesterol, that determine whether your cholesterol is cause for concern.* People with lots of healthy HDL cholesterol usually don't need to worry, even if they have high total cholesterol. In contrast, people with lower total cholesterol but very little HDL should be concerned. Triglycerides above 200 are also a warning sign. So forget about the total cholesterol, and look at your LDL, HDL, and triglyceride levels.

A comparison of June and Joe's lipid profiles explains why the two received very different recommendations:

	June	Joe
Total cholesterol	242	190
LDL cholesterol	128	140
HDL cholesterol	86	25
Triglycerides	140	125

June has lots and lots of healthy HDL (see table 10.1), and fairly low levels of potentially harmful LDL and triglycerides. Because of the protective effect of HDL, she really has little to worry about, and this would be true even if her LDL was quite a bit higher.

Joe, on the other hand, has very little protective HDL. Thus, even his mildly high LDL is concerning. Since Joe had a recent heart attack, evidence that he already suffers from heart disease, I'd like to see his LDL level below 100 mg/dL.

As you can see from June and Joe's examples, total cholesterol is not very helpful and can even be misleading in determining whether someone has cholesterol trouble. To get the full story, it is crucial to look at how much harmful LDL is present, compared with the amount of helpful HDL, followed by a quick peek to be sure triglycerides are not out of control.

Table 10.1: Lipid levels: Where do you stand?

Lipid category	What the number means
Total Cholesterol:	Ignore it!
LDL cholesterol:	(The lower the better)
< 100 mg/dL	Perfect! Goal for people with heart disease or diabetes.
100–129 mg/dL	Healthy. Great goal for most people.
130–159 mg/dL	So-so. Okay if you have fewer than two risk factors.
> 160 mg/dL	Not good. Needs attention.
HDL cholesterol:	(The higher the better)
< 35 mg/dL	Very low.
36–40 mg/dL	Lower than it should be.
> 40 mg/dl	Healthy goal for men.
> 50 mg/dL	Healthy goal for women.
> 60 mg/dL	Fantastic! Considered protective against heart disease.
Triglycerides: (Lower is better, but less important than LDL)	
< 150 mg/dL	Perfect!
150–199 mg/dL	Not bad.
200–399 mg/dL	High.
> 400 mg/dL	Very high. Lab cannot calculate your LDL level. Definitely needs attention.

✋ *Personal action plan:* Get a copy of your most recent lipid profile. If it's been more than five years since your last profile or you've never had lipids checked, ask for a new test. Once you have your results, ignore the total cholesterol number, but take a careful look at your LDL, HDL, and triglyceride levels. Now see where you stand based on table 10.1.

Do you need treatment?

Table 10.1 should help you determine whether your current cholesterol levels are healthy, worrisome, or somewhere in between. If all of your numbers are excellent, congratulations, but if not, you might need lifestyle changes or medication to improve your numbers. This depends largely on your LDL cholesterol level and number of cardiac risk factors. High LDL cholesterol is the biggest risk factor for heart disease, and lowering LDL prevents heart attacks.[1] The big question is how low is good enough?

In 2001, the National Cholesterol Education Program (NCEP) came out with new guidelines that help clarify who needs LDL-lowering treatment and what the goals of treatment should be.[2] (The NCEP is a group of experts convened by the National Institutes of Health.) The NCEP recommendations vary dramatically depending on a person's cardiac risk factors. For example, the group advises aggressive treatment of even mildly elevated LDL cholesterol levels (greater than 100 mg/dL) in people at greatest risk of dying from heart disease—such as diabetics and individuals like Joe who already have heart disease (indicated by previous heart attacks, bypass surgery, or coronary artery stents). For those like June who have few risk factors, however, treatment is not necessary unless LDL rises above 160 mg/dL.

Of course, each person's situation is different. To figure out whether you need lifestyle changes or medication to control your cholesterol, proceed through the following steps:

1) Add up your cardiac risk factors. Table 10.2 lists the commonly accepted risk factors for heart disease. Count how many apply to you, and subtract one if your HDL cholesterol is greater than 60 mg/dL:_____.

Table 10.2: Risk factors for heart disease
- Smoking
- High blood pressure (or taking blood pressure medication)
- Age > 45 for men or > 55 for women
- Family history of early heart disease (father or brother < age 55; mother or sister < age 65)
- Low HDL cholesterol level (< 40 mg/dL)
- BONUS: high HDL cholesterol level > 60 mg/dL lets you *subtract* one from your total number of risk factors!

2) Use table 10.3 to determine whether your risk of developing heart disease is low, medium, or high based on your number of cardiac risk factors. If you have zero or one cardiac risk factor, you are considered low-risk. If you have two cardiac risk factors, you are medium-risk; and if you have three or more you are generally considered high-risk. People with diabetes or a history of heart disease (prior heart attack, angina, coronary artery stent or bypass) are always considered high-risk.

Table 10.3: LDL cholesterol goals based on cardiac risk factors and 10-yr risk

Risk factors	RISK GROUP	LDL goal	High: Try diet, exercise	Too high: Consider drug therapy
0 or 1 risk factors	LOW	<160 mg/dL	160–189 mg/dL	> 190 mg/dL
2 risk factors	MEDIUM	<130 mg/dL	130–159 mg/dL	> 160 mg/dL
3 to 5 risk factors, heart disease or diabetes	HIGH	<100 mg/dL	100–129 mg/dL	> 130 mg/dL

3) Knowing your risk group and current LDL cholesterol level, use table 10.3 again to find out whether your LDL meets the goal for preventing heart disease, or whether you need to try diet and exercise or drug therapy to bring it into the recommended range. Back to the earlier examples, June is in the low-risk group because she has no cardiac risk factors. Thus, her LDL of 128 is quite acceptable. Joe, on the other hand, is in the high-risk group because of his heart attack, so his LDL of 140 needs medication.

✋ *Personal action plan:* Figure whether you are at low, medium, or high risk for developing heart disease and use table 10.3 to see how your LDL cholesterol level measures up.

Goals of treatment

When cholesterol treatment is recommended, the main goal is to lower *LDL cholesterol* into the healthy ranges described in table 10.3. Studies have proved that lowering LDL prevents heart attacks and saves lives in high-risk individuals.[3,4] Thus the lifestyle changes and medications described further on are aimed primarily at reducing LDL.

Though lowering LDL cholesterol is the top priority of treatment, high or very high *triglyceride* levels should not be ignored. High triglycerides contribute to heart disease and can cause pancreatitis, both good reasons to attempt to control them. If your triglyceride level is higher than 200 mg/dL, eat a lower-fat diet and begin regular exercise (or exercise more often) to try to bring the number down. People at high cardiac risk should be especially aggressive in their efforts. Poorly controlled diabetes and heavy drinking are two significant and treatable causes of high triglycerides. If you are diabetic, take steps to bring your blood sugar under control. If you're a heavy drinker, reduce alcohol consumption to one or two drinks per day (or none at all).

Finally, since we know that good *HDL cholesterol* can neutralize bad LDL cholesterol, you might be wondering why the NCEP treatment guidelines don't focus more on *increasing* HDL cholesterol in high-risk people. This is indeed a noble goal, but it can be hard to achieve. People who successfully lower their triglycerides through lifestyle changes (i.e., a healthier diet and more exercise) will often see an increase in HDL cholesterol.

Unfortunately, in people with low HDL cholesterol and normal triglycerides (isolated low HDL), it is very difficult to increase the HDL level. One exception is in people who smoke. *Simply quitting smoking can increase HDL levels by 30 percent.* Weight loss and exercise also help. Medications are not very effective in raising isolated low HDL, but they can help lower LDL in order to improve the ratio of harmful LDL to healthy HDL.

> *Key point:* A major goal of cholesterol treatment is the aggressive reduction of LDL cholesterol in people at high cardiac risk, especially those who already have heart disease or diabetes. Efforts to lower triglycerides and raise HDL cholesterol can also be beneficial.

BETTER LIPIDS THROUGH HEALTHY LIVING

A matter of TLC

Medications and lifestyle changes are the two main ways to lower harmful LDL cholesterol levels. In addressing lifestyle, the NCEP guidelines coined a new acronym, *TLC*, which stands for *Therapeutic Lifestyle Change*. As you would expect, TLC includes a healthy diet, increased physical activity, and weight loss for people who are overweight or obese. Depending on your current diet and exercise patterns, TLC can have modest to fairly impressive results when it comes to lowering LDL cholesterol.

Cholesterol is a lifelong issue, and most people have plenty of time to experiment with different diet and exercise approaches to see what works best for maintaining healthy lipid levels. Individuals with known coronary heart disease do not have the luxury of time, however. Most will need medication as well as TLC to prevent further problems.

The diet

The NCEP used to recommend one diet for most adults and a stricter "step 2" diet for those with hard-to-treat high cholesterol. The group's new guidelines recommend the following healthy diet for all Americans:

- Eat more monounsaturated fats (found in olive, canola, and sunflower oils; and avocados, walnuts, and almonds), up to 20 percent of total daily calories (about 40 to 50 grams).
- Eat some polyunsaturated fats (found in corn, soybean, cottonseed, and peanut oils, and most nuts), up to 10 percent of total daily calories (roughly 20 to 25 grams).
- Restrict saturated fats (found in red meats, whole milk, and cheese) and trans fats (found in hydrogenated and partially hydrogenated oils) to less than 7 percent of total daily calories (about 15 to 20 grams). Trans fats are particularly nasty because they raise LDL, lower HDL, and amounts are not clearly listed on food labels.
- Restrict cholesterol to 200 mg per day (about one egg).
- Get 50–60 percent of daily calories from carbohydrates (primarily from fruit, vegetables, and whole grains). An even higher carbohydrate diet can lower harmful LDL levels further, but unfortunately tends to raise triglycerides and reduce HDL levels.
- Get 15 percent of calories from protein (found in meats, fish, dairy products, soy products, and nuts).
- Eat 20–30 grams per day of fiber (plentiful in fruit, vegetables and whole grains).

So how does a person actually follow this diet? If you adopt the four-step plan for healthier eating outlined in Chapter 2, you should be well on your way. Once you've improved your diet, your LDL level will not drop overnight. Cholesterol levels change gradually, over several weeks. Eat a healthy diet and exercise (see below) for three months before having lipid levels rechecked.

Exercise

Even modest increases in physical activity can dramatically reduce high triglyceride levels and help to lower LDL cholesterol. The effect can be strong and fairly fast (a few weeks makes a big difference). Exercise can also increase HDL levels, but it takes quite a bit of consistent aerobic activity for a significant HDL increase to occur.

Besides improving your lipids, becoming more active can make you feel better, have more energy and stamina, concentrate better, and sleep more soundly. It can also help reduce blood pressure, strengthen bones, and lower your risk of developing heart disease, diabetes, colon cancer, and breast cancer. If you are currently sedentary or get little exercise, set a goal of walking for 20 minutes, three times a week.

You might only be able to walk for 10 minutes at first, but that's OK. With regular exercise, your fitness level will improve and you'll be able to increase the length and speed of your walks. For more ideas about exercise and details about its benefits, review Chapter 3.

> *Key point:* Almost everyone would benefit from a little TLC (therapeutic lifestyle change), which mainly involves eating fewer saturated fats and trans fats while getting more exercise.

BETTER MEASUREMENTS WITH MEDICATION

When do you need drug treatment?

For most high-risk people (those with known heart disease or diabetes), the LDL goal is so strict (< 100 mg/dL), and the benefits of treatment are so great, that LDL-lowering medication is usually recommended. In fact, studies have found that heart-attack survivors who are started on cholesterol-lowering medication right away are less likely to die in the next six months than those who are not.[5]

For low-risk people with elevated LDL, the benefits of medication are not as great. Remember the "number needed to treat" (NNT from sidebar 9.2)? For men without heart disease, but with moderately high LDL cholesterol levels, the NNT to prevent one heart attack is estimated at 44.[6] In other words, 44 men need to take drug treatment for five years to prevent one heart attack. Medication is somewhat worthwhile, but it's certainly not a slam-dunk. For this group, HDL cholesterol level could be a deciding factor. Those with high levels of protective HDL probably don't need LDL-lowering medication.

Generally, medium-risk people whose LDL cholesterol remains greater than 160 mg/dL and low-risk individuals whose LDL level remains higher than 190 mg/dL despite lifestyle changes are good candidates for drug therapy (see table 10.3). If you think you might need medication, consult your physician for a careful assessment of your unique situation.

The lipid-lowering drugs

Although there is no "cure" for high cholesterol, a number of LDL- and triglyceride-lowering drugs work very well—as long as you stay on them. All of the medications work best when you are physically active and eat a healthy diet. Following is a rundown of the different types of lipid-lowering drugs:

Statins, technically known as "HMG-Co A reductase inhibitors," are the workhorse drugs for treating cholesterol. The statins include lovastatin (Mevacor), pravastatin (Pravacol), simvistatin (Zocor), fluvastatin (Lescol), atorvastatin (Lipitor), and rosuvastatin (Crestor). These drugs are incredibly effective, often lowering LDL cholesterol by 40 or 50 percent. They work by cutting down the amount of cholesterol made in the liver.

Statins may also help prevent heart attacks by stabilizing plaque already present in arteries, making it less prone to rupture and cause blockage. Statins lower triglycerides a bit and raise HDL levels a little, but their main effect is to lower LDL cholesterol. Overall, they are well tolerated and convenient to take.

Statins do have some drawbacks: they are expensive and require periodic blood tests to make sure they're not causing an abnormality in liver function tests (this occurs in 1–2 percent of people on statins). Fortunately, when this happens the liver usually recovers completely once the drug is stopped.

People on statins also need to tell their doctor if unexplained muscle soreness develops. Although it's uncommon, statins can cause serious muscle inflammation, which can lead to kidney damage. This is more common if statins are used in combination with niacin or fibrate drugs. Again, most people recover once the drug is stopped.

Niacin is one of several B vitamins found in normal diets. In "mega-vitamin" amounts, niacin becomes a potent drug for treating problem cholesterol. Niacin does it all: lowers harmful LDL cholesterol levels by 20 to 40 percent, lowers elevated triglyceride levels, and raises good HDL cholesterol levels. In addition, niacin can be purchased without a prescription and is inexpensive. Its effectiveness and convenience make niacin an excellent drug for treating cholesterol, but in treatment doses it requires careful medical monitoring.

The most common side effect of niacin is a harmless, but annoying flushing of the skin soon after a dose. Many people stop "turning red" after they have been on niacin for several weeks. Taking one aspirin (325 mg) 30 minutes before a niacin dose can help prevent flushing. (A form of niacin called niacinamide doesn't cause flushing but shouldn't be used because it also doesn't lower cholesterol.)

Upset stomach is another possible side effect of niacin, but is less likely if the medicine is taken with meals. Niacin should be used cautiously by people with gout, diabetes, chronic hepatitis, or peptic ulcer disease because it could aggravate those conditions. Like statins, niacin can cause abnormal liver-function readings. People on niacin need periodic blood tests to make sure the drug is working without harmful side effects. Niacin should generally not be taken with statins or fibrate drugs due to the risk of muscle inflammation.

Niacin is usually started at a low dose and increased slowly to an effective amount. For the first week, I recommend one 500 mg niacin pill per day taken with a meal. Increase to one pill, twice a day during the second week. If all is going well, take one pill, three times a day from the third week on. Your doctor will want to order a blood test after you are on this dose for a few weeks, and may raise your dose further if the test results are good.

Resins, also called "bile acid sequestrants," lower LDL cholesterol by binding it and trapping it in the intestines. The resins include cholestyramine (Questran), colestipol (Colestid), and colesevelam (WelChol). They are pretty good at lowering LDL cholesterol, but have no effect on triglycerides or HDL cholesterol. Resins are very safe drugs since they are not absorbed into the blood or used by the liver. Resins can safely be used in combination with any of the other cholesterol-lowering medications. Unfortunately, they sometimes cause unpleasant side effects, including constipation, bloating, nausea, and heartburn.

Ezetimibe (Zetia) is a novel new drug that prevents cholesterol absorption in the small intestines. Taken by itself, it mainly lowers LDL cholesterol levels. When taken with a statin, however, ezetimibe appears to lower triglycerides and raise HDL levels a little more than the statin taken alone. Ezetimbe appears to be safe when used in combination with other cholesterol-lowering drugs, but results of long-term studies on safety and benefit are not yet available.

Fibrate drugs are mainly used in people who have very high triglyceride levels despite positive lifestyle changes. Fibrates include gemfibrozil (Lopid) and fenofibrate (Tricor). These drugs are very good at lowering high triglycerides and increasing HDL cholesterol levels, but have little effect on LDL cholesterol. Fibrates should be used cautiously if people have liver, kidney, or gallbladder problems. They should generally not be used with statins or niacin due to the increased risk of muscle inflammation.

Key point: The statins have revolutionized the treatment of problem cholesterol. They are safe and effective in the majority of people who need medication to help lower LDL cholesterol. They also clearly save lives among people at high risk of dying from heart disease.

SUMMARY

High levels of harmful LDL cholesterol are one of the main risk factors for developing coronary heart disease. High levels of triglycerides and low levels of helpful HDL cholesterol also cause problems. All adults should have a fasting lipid profile to help assess their risk of developing heart disease. People who already have heart disease, diabetes, or multiple other risk factors for heart disease will benefit the most from efforts to lower LDL cholesterol. Eating foods low in saturated fats and trans fats, increasing exercise, and losing weight all help keep lipids in the healthy range. In high-risk individuals and when lifestyle efforts are not enough, very effective medications can usually keep cholesterol under control.

CHAPTER ELEVEN

Diabetes: The Plague of Plenty

"One out of every three children born in 2000 in the United States will develop diabetes unless Americans make major improvements in their diet and exercise habits."

—National Diabetes Education Program,
National Institutes of Health

EPIDEMIC IN AMERICA

Younger and younger

My friend John had gained a few pounds since college, but we were all surprised when he was diagnosed with diabetes several years ago at age 38. I was also shocked 10 years ago when my patient Lynn developed diabetes at age 35. Since then, however, I have seen adult-type diabetes diagnosed in 20-year-olds, teenagers, and even in a 12-year-old.

It's a very sobering statistic: at least 18 million Americans have diabetes. More than 90 percent of them have *adult-onset* diabetes, also known as *type 2* or *non-insulin dependent* diabetes. Adult-onset diabetes used to be diagnosed mainly in people past middle age, but in recent years the disease has been found in younger and younger people.

In fact, rates of type 2 diabetes have tripled in the last 30 years, according to the U.S. Centers for Disease Control and Prevention. The reason is no mystery. The increase in diabetes in America coincides perfectly with the country's epidemic of overweight and obesity. The two are so closely linked that some health professionals have started to use the term "diabesity."[1]

The message is clear: The heavier and less physically active Americans become, the greater their risk of developing type 2 diabetes, and all of the health problems that can go along with it. Public health officials fear that diabetes' upward trend may reverse gains in life expectancy Americans have enjoyed thanks to improved hygiene, sanitation, and medical advances. In the next two decades, baby boomers may see more diabetes-related chronic illness and early death not only among their peers, but also among their grown children who should be in the prime of their lives.

What is diabetes anyway?

Medically, there are two distinct types of diabetes. *Type 1* or *juvenile-onset* diabetes starts in childhood or sometimes in early adulthood. It strikes rather suddenly, causing increased thirst, frequent urination, and a fruity odor to the breath. These symptoms occur when the body—actually the pancreas—stops making insulin. Type 1 is also called *insulin-dependent* diabetes because those who have the disease require insulin shots to stay alive; oral diabetes medicines will not work.

Becoming overweight or physically inactive does not bring on Type 1 diabetes. Rather, experts believe it is caused by an unlucky mix of genetic tendency and some kind of infection or other trigger in the environment. Insulin treatment, a miracle of modern medicine developed several decades ago, has allowed several generations of type 1 diabetics to live fairly normal lives. New technology such as insulin pumps and better blood-sugar monitors are improving their outlook even more. Fortunately, type 1 diabetes is not very common and does not seem to be on the rise. The issues surrounding type 1 diabetes are beyond the scope of this book.

Type 2 diabetes is a very different story. Affecting 90 to 95 percent of diabetic Americans, it runs in families and is most common in people who are overweight and inactive. As noted above, type 2 is being diagnosed more often and at younger ages than in the past. Unlike type 1 diabetics, people with type 2 usually *do* make insulin. The problem is that their body does not use the insulin properly, a condition called "insulin resistance."

When people eat, sugar levels in the blood rise and insulin is released from the pancreas. Insulin is a hormone that allows muscle cells to use sugar (glucose) for energy. Normally, there is a nice balance between glucose available and glucose used, so the cells get plenty of energy while levels of sugar in the blood stay in a healthy range.

With insulin resistance, cells "resist" the action of insulin and take up less sugar from the blood. Since less sugar is used by muscle cells, levels of sugar stay too high in the blood. Over time, high blood sugar damages arteries and the nervous system.

At first, people with type 2 have no symptoms, but blood-sugar levels gradually creep higher. By the time these diabetics experience the telltale signs—increased thirst and urination, infections, and weight loss—their blood sugar has been very high and doing them harm for years.

> ✒✒ *Key point:* Type 2 or adult-onset diabetes is reaching epidemic proportions in modern America. Heredity, lack of exercise, and overweight all contribute, but a great deal can be done to treat the disease and prevent complications.

Why worry?

If you can have high blood sugar and not even be aware of it, why should you worry about it? Unfortunately, even mildly high blood sugar causes damage to both small and large arteries throughout the body. The retinas of the eyes, the kidneys, and nerves in the feet are especially vulnerable to *small-artery* or *micro-vascular* disease. This gradual but relentless process can lead to blindness, kidney failure, and amputation of feet or legs.

An even bigger threat for individuals with high blood sugar comes from *large-artery* or *macro-vascular* disease, which affects the heart and brain. Diabetics have a much higher risk of heart attacks and strokes than non-diabetics. In fact, diabetics are at about the same risk for a heart attack as non-diabetics who have already suffered a first heart attack.[2]

Diabetes can be scary, but there is some good news. Most of these complications can be prevented by aggressive treatment of the disease. With good control of blood sugar, people with diabetes can live long, healthy lives.

> ❉ *Key point:* Diabetes can cause some nasty complica-
> tions, but early diagnosis and active treatment of the
> disease can greatly improve the outlook for diabetics.

EARLY-WARNING SYSTEM

Prediabetes

For every American adult with type 2 diabetes, there is another who has blood sugar higher than normal, but not quite in the diabetic range. For years this condition was called "borderline diabetes" or "glucose intolerance," and little was done for those who had it. In 2002, however, experts coined a new term for mildly elevated blood sugar: *prediabetes*. At the same time, diabetes educators launched a campaign to increase awareness of the importance of identifying people with prediabetes.

Without intervention, prediabetes is very likely to progress to full-blown diabetes within 10 years. However, several recent studies have shown that certain strategies can help prevent or at least slow the progression of prediabetes to diabetes. Exercise appears to be the most potent weapon in the fight against diabetes.[3] Moderate amounts of weight loss are beneficial as well, but exercise even without weight loss helps control blood sugar. For people with pre-diabetes, medications are not as effective as diet and exercise in preventing full-blown diabetes. See the section on dodging diabetes for more details on these studies.

> ✋ *Personal action plan:* If your fasting blood sugar level is between 100 and 125 mg/dL, you may have prediabetes. Consult your doctor, exercise, and be sure to have another test in the next 6–12 months.

Screening: How sweet are you?

Along with the new term "prediabetes" has come a national effort to screen people at high risk for elevated blood sugar. Screening guidelines introduced in 2002 recommend a fasting blood sugar test every couple years for high-risk people over age 45. You are "high risk" if you are overweight or obese, or have a family history of diabetes.

You're also extremely high-risk if you've had gestational (pregnancy-caused) diabetes. Most pregnant women are screened for high blood sugar around the seventh month of pregnancy. A fair number have levels high enough to require dietary changes or even insulin during the pregnancy, but their blood sugar usually returns to normal once the baby is born. Unfortunately, a whopping 50 to 80 percent of these women will develop type 2 diabetes later in life. If you've had gestational diabetes, you should have your fasting blood sugar level checked every couple of years.

If you have prediabetes, you should be tested at least once a year to see how well you are controlling your blood sugar and whether you have progressed to diabetes. Table 11.1 explains the meaning of blood-sugar (also called glucose) screening results.

Table II.I: Blood-sugar (a.k.a. glucose) screening

Fasting blood sugar	What the number means
60–99 mg/dL	Normal
100–125 mg/dL	Prediabetes
> 126 mg/dL	Diabetic (2 tests > 126 mg/dL confirm diabetes)
> 140 mg/dL	Old cut-off for diabetes diagnosis
> 200 mg/dL	Diabetes out of control

Health tip: Ask for a fasting blood sugar test if you have any of these risk factors for diabetes: a history of gestational (pregnancy-caused) diabetes; over age 45 and diabetes runs in your family; or over 45 and overweight.

DODGING DIABETES

An ounce of prevention

When it comes to diabetes, early recognition and treatment is the key to preventing serious problems down the road. Far too many people have diabetes for several years before it is discovered, and oftentimes they pay a price.

Vanna is a good example. She was told 12 years ago that her blood sugar was "borderline." Then she moved and never got around to having it rechecked. Vanna felt fine and figured she was OK, but last year, at age 55, she experienced increased thirst, frequent urination, weight loss, and several yeast infections. When she came to see me, her blood sugar was sky high.

Together, we have managed to bring her blood sugar down to healthy levels, and she is feeling much better. Unfortunately, some irreversible diabetic complications developed during those long years of silent diabetes. Vanna has damage to the retinas of both eyes that threatens her vision, and signs of kidney damage. Vanna's long-term outlook is not as bright as it would have been had her diabetes been diagnosed and treated years ago. Her experience shows the importance of yearly blood sugar checks for people with borderline high blood sugar or prediabetes.

The magic of exercise

If you have prediabetes, two large studies indicate that a few lifestyle changes could keep you from becoming diabetic. Conducted in the United States[4] and Finland,[5] the studies focused on overweight people with prediabetes and found that regular exercise and modest amounts of weight loss cut the risk of progressing to diabetes by almost 60 percent.

People in these studies tried to exercise 150 minutes each week, or about 30 minutes a day. The weight-loss goal was 5 percent in the Finnish study and 7 percent in the U.S. study, but fewer than half of the study participants actually met these goals. The tremendous reduction in progression to diabetes occurred with very modest weight loss, in the 10-to-20-pound range.

Other studies have confirmed that exercise alone, even when people don't lose weight, is a powerful protector against diabetes. Harvard School of Public Health's Physician's Health Study, for example, found that male doctors who exercised enough to "break a sweat" two to four times a week reduced their risk of type 2 diabetes by almost 40 percent over a five-year period compared with those who did not exercise.[6]

Diabetic medications have also been tested in prevention studies focusing on people with prediabetes. In the Diabetes Prevention Program, the drug metformin lowered the risk of developing diabetes by 31 percent over three years. Drug treatment was most effective among younger people (ages 25–40) who were 50 to 80 pounds overweight.[4] Drugs generally have not been recommended for prediabetics, however, because exercise and weight loss are more effective, free of side effects, and have other health benefits.

> ✋ *Personal action plan:* For some simple insurance against developing diabetes, work out enough to break a sweat a couple of times each week. For exercise ideas, see Chapter 3.

The American diet and diabetes

We know that many Americans become diabetic, but why? As noted earlier, Americans' increasing tendency to put on weight is a big part of the problem. According to the Health Professionals Follow-Up Study, another part of the problem may be our love affair with hot dogs and other processed meats. Sponsored by Harvard School of Public Health, the study looked at the dietary habits of thousands of male health professionals for more than a decade. The men who ate processed meats five or more times per week were 50 percent more likely to develop diabetes.[7] This effect was found after other risk factors like obesity and lack of exercise were accounted for. In other words, all else being the same, the more processed meats men ate, the higher their risk of diabetes. Popular processed meats included hot dogs, baloney, bacon, and sausage.

To prevent diabetes, your best bet is to consume more fruit and vegetables; eat more fish, poultry, or tofu and less red meat and processed meats; and take in plenty of whole-grain or high-fiber foods. An occasional hot dog won't hurt, but daily bacon, sausage, baloney, or a dog is asking for trouble. Consumption of junk foods such as pizza, chips, and sweets should also be kept to a minimum.

> ✋ *Personal action plan:* For diabetes prevention, limit processed meats like hot dogs, bacon, sausage, and baloney to a couple of times a week at most. Also cut down on high-calorie junk foods.

❄ *Key point:* Regular exercise and healthier eating habits could help many Americans avoid diabetes. Those at risk for the disease should have their blood sugar tested every couple of years. Early detection and treatment of prediabetes and diabetes are the key to preventing serious complications.

DEALING WITH DIABETES

Despite efforts at prevention, millions of Americans already have type 2 diabetes, and millions more will be diagnosed during the next decade. The treatment of type 2 diabetes is a complex and evolving field. This section highlights some of the key goals and principles of managing the disease, but a close working relationship with a personal physician and professional diabetes educators is crucial for long-term success.

Treatment goals

During the past two decades, studies have found that many complications of diabetes can be prevented by intensive treatment to keep blood sugar as close to normal as possible. The widely accepted standard for measuring control of diabetes is a blood test called the hemoglobin A1c, abbreviated A1C. The A1C measures the amount of sugar that is binding to your red blood cells. The higher your blood sugar throughout the day, the more sugar attaches to your red blood cells, and the higher your A1C. This test does not require an overnight fast. It can be thought of as a report card reflecting your average blood sugar during the six weeks preceding the test. Table 11.2 explains what the results of an A1C test mean.

Alcohol and diabetes

My diabetic patients often ask whether it's OK to drink alcohol. They are concerned that alcohol might *raise* their blood sugar. Strangely, the opposite is actually true. The ethanol in alcoholic beverages is digested like fat, not carbohydrate. Alcohol also increases the action of insulin. The risk of drinking alcohol without eating is that blood sugar can go too *low*. Alcohol also contains a lot of empty calories, so too much can cause weight gain and high triglycerides in the blood. As with most things, the bottom line is moderation. Up to one drink a day is usually no problem for diabetics. If more than one drink is consumed at a sitting, it should be with or following a meal to avoid low blood sugar. ■

An A1C test every three to six months is a great way to monitor the success of treatment. It is a good motivator as well, because people know they have to make a sustained effort to improve their reading. The goal for "excellent control" of diabetes recently was revised downward from "below 7.0" to "below 6.5." The new goal is very strict, but is thought to be the best way to prevent complications from diabetes.

Table 11.2: Hemoglobin A1c (A1C) results

A1C	Average blood sugar	What it means
4.2–6.0	< 100 mg/dL	Normal, non-diabetic.
6.1–6.5	125 mg/dL	Excellent control, current goal.
6.6–7.0	140 mg/dL	Good control.
7.1–8.0	165 mg/dL	Fair control.
8.1–9.0	200 mg/dL	Too high, needs action.
9.1–10.0	230 mg/dL	Poor control.
> 10.0	> 240 mg/dL	Out of control.

Personal action plan: If you have diabetes, the A1C blood test is your report card. It is the best way to see how well you have controlled your blood sugar during the past six to eight weeks.

The glycemic index: How sweet are your carbs?

Many nutritionists and their diabetic patients now use a tool called the glycemic index (GI) to help with food selection. The GI is a number system that ranks carbohydrate foods according to how fast they raise your blood sugar in the 2–3 hours after you've eaten them. High-GI foods (i.e., white bread, mashed potatoes, white rice, most cereals, doughnuts, Kaiser rolls, bagels) raise your blood sugar the fastest; lower-GI foods (i.e., artificially sweetened low-fat yogurt; dried apricots, plums, or peaches; All-Bran cereal; 100% wheat bread; fat-free milk) raise blood sugar more gradually. As a rule, processing grains removes natural fiber and raises the GI. Less processed, whole-grain foods have a lower GI. Choosing more low-GI foods may help diabetics shed excess weight and control their blood sugar. Glycemic index charts are now widely available. Consult your nutritionist or check the Internet (www.glycemicindex.com). ■

Diet and exercise

A healthy diet and regular exercise are the foundation for effective treatment of type 2 diabetes. As Lynn's story in Chapter 8 shows, even modest amounts of weight loss (brought on by healthier eating and increased activity) can greatly improve control of diabetes.

Regular physical activity helps the body to burn excess sugar and use sugar more efficiently. A recent study of 2,900 American adults with diabetes found much lower death rates among those who walked regularly. Over an eight-year period, diabetics who walked 3–4 hours per week were half as likely to die compared with those who were inactive, and walking just two hours per week decreased death rates by 40 percent.[8] For more ideas on how to increase physical activity, see Chapter 3 on exercise.

A healthy diabetic diet is similar to the four-step plan described in Chapter 2. One difference, however, is that diabetics need to limit their intake of carbohydrates. Because the body eventually converts all carbohydrates into glucose (blood sugar), eating too many carbs can flood the body with more glucose than it needs. For non-diabetics, who use insulin efficiently, this isn't a problem. But for type 2 diabetics, whose cells are resistant to the insulin that allows glucose to enter from the bloodstream, too many carbohydrates can lead to skyrocketing blood sugar.

In a diabetic diet, only about half of the calories should come from carbohydrates, with an emphasis on "good" carbs such as vegetables and whole grains (see the sidebar "The glycemic index: How sweet are your carbs?"). The other half of the calories should be supplied from lean protein—i.e. tuna, salmon, or chicken—and healthy fats—like olive oil.

Carbohydrates are measured in grams and listed on food labels. One "serving" contains 15 grams, and will raise blood sugar by about 30 mg/dL. Examples of a carbohydrate serving include:

- a small-to-medium piece of fruit
- ½ cup canned fruit, or ¼ cup dried fruit
- ½ cup of raw, chopped or cooked vegetables
- ½ cup of cooked pasta, brown rice, beans, potatoes, or corn
- 1 cup of fat-free milk or plain yogurt, or ½ cup of low-fat cottage cheese
- 1 oz. of shelled nuts
- 2 tablespoons of peanut butter or sour cream
- 1 teaspoon of oil, butter or regular mayonnaise
- 1 tablespoon of low-fat mayonnaise or cream cheese
- 1 slice of whole-wheat bread.

Diabetics generally should limit carbohydrate servings to three or four with each meal, with another one or two included in snacks. A larger or very active person could increase this to four or five servings per meal. Carbs are best metabolized when eaten with servings of protein and healthy fats. Most diabetics should see a registered dietitian or certified diabetic educator for expert advice and fine-tuning of their diet.

> ✖✖ *Key point:* People with diabetes should get regular
> ✖✖ exercise and keep track of the carbohydrate servings
> in their diet.

Blood-sugar monitoring

Like computers, blood-sugar monitors keep getting better, smaller, and cheaper. I believe that all people diagnosed with diabetes or prediabetes should get a reliable blood-glucose testing machine and learn how to use it.

For type 2 diabetics, a fasting test first thing in the morning gives a good snapshot of how much sugar the liver made over night. A fasting sugar less than 120 mg/dL is excellent and a reading between 121 and 140 mg/dL is not bad. Readings greater than 140 mg/dL usually mean that the person needs to lose weight or take more medication or insulin.

Blood-sugar monitors are also a great way for people with type 2 diabetes to learn what types of meals they should or should not eat. Once diabetes is reasonably well-controlled, a home blood-sugar test two hours after a meal gives instant feedback on that meal. A sugar of less than 140 mg/dL is fantastic, and means that the body handled that particular combination of foods quite nicely. A sugar of 160 mg/dL is not bad, but a reading above 180 mg/dL means the meal was not healthy and likely contained too many carbohydrates.

> **Personal action plan:** People with diabetes and pre-diabetes should get a blood-sugar testing device and periodically test their blood sugar two hours after eating to get feedback on the impact of that particular meal.

Medications for type 2 diabetes

When diet and exercise are not enough to control type 2 diabetes, a number of medications can help. *Metformin* is the first-line drug many doctors recommend. It is the only available drug in its class, and works mostly by telling the liver to make less sugar. It also helps the body use insulin more efficiently. Unlike insulin shots or some of the other drugs, metformin alone will not cause blood sugar to go below normal (hypoglycemia). Metformin does not cause weight gain, and even helps some people to lose weight. The most annoying side effect can be loose stools or diarrhea. A rare but serious side effect is the build up of acid in the blood called lactic acidosis. To prevent lactic acidosis, doctors usually stop metformin for a few days after a major operation, serious injury, or x-ray study that needs intravenous dye. People taking metformin should contact their doctor if they get ill with vomiting or weakness.

The *sulfonylureas*, including glipizide and glyburide, are a class of drugs that has been used for many years for type 2 diabetes. Sulfonylureas stimulate the pancreas to make more insulin, which lowers blood sugar pretty quickly. These drugs can cause hypoglycemia (low blood sugar) and some weight gain, but overall are tolerated fairly well.

When diet, exercise, and first-line pills fail to control type 2 diabetes, adding *insulin shots* can be quite effective. A single shot of long-acting insulin at bedtime will often suffice. This helps fight the buildup of sugar in the blood during the night caused when the liver makes too much sugar.

Acarbose is an interesting one-of-a-kind drug that slows the absorption of sugar from the intestines, preventing sky-high sugar readings that can occur after eating. It is quite safe, but has to be taken before each meal and can cause a lot of gas and loose stools.

The *thiazolidinediones* are second-line drugs that include rosiglitazone and pioglitazone. They work slowly by helping the body to use insulin better (improved insulin sensitivity). In theory this is a great idea, but there are some safety concerns with these drugs. An earlier version, troglitazone, was taken off the market because of a small number of deaths due to liver failure. The newer drugs can cause fluid retention, swollen legs, and—rarely—heart failure. People with heart failure should not use these drugs.

> *Key point:* Combined with a healthy diet and exercise program, modern medications can help virtually all diabetics achieve their treatment goals.

PREVENTING COMPLICATIONS

Feet

Every exam room in my office has a sign that says, "If you are diabetic, please remove your shoes." These signs generate lots of good questions, but mainly remind my diabetic patients that I want to examine their feet at every visit. Over time, many people with diabetes lose sensation or feeling in their feet. This gradual process is called peripheral neuropathy, and is one of the small-blood vessel disease problems that can occur with diabetes. Feet that can't feel pain are very vulnerable to blisters, cuts, and foreign objects penetrating the skin. Add poor circulation into the mix and you have a recipe for potentially disastrous infections.

People with diabetes should not walk barefoot and should check their feet for cuts or infections once a day. They need soft, well-fitting shoes and should keep their toenails carefully trimmed. Doctors can easily check the feeling in the feet with a plastic thread that looks like a hair-brush bristle. This should be done once a year. Diabetics who lose feeling need to take extra care and may wish to see a podiatrist with expertise in the care of diabetic feet.

Personal action plan: If you have diabetes, wear well-fitted shoes all day and check your feet for problems every night.

Eyes

Diabetes remains one of the leading causes of blindness in the United States. Like nerves in the feet, the retinas of the eyes can be damaged over the years by small-blood vessel disease. Most of the time, vision is completely normal until eye disease (called retinopathy) is pretty advanced. At that stage, decreased vision or blindness can occur without warning.

The best prevention against retinopathy is to keep A1C readings in the "excellent control" or "good control" range. For every four type 2 diabetics who achieve excellent control of their diabetes, one case of diabetic eye disease will be prevented. Meanwhile, people with any type of diabetes should have their eyes examined once a year by an eye doctor experienced in diagnosing diabetic retinopathy.

> *Key point:* People with diabetes should have an eye exam every year.

Kidneys

The kidneys are another area vulnerable to damage from small-vessel disease. Diabetic kidney disease, or nephropathy, is a leading cause of kidney failure requiring dialysis or a kidney transplant. Tight control of diabetes is a potent way to prevent this problem. For every five adults with type 2 diabetes that is well-controlled, one case of diabetic kidney disease is prevented.

There are no physical symptoms caused by early kidney disease, but the kidneys start to leak protein into the urine. A urine test for microalbumin (small amounts of protein) is therefore a good early warning system for kidney damage. If protein is present, ACE inhibitor medications (see Chapter 9) are quite good at slowing damage and protecting the kidneys. ACE inhibitors are also great first-line drugs to treat high blood pressure in people with diabetes. Any degree of high blood pressure greatly increases the risk of kidney damage, so the goal for blood pressure control in diabetics is very strict (<130/80).

> *Personal action plan:* If you have diabetes and do not take an ACE inhibitor, ask you doctor about an annual urine microalbumin test. If your blood pressure is >135/85, ask whether an ACE inhibitor is right for you.

Heart

The most serious risk for people with diabetes may be coronary heart disease. If all else is equal, a person with diabetes is two to four *times* as likely to have a heart attack as a person without diabetes. Strokes and poor circulation to the legs are other complications related to large-blood vessel disease worsened by diabetes. All this makes the heart attack-prevention measures in chapters 7 through 12 even more crucial if you have diabetes. The good news is that a diabetic's risk of heart disease can be greatly reduced by the following measures:

- Never, ever smoke!
- Do some physical activity 20–30 minutes most days
- Take aspirin (81 to 325 mg) daily unless there's a good reason not to
- Take 0.4 mg of folic acid or a multiple vitamin without iron daily
- Keep your LDL cholesterol under 100 mg/dL (medication often needed)
- Keep your blood pressure as close to normal as possible (medication often needed)
- Keep your diabetes under good control (medication often needed)

> Q *Health tip:* People with diabetes can help their heart by paying close attention to cholesterol and blood pressure.

SUMMARY

Type 2, or adult-onset, diabetes is an epidemic affecting millions of Americans. Diabetes causes untold suffering and early death from heart disease, kidney failure, loss of limbs, and blindness. Early detection and aggressive treatment of diabetes can help prevent many of these tragedies. People at high risk (those who are overweight or obese, or have a family history of diabetes) should be screened for diabetes. People diagnosed with prediabetes or diabetes should adopt healthy diet and exercise routines and work closely with health-care professionals to control their blood sugar. With regular follow-up visits and a healthy lifestyle, people with diabetes can live long, productive lives.

CHAPTER TWELVE

Arterial Disease: Avoiding Stroke and Other Calamities

"A man is as old as his arteries."

—Elie Metchnikoff, Russian-French scientist

STOMPING OUT STROKE

Wake-up call

At age 47, my patient Marilyn never dreamed she might have a stroke. One day last year, she woke up with an unusual headache. When she tried to get ready for work, she noticed that her left hand was clumsy and she couldn't button her shirt. She laid down for a little while, and when she tried to get up, her left leg felt very heavy and weak. Marilyn had to crawl to the phone to call for help. In the hospital, she was very fortunate that her symptoms completely went away during the next 24 hours. Marilyn survived a scary warning without permanent harm.

It turns out that Marilyn was supposed to be taking blood pressure medication. She was diagnosed with high blood pressure many years ago, but stopped taking her medications because she felt good. She learned in dramatic fashion how important it is to stay on blood pressure medication. Marilyn was lucky to avoid permanent damage from a stroke, but many others are not so fortunate.

What is a stroke, anyway?

In simple terms, a stroke occurs when the blood supply to part of the brain is cut off. Just as a heart attack causes some dead heart muscle, a stroke, or "brain attack," causes some dead brain tissue. There are, however, lots of differences between heart attacks and strokes. The two main kinds of stroke are caused by two very different events in the brain. The most common type is caused when a blood clot, or "embolus," blocks blood flow to part of the brain. Medically, this is called an *ischemic* stroke. The less common type is called a *bleeding* stroke, or brain hemorrhage, where damage is caused by bleeding directly into brain tissue. Most bleeding strokes occur when small aneurysms in the brain rupture.

Why do people get strokes?

Drugs: A 23-year-old exotic dancer was admitted to our hospital a few years ago with a stroke. She had weakness of one arm, a leg, and facial muscles. The cause was a mystery until she admitted to using cocaine the night before. Cocaine and methamphetamines ("crystal meth") are potent blood-vessel constrictors. They can cause strokes or heart attacks even in healthy people by squeezing shut the arteries in the brain or heart and by raising blood pressure to alarming levels.

Some diet medications and decongestants can do the same thing. A popular decongestant and appetite suppressant, phenylpropanolamine (abbreviated PPA), was removed from the market after several young women had strokes while using it. Another scary drug, ephedra (a.k.a. ma-huang), is used in many herbal weight loss products. Ephedra was banned in the United States in 2004 after large doses were linked to strokes and a number of deaths.

Stroke and Woodrow Wilson

Stroke has caused some tragic but fascinating drama in American politics. While serving as president in October 1919, Woodrow Wilson suffered a devastating stroke that left him paralyzed on his left side. President Wilson had suffered from extremely high blood pressure long before doctors had any good medications to help control it. This caused bouts of debilitating headaches for which the only treatment was rest. Just prior to his stroke, Wilson had embarked on an exhausting 8,000-mile train trip around the country to support the proposed League of Nations.

Amazingly, Wilson's condition after the stroke was kept secret from the public, his Cabinet, and even the vice president. According to many accounts, Mrs. Wilson ran the country as her husband slowly recovered. He finished his term in 1921 and died in seclusion a few years later at the age of 67. Modern high blood pressure medications probably could have prevented the stroke that felled President Wilson. ■

High blood pressure: Although drugs do cause some strokes, the single biggest risk factor for stroke is untreated high blood pressure. Over several years, high pressure in the arteries weakens the arterial walls and causes build up of fatty plaque. Treating high blood pressure prevents much of this damage. Since the 1920s, stroke rates have actually dropped in half, mainly due to good treatments for high blood pressure. Other risk factors for stroke include diabetes, smoking, heavy alcohol drinking, and high cholesterol.

Despite great progress in stroke prevention, stroke remains the third-leading cause of death in the United States (behind heart disease and cancer). Almost 1 million strokes per year occur in America, causing a huge burden of caring for stroke survivors. Fortunately, you can do a lot to lower your risk of having a stroke.

Q *Health tip:* Avoid stimulants or appetite suppressants that contain ephedra or ma-huang. Don't use cocaine or methamphetamines either. Any of these drugs can cause a stroke.

Atrial fibrillation

My mother has had atrial fibrillation for many years, but for a long time she refused her doctor's advice to take a blood-thinning medication called warfarin (brand name Coumadin). A few years ago while babysitting her three-year-old granddaughter, she slumped over unable to speak or move the right side of her body. She feared the worst, but the symptoms slowly disappeared over about 30 minutes. A blood clot likely triggered this warning event, but did not stay lodged in a dangerous area. Mom received blood thinners in the hospital, and she has done very well on warfarin since that episode.

People with atrial fibrillation are at especially high risk of having a stroke. Atrial fibrillation is a heart condition in which the two small, thin-walled chambers of the heart—the atria—stop beating at a regular pace, but merely wiggle or "fibrillate." The two powerful chambers of the heart—the ventricles—continue to beat, but may be somewhat irregular. Atrial fibrillation is more common as people get older, and occurs in as many as 10 percent of people over age 80.

With atrial fibrillation, blood clots are more prone to develop in the fibrillating chambers, where the blood moves slowly. Clots that break away and go up to the brain cause a stroke. People with atrial fibrillation have up to a five times greater risk of a stroke than people without it. Fortunately, this risk can be greatly reduced by using the blood-thinning medication warfarin. People who cannot take warfarin will get some stroke-reducing benefit from aspirin. If you or someone you care about has atrial fibrillation, please ask about blood thinners as a way to prevent a stroke.

Health tip: People with atrial fibrillation should take the blood-thinning medication warfarin to prevent strokes unless there is a good reason not to. ∎

> *Key point:* High blood pressure is still the main, preventable cause of stroke.

Reducing your stroke risk

Once again, lifestyle is the key to prevention. The following steps will greatly decrease your risk of a stroke:

- If you have high blood pressure, take medication if needed to lower it into the normal range.
- Avoid diet aids and stimulants that contain ephedra or mahuang. Avoid cocaine and methamphetamines.
- Avoid all tobacco.
- If you have diabetes, work closely with your health-care team to keep your blood sugar under control.
- Limit alcohol to one to two drinks per day.[1]
- Keep your cholesterol in a healthy range (see Chapter 10).
- Don't ignore a warning sign of stroke: unexplained numbness or weakness in one arm or leg or on one side of the face; slurred speech; blindness in one eye (see carotid artery blockage section).
- If you have atrial fibrillation, take blood thinners (see sidebar on atrial fibrillation).
- If you have survived a stroke, ask your doctor about aspirin or other blood thinners to prevent further problems.

> *Key point:* Successful treatment of high blood pressure has helped to lower the risk of stroke in America. Limiting alcohol, avoiding tobacco, treating diabetes, and lowering cholesterol can all help to reduce the risk even more.

CAROTID ARTERY BLOCKAGE

Carotid artery screening

Patients often wonder whether they should have screening tests to look for blockage of arteries in various parts of their body. Hank came in to see me a couple of years ago with the results of an ultrasound of his carotid arteries. The test had been done at his church as part of a stroke-awareness program. The carotid arteries are the big arteries in the neck that supply most of the blood to the brain.

Hank had been feeling great, but now he was worried sick. He was told he needed to see his doctor because the test showed some blockage in one of his carotid arteries. Hank's left side had a 40 to 50 percent blockage, and the test result said he was at increased risk of having a stroke. Hank wanted to know if he should get his affairs in order, schedule an operation to "clean out" the artery, or try to forget the whole thing.

Although a 40 to 50 percent blockage may sound scary, medically it is considered mild to moderate. I reminded Hank that he was doing all the right things to prevent strokes and heart attacks. He quit smoking years ago, walked daily, took a baby aspirin, and had good cholesterol and blood pressure readings. With no warning symptoms, Hank really had no reason to worry. In fact, he could have avoided all the anxiety by not having an unnecessary screening test in the first place.

Transient ischemic attack (TIA)

Ray was another story. At 62 he had smoked for many years and was on medication for high blood pressure. One Saturday, he felt numbness in his left arm and on the left side of his face. His hand and arm felt heavy, clumsy, and useless. He thought about calling 911, but the symptoms started to get better. They completely went away after about one hour.

Transient ischemic attack (TIA)

A TIA is a disturbance of nervous-system function that lasts less than 24 hours, and usually less than one hour. The symptoms are the same as those of a stroke, except that they go away quickly. They can include the following:
- Blindness in one eye
- Slurred speech or trouble finding words
- Unexplained numbness of one side of the face, one arm, or one leg
- Weakness or paralysis of a hand, arm, or leg

If you have any of these symptoms, seek medical attention immediately. If it turns out to be a TIA, you are at high risk for having a subsequent stroke. You should have tests to see if blockage in a carotid artery could have caused the problem. If so, surgery to remove the blockage or a stent to keep the artery open could prevent a stroke. If no blockage is found, blood thinners like aspirin (or warfarin, if atrial fibrillation is also present) will reduce the risk of a stroke in the future. ■

Ray had an ultrasound that found severe blockage in his right carotid artery. A blood clot or piece of plaque had broken off from Ray's right carotid artery and gone to the right side of his brain, causing stroke-like symptoms on the left side of his body. Ray was lucky to have had a transient ischemic attack (TIA), an episode whose effects are only temporary but serve as a warning. Ray had a successful operation to remove the blockage from the artery. The shock of the experience convinced him to quit smoking, and with some aspirin as a blood-thinner he has managed to avoid a stroke so far.

Key point: Do not ignore a warning symptom that could be a TIA (transient ischemic attack). Ask your doctor about any unexplained neurological symptoms.

To screen or not to screen

Physicians and researchers debate whether people should be screened for blockage of the carotid arteries using ultrasound. Research shows that people with no symptoms, even those who have risk factors for a stroke, benefit little from screening. Folks with severe blockage and no symptoms do just about as well with medical treatment—such as taking an aspirin a day—as they do with surgery.[2] Lots of people with mild blockage will end up worried like Hank, with no true benefit.

Individuals who have a warning event like a TIA are a very different matter. They clearly benefit from surgery if tests find a moderate or severe blockage of the carotid artery on the side that caused their TIA.[3]

Key point: Don't bother with an ultrasound of your carotid arteries if you have no symptoms.

Personal action plan: The best way to avoid a stroke is to take blood pressure medication if you need it, avoid tobacco, limit alcohol to one or two drinks a day, and don't ignore warning symptoms.

ABDOMINAL AORTIC ANEURYSM

A deadly bulge

Dan was 68 years old when he developed severe low-back and belly pain. He went to the emergency room and a CT scan found a large aneurysm in the aorta in his abdomen (the aorta is the large artery that carries blood from the heart down toward the legs). Dan's aortic wall was "dissecting", kind of like a layer of rubber separating from a bulging area on a car tire. Fortunately, the outer layer had not fully ruptured and Don survived an emergency operation to repair his aneurysm.

Why did this happen to Dan? The cause of most abdominal aneurysms is atherosclerosis, which wears out the layers of the aorta and eventually allows it to bulge outward. Some people have a genetic tendency toward this condition, but being male, getting older, smoking, and having high blood pressure all increase the risk. Dan had smoked for many years and was taking medication for high blood pressure.

Aneurysms tend to grow slowly, and the bigger they get the more likely they are to rupture. When an abdominal aneurysm reaches 5 to 6 centimeters in width, it is considered dangerous enough to warrant elective (non-emergency) surgery to fix it. Aneurysms often cause no symptoms at all. When they start to rupture or dissect, they may give some warning, as in Dan's case, or it can be sudden and catastrophic. If an abdominal aneurysm does rupture, the death rate is very high.

> ✹✹ *Key point:* A dissecting abdominal aneurysm can be
> ✹✹ deadly. Don't ignore new, unexplained pain in the
> low back or abdomen.

Saving lives

With elective repairs of abdominal aneurysm getting better and better, some physicians think it makes sense to screen all older male patients for aneurysms. A large study in Great Britain found that most deaths from abdominal aneurysms could be prevented by screening men at age 65 with an abdominal ultrasound.[4] Unfortunately, overall life expectancy did not really change because the men with aneurysms often died of other cardiovascular diseases.

The bottom line: men with risk factors for aneurysm, such as family history, high blood pressure, or a history of smoking, should consider a screening ultrasound at age 65. If an aneurysm is detected, it should be followed closely and repaired if it gets larger than 5 centimeters in diameter. Men with aneurysms of any size should try their best to lower their risk of heart disease by avoiding tobacco, exercising, and maintaining healthy cholesterol and blood pressure readings.

> ✋ *Personal action plan:* Men with risk factors for heart disease or a family history of aortic aneurysm should consider a screening abdominal ultrasound at age 65.

PERIPHERAL VASCULAR DISEASE

Poor circulation

Blockage of the big arteries that supply blood to the legs is called peripheral vascular disease (PVD). People who develop PVD often complain of an aching pain in their calf or thigh muscles while walking. This pain, medically known as claudication, is caused when the exercising muscles cannot get enough oxygen because of poor circulation. When the muscle rests, the pain usually goes away. How much exercise a person can do is a pretty good indicator of whether there is blockage, and how severe it is.

My patient Bob, for example, walks a couple of miles each day. About one mile into his walk, his calves start to ache. He rests for a minute, and then is able to go another mile at a slightly slower pace. Bob has very mild PVD compared with another patient, Marge. Marge gets leg pain when she walks out to the curb to get her mail.

Who is at risk

The risk factors for peripheral vascular disease are the same as those for heart disease and strokes. Smoking, diabetes, high blood pressure, high cholesterol, and lack of exercise all contribute. For smokers who develop PVD, stopping smoking is the key to halting the process and saving the legs. People who drink moderately (one to two drinks per day) seem to have some protection against PVD.[5]

To screen or not to screen

An ultrasound test can be used to measure blood flow through the big arteries to the legs. If you have aching pain in your calf or thigh muscles while walking, you should have this test. So far, however, there is no proven benefit to screening people who have risk factors for PVD but no symptoms.[6] If you are at risk for PVD but don't have pain, forget about those screening tests and work on lifestyle choices that will help prevent all kinds of vascular disease.

Management of peripheral vascular disease

The mainstays of treatment for PVD are smoking cessation, exercise, and blood-thinning medication such as aspirin. Quitting smoking is critical. Patients who manage to stop do very well, but those who keep smoking often worsen to the point of losing toes or even a leg. Aspirin helps prevent clots that can totally block the circulation, and also helps protect against heart attacks and strokes.

Exercise is a great way to stimulate the body to restore circulation. People with claudication are encouraged to walk to the point of mild discomfort, rest until pain improves, and repeat the cycle. With regular walking, most people can greatly increase how far they can go without pain. Control of high blood pressure and cholesterol is also important for people with PVD.

Surgery or stents to restore circulation are helpful for people who worsen despite these measures. Emergency intervention may be required if a leg becomes painful at rest, cold, or discolored.

> ✖✖ *Key point:* Pain in the leg muscles that occurs while
> ✖✖ walking and goes away with rest could be a sign of blockage in the arteries to the legs (peripheral vascular disease).

SUMMARY

Stroke is the third-leading cause of death in the United States and creates a great deal of disability. Efforts to treat high blood pressure have helped prevent many strokes. Renewed efforts to control diabetes, cholesterol, and blood pressure should further reduce the incidence of stroke. People who experience stroke-like symptoms (unexplained numbness or weakness in one arm or leg or on one side of the face; slurred speech; blindness in one eye) should seek medical care immediately. Those with atrial fibrillation (see sidebar) should take blood thinners like warfarin unless there is a good reason not to. Stimulants such as ephedra, cocaine, methamphetamines, and nicotine can cause a stroke and should be avoided. Screening tests that check for blockage of arteries leading to the brain or legs have not been beneficial to people with no symptoms. Men with risk factors for heart disease should consider an abdominal ultrasound at age 65 to screen for aortic aneurism.

PART III

Cancer Control

....

CHAPTER THIRTEEN

Controlling Cancer: Healthy Habits Can Lower Your Risk

"It's been widely claimed that 80 to 90 percent of all cancer is related to environmental influences, particularly...lifestyle practices."
—Cecil Textbook of Medicine, 18th Edition

CANCER—BIOLOGY AND PREVENTION

The mere thought of cancer frightens most Americans, and for good reason. Despite advances in treatment, one out of four Americans will ultimately die of cancer. Because we hear that cancer-causing agents are present in our air, food, and water supplies, many of us believe that fate alone determines who will get cancer. Fortunately, reality is not so bleak. Studies have shown that people can do a great deal to reduce their risk of developing the dreaded disease.

What is cancer?

Although cancer is listed as the second-leading cause of death in the United States, it is not a single disease. Cancer actually encompasses a large number of different diseases and subtypes. All cancers have abnormal cells that grow in an uncontrolled manner, but they are classified according to the organ in which the cancerous cells start to grow, such as breast, colon, or lung. A cancer's rate of growth and impact on a person's health varies tremendously depending on its type and subtype.

Table 13.1 (see below) estimates the number of Americans diagnosed with the most common types of cancer in 2003.[1] It also shows which cancers took the most lives. As you can see, cancers vary greatly in terms of deadliness. My patient Frank has lived with a slow-growing form of prostate cancer for 15 years, for example, while his unlucky friend Lou died of lung cancer within six months. In fact, the majority of men who develop prostate cancer actually die of other causes, like heart attacks or strokes. At the other end of the spectrum is pancreatic cancer, which tends to be fast growing and highly lethal. Most people who get pancreatic cancer die from it within a year.

Table 13.1: Estimates of new cancer cases and deaths in the United States in 2003

New cases in 2003		Deaths in 2003	
Prostate	221,000	Lung	157,000
Breast	213,000	Colon	58,000
Lung	172,000	Breast	40,000
Colon	152,000	Pancreas	30,000
Lymphoma	61,000	Prostate	29,000
Bladder	57,000	Lymphoma	25,000
Melanoma	54,000	Leukemia	22,000
Uterus	40,000	Liver	14,000
Pancreas	31,000	Ovary	14,000
Cervix	12,000	Cervix	4,000

Data from the American Cancer Society

Each type of cancer has its own causative factors and strategies for prevention or early detection. Specific prevention strategies and screening tests for common types of cancers are discussed in subsequent chapters. The rest of this chapter focuses on the general themes and prevention strategies that apply to all cancers. Read on to learn the simple steps you can take to lower your risk of developing "the big C."

What causes cancer?

Researchers believe an ongoing battle is being waged inside our bodies between cancer causers and cancer fighters. Cancer causers include chemical carcinogens that damage the DNA inside our cells and promote abnormal cell growth. Human beings inevitably come in contact with carcinogens. Following are some examples:

- Water supplies with naturally occurring *arsenic*
- Foods containing *aflatoxin* (a toxin made by molds that contaminate certain foods)
- Foods containing *nitrosamines* (created when chemicals react during high-temperature cooking)
- Airborne *asbestos* or tiny *particulate pollution*
- Cigarette smoke loaded with *tar* and *benzene*

Cancer-promoting damage to cells can also be caused by radiation exposure and some viral infections. Radiation occurs in nature (from the sun and radioactive gases like radon) and from man-made sources (like x-rays and nuclear power plants). Viral infections—including human immunodeficiency virus (HIV), hepatitis B, and human papilloma virus (HPV)—can cause abnormal cell growth that increases cancer risk.

Researchers believe it often takes 10 or more years for damaged cells to grow into a tumor large enough to diagnose as cancer. Various factors either promote or inhibit the transformation of damaged cells into cancer. One factor beyond our control is a genetic tendency for tumor formation. More often, however, unhealthy lifestyle choices create a ripe breeding ground where precancerous cells can grow into full-blown cancers. Overeating (including too many unhealthy foods), drinking too much alcohol, and smoking are the three lifestyle factors most strongly linked with cancer development.

> ❀ *Key point:* Cancer can be caused by one or more of the following: exposure to natural and man-made carcinogens (including toxins, radiation, and viral infections) that induce cell damage, lifestyle choices that promote cancer growth, and genetic tendency.

Can we prevent cancer?

Despite all the cancer causers and promoters in the environment, most people *do not* get cancer. Researchers believe that a healthy immune system is often able to remove early stage cancerous cells before they can take hold or spread. This microscopic cancer control occurs numerous times during a normal lifespan. By establishing healthy habits—eating a balanced diet, exercising regularly, not smoking, and avoiding excess alcohol—you can strengthen your immune system and literally fight off cancer.

When precancerous cells are not removed, healthy dietary and exercise habits create an internal environment that helps inhibit their growth and prevent tumor formation. In fact, it is estimated that more than half of all new cancer cases could be prevented if Americans adopted healthier lifestyle habits.[2]

> ⌕ *Health tip:* More than half of all new cancer cases in the United States could be prevented if people never smoked, ate healthy diets, exercised regularly, and limited alcohol consumption.

THE CANCER PREVENTION LIFESTYLE

Diet

Fruit and vegetables: The high-fat, high-calorie, super-sized American diet is likely responsible for one third of all cancer deaths.[2] As scary as that sounds, cancer risk in the United States could be drastically reduced if people made some simple dietary changes. Researchers believe that 20 percent or more of all cancers could be prevented if Americans would just add fruits and vegetables to their diet.[3]

In 1991, the National Cancer Institute started a nationwide health campaign called "Five-a-day for better health." The message was direct and powerful: eat five or more servings of fruit or vegetables each day to prevent cancer. The cancer-preventing punch comes from eating the right blend of vitamins, minerals, antioxidants, phytochemicals (plant chemicals), and fiber that come in these healthy foods. Phytochemicals protect plants from too much sun, pollution, and disease. Researchers think that phytochemicals may have a similar protective effect on humans, boosting our immune systems and helping to remove damaged, precancerous cells.

If your diet is heavier on meats and dairy products than fruits and vegetables, consider making a change. A diet with more foods from plants than from animals is the best bet for cancer prevention. Fruits and vegetables rich in vitamins A and C may offer the greatest benefit, including citrus and cruciferous vegetables like broccoli and cauliflower. Unfortunately, vitamins and antioxidants in pill form have never shown the same benefit for cancer prevention as the healthy foods themselves.

A fun way to assure a healthy blend of cancer-fighting nutrients is to choose fruits and vegetables from throughout the color spectrum—

Cancer-prevention tips

- Eat five or more servings of fruit or vegetables each day. Try for a healthy mix of colors—yellow, orange, red, green, blue, and purple.
- Increase high-fiber foods in your diet, including whole grains, beans, and nuts.
- Limit red meat and nitrite-cured, salt-cured, pickled, or smoked foods.
- Be physically active—30 minutes a day of moderate exercise dramatically lowers your cancer risk. Just taking a walk three days a week will help.
- Avoid alcohol or limit yourself to one drink per day.
- If you smoke, please quit. Avoid second-hand smoke whenever possible.
- When outdoors, wear a hat with a brim and use sunscreen with an SPF of 15 or higher. Avoid being outdoors during the middle of the day.
- Get a hepatitis B vaccine to lower your risk of liver cancer.
- Practice "safe sex" and always use a condom unless you are in a long-term monogamous relationship. This can lower your risk of cervical cancer (see Chapter 14) and HIV-related cancers. ■

yellow, orange, red, green, blue, and purple. "Five-a-day" is a reachable goal for most people. One fruit or vegetable serving is described as follows:

Fruit	One medium piece
	½ cup cut-up
	¼ cup dried
	6 ounces of 100% fruit juice
Vegetable	One cup raw, leafy vegetables
	½ cup raw or cooked vegetables
	½ cup dried, cooked or canned peas or beans
	6 ounces of 100% vegetable juice

Make sure your breakfast contains fruit. One salad during your day can provide a couple of vegetable servings and is a healthy choice at a fast-food restaurant. Include vegetables, like carrots or celery, in your snacks. Be sure your dinner includes a vegetable serving, and consider some fruit for an after-dinner treat.

Fiber: Other benefits of eating five fruits and vegetables each day are that you will consume fewer harmful fats and a lot more healthy fiber. Colon cancer is virtually unheard of in African cultures with primarily vegetarian, high-fiber diets. Researchers theorize that a lack of fiber, or roughage, in the American diet slows down passage of stool through the colon, allowing cancer-causing chemicals to spend more time there. This causes the growth of polyps, which eventually turn into colon cancers. Two recent studies suggest that high-fiber diets could reduce colon cancer rates by up to 40 percent.[4,5] The National Cancer Institute recommends fiber intake of 20 to 30 grams each day, although most Americans eat far less.

For some good sources of fiber, refer to Table 2.1, found in Chapter 2. Fruits and vegetables contain fiber naturally. Each fruit or vegetable serving contains about 2–3 grams of fiber, a little more if you eat the peel. Beans are another rich fiber source, with 4–8 grams per half-cup serving. If you achieve the five-fruits-and-vegetables-a-day goal, you are well on your way to a healthy fiber intake.

Breakfast is a great time to get some fiber. Checking labels makes it easy to determine high-fiber choices. Cereals vary a lot, but tasty whole-grain cereals often have 4 or more grams of fiber per serving. Whole-wheat toast has 2–3 grams per slice. One-third cup of oatmeal contains 3 grams of fiber, while the same amount of 100% oat bran cereal packs 6 grams. If you want more fiber, bran cereals supply 8–12 grams per serving, and prunes provide 1 gram each.

Cancer prevention plan: Make a point to eat five or more servings of fruit or vegetables every day. Add in a high-fiber breakfast, and you should be well on your way to a healthy, high-fiber cancer-preventing diet.

Exercise

One of the many benefits of exercise is cancer prevention. A number of studies have found that people who do moderate or vigorous exercise have half as many colon polyps and colon cancers as sedentary people.[6,7] In addition, one recently completed study found that men and women who walked or hiked four hours each week had a 54 percent lower risk of developing pancreatic cancer, one of the deadliest cancer types.[8] Exercise might also help reduce your risk of developing cancers of the breast, uterus, and lung.

No one knows for sure why exercise prevents cancer, but a variety of factors likely come into play. For colon health, physical activity speeds up the transit time of stool through the colon. This reduces the time that cancer-causing chemicals stay in contact with the colon walls.

Exercise also boosts your immune system (making your body better able to battle cancer causers) and keeps your muscles in good shape. In addition, when you build muscle through physical activity, you reduce the amount of fat on your body. In animal studies, fat, sedentary rats develop many more tumors than lean, fit rats. Experts believe that in humans, as in rats, too much fat prevents proper regulation of hormones like estrogen, and encourages tumor formation. Physical activity helps people maintain a healthy weight, but regular exercisers who remain overweight still receive cancer-fighting benefits. The take home message is to start exercising.

> *Health tip:* If you are sedentary, one hour of exercise a week (three 20-minute walks) will go a long way toward improving your overall health and lowering your cancer risk.

Alcohol

Health-care professionals have long known that alcoholics suffer from much higher cancer rates than non-alcoholics. In fact, alcohol is listed as a carcinogen by the U.S. Department of Health and Human Services. Heavy drinkers have much higher rates of cancer of the mouth, pharynx (throat), larynx (voice-box), and esophagus (swallowing tube) than non-drinkers. Unfortunately, heavy drinkers often elevate their cancer risk even more by smoking.

Though the connection is not as strong, alcohol also has been linked to liver, breast, and colon cancers. For women who drink daily, the risk of breast cancer rises slightly (about 10 percent). For those who drink daily and have a strong family history of breast cancer, however, the risk rises dramatically: A recent Mayo Clinic study looked at the risk of breast cancer among women whose mother, sister, or daughter had breast cancer.[9] Members of this already high-risk group who drank alcohol daily had twice the rate of breast cancer compared with non-drinkers.

For cancer prevention, the safest strategy is to avoid alcohol completely. However, you have to weigh this information against the overall health benefit (less incidence of heart disease) of drinking in moderation. Unless you're a smoker, one drink a day should pose little overall cancer risk.

> ❧❧ *Key point:* Alcohol is a carcinogen and a significant
> ➚➘ cause of cancers of the head and neck among heavy
> drinkers. When it comes to cancer, abstinence is best, but
> one drink a day for non-smokers should pose little risk.

Tobacco

Tobacco is by far the deadliest carcinogen to humans. Lung cancers kill far more Americans than any other kind of cancer (see table 13.1), and the vast majority are caused by smoking. Cigarette smoke is loaded with tar, arsenic, benzene, cadmium and other cancer-causing chemicals. Cancers form wherever these chemicals contact the body—in the mouth, throat, voice box, esophagus, and, of course, the lungs. Smokers even have higher rates of kidney and bladder cancers because kidneys filter the carcinogenic chemicals from the blood and the bladder stores the chemical-filled urine. And that's not all: Smokers are more likely to develop pancreatic cancer; and young women smokers have an increased risk of cervical cancer. All told, smoking causes one-third of all cancer deaths in the United States (more than 150,000 each year).

> Q *Health tip:* If you smoke, the best thing you can do to lower your cancer risk is quit.

Sun exposure

Skin cancer, including the deadly form known as melanoma, has increased at an alarming rate during the past few decades. Experts believe there are several reasons for the increase, including the large migration of Americans to the Sun Belt, the popularity of sun tanning, and the depletion of protective ozone from the atmosphere. Fair-skinned individuals who burn easily are the most susceptible to skin cancer. Cancer occurs most often in skin that has been damaged by repeated sunburns. Severe sunburns during the teen years increase the skin cancer risk for the rest of a person's life.

On a more positive note, you can do a lot to reduce your sun exposure and prevent sunburns:

- Avoid midday sun and limit time spent exposed to sunlight.
- Wear protective hats and clothing in intense sunlight and especially at higher altitudes (where the air is thinner and you'll burn faster).
- Never use tanning booths.
- Use waterproof sunscreen with an SPF factor of at least 15 (30 or 45 SPF if you are fair-skinned or plan to be in the sun for more than 30 minutes). Get your children in the sunscreen habit, as well.

Cancer warning signs

Some cancers will occur despite prevention efforts. Early detection generally improves the chance for cure. There are as many possible warning signs as there are different types of cancers. Following are some symptoms that could indicate a problem and should be discussed with your doctor. (This is by no means a complete list; you should consult your physician anytime you experience unusual or persistent symptoms.):

- Blood in the urine
- A breast lump or thickening of lumps, itching, redness, or soreness of the nipples that is not related to pregnancy, breast feeding, or menstruation
- Menstrual bleeding between periods or any vaginal bleeding after menopause
- Blood in the stool or changes in bowel habits such as pencil-thin stools or unexplained constipation
- Persistent hoarseness of the voice
- Unexplained weight loss or fatigue
- Unexplained bleeding or easy bruising
- Persistent unexplained cough (greater than three weeks) or coughing up blood
- Enlarged, rubbery lymph nodes larger than a dime and present more than a couple of weeks
- Night sweats or unexplained fever for more than a week
- Any ulcer (sore) of the mouth, tongue, or throat that does not heal; any growths or persistent white areas in the mouth
- Moles that change color, size, or shape; or any sores or ulcers on the skin that fail to heal
- Frequent indigestion and pain after eating, especially with weight loss
- Trouble swallowing or vomiting of blood ■

Skin cancer is the only type of cancer readily apparent to the naked eye. Ask your doctor to check any mole that has an odd shape, irregular edge, or different colors.

Personal action plan: Avoid or limit sun exposure. Cover up or wear sunscreen when you are outdoors; and report any odd or changing moles to your doctor.

SUMMARY

Americans fear cancer more than any other medical condition. Despite advances in detection and treatment, cancer remains the second-leading cause of death in the United States. Some contact with cancer-causing agents (carcinogens) is inevitable, but avoiding tobacco and keeping alcohol intake moderate will greatly reduce your exposure. A high-fiber diet rich in fruits and vegetables provides a healthy mix of cancer fighting nutrients. Regular physical activity helps maintain a strong, cancer-fighting immune system. Limiting sun exposure protects against skin cancer. Overall, adopting a healthy, cancer-prevention lifestyle can cut your risk of developing cancer in half.

CHAPTER FOURTEEN

Cervical Cancer: A Success Story

"The PAP test has been more effective than any other screening test in preventing a cancer."
—American Cancer Society

THE PAP SMEAR AND CERVICAL CANCER

The PAP smear—truly a lifesaver

Maria was a 34-year-old mother of four who'd never had a PAP smear. She grew up in a poor rural area in Mexico, but had lived in Arizona for a year. She came to my office as part of a community program that encouraged uninsured women to get a well-woman check-up and PAP smear. The report from Maria's first and only PAP smear was alarming—cervical cancer cells were present. Maria had a biopsy that confirmed cervical cancer. Fortunately, it was in an early stage and had not spread beyond the end of her cervix.

Maria had surgery that cured the cancer. Her decision to have a PAP test probably saved her life. By the time her cancer would have caused symptoms such as pain or bleeding, it likely would have spread too far to cure. Most American women know they should "get a PAP smear" every year or two, but few may realize what a powerful weapon this test has been in the battle against cervical cancer.

Eureka! Dr. Papanicolaou's discovery

The PAP smear was developed by Dr. George Papanicolaou in the 1950s. Working at Cornell Medical School, Papanicolaou studied "swabs," or gentle scrapings, taken from inside a woman's vagina at the surface of the cervix. While examining cells from the cervix under the microscope, he realized that most women had normal cells, but some had precancerous cells, and a few had actual cancer cells on their cervix. He soon proposed using swabs of the cervix (now widely known as PAP smears) to check women for cervical cancer.

The PAP smear turned out to be the most successful cancer-screening test ever developed. Death rates from cervical cancer have dropped by an astounding 80 percent since the test's widespread use. Through PAP smears, early cervical cancers like Maria's can be found and cured. Most women who die of cervical cancer today have never had a PAP smear or have gone more than five years without one.

Why PAP smears work

In one sense, Dr. Papanicolaou was lucky. The slow-growing nature of cervical cancer makes it ideal for screening (see sidebar on biology and cancer screening). Prior to PAP smears, a woman unfortunate enough to die from cervical cancer would typically be in her 40s. She would have developed precancerous cells on her cervix much earlier, usually during her 20s. Over five to 10 years, the cells on the surface of her cervix would have slowly progressed from abnormal to early cancer (carcinoma in situ) with no warning symptoms. At this point, surgery would still be curative. Undetected by a PAP smear, however, the cancer would eventually invade deeper, spread to nearby lymph nodes, and declare itself with pain and abnormal bleeding. At this advanced stage, the cancer would not be curable.

Biology and cancer screening

When it comes to screening, not all cancers are alike. The following bullet points highlight some reasons why screening efforts are successful for some cancer types, but not others:

- Ideal for screening programs (cervix, breast, colon, maybe prostate)
  - Long phase where people have no warning symptoms
  - Good screening tests to find early disease
  - Proven treatments that save lives
- Screening not needed (bladder, uterus cancer)
  - Warning symptoms develop early (red blood in urine for bladder cancer or vaginal bleeding after menopause for uterus cancer)
  - Treatments still save lives after person has warning symptoms
- Screening not likely to help (pancreas, ovary, maybe lung cancer)
  - Fast growing, aggressive, deadly types of cancer
  - Cancers tend to spread (or metastasize) early
  - Treatments not very effective, even when cancers are found early ∎

This scary scenario should provide plenty of motivation for women to get PAP smears regularly. If it's been a few years since your last one, make an appointment. Even though PAP tests are not perfect, women who get them at least every three years tremendously reduce their chance of dying of cervical cancer.

> *Key point:* The PAP smear is a life-saving screening test that has helped to lower death rates from cervical cancer by 80 percent.

HUMAN PAPILLOMA VIRUS (HPV) AND CERVICAL CANCER

HPV and abnormal PAP smears

Ann was a 21-year-old college student with an abnormal PAP smear. She was very surprised and upset when I told her it was caused by a sexually transmitted disease, human papilloma virus (HPV). When people hear the words "sexually transmitted disease," they think of chlamydia, gonorrhea, syphilis, herpes, and HIV/AIDS. Few people realize that HPV is actually the most common of the sexually transmitted diseases, and currently affects at least 20 million Americans.

More than 100 different types of HPV affect humans. Many cause common warts on the skin or plantar warts on the feet. About 30 types can infect the genital area and are spread through sexual contact. Some of these cause visible "venereal warts" on the penis or around the anus or vagina. Other types infect cells on the surface of the cervix but are invisible to the naked eye. Most people with HPV infections have no warts and no idea that they carry the virus. The problem with HPV is that a few of its strains tend to cause precancerous changes on the cervix. If a dangerous HPV type infects the cervix and is not cured by the immune system, cell changes could progress into cervical cancer.

> *Key point:* A few dangerous strains of human papilloma virus (HPV) are the major cause of cervical cancer.

HPV treatment: some bad news, some good news

When Ann heard that she had HPV, her first question was, "What can I do to get rid of it?" The bad news is that there are no effective *medical* treatments to eliminate HPV infection from the cervix. The good news is that your own immune system will often fight off and eliminate an HPV infection within six to 12 months. Eating a diet rich in fruits and vegetables and not smoking can help eliminate HPV (see the sidebar on natural therapy for cervical dysplasia and HPV). There is also good news for people with visible, cosmetically concerning venereal warts. The HPV strains that cause these external warts rarely if ever cause abnormal PAP smears or cervical cancer, and there are good treatments to remove them.

Natural therapy for cervical dysplasia and HPV

Your body's own immune system is your best defense against cervical dysplasia and human papilloma virus (HPV, the virus that causes genital warts and most abnormal PAP smears). The following measures will strengthen your immune system to fight HPV and increase your odds of healing cervical dysplasia.

- If you smoke, *STOP!* This is the most important step you can take to help your cervix heal and prevent cervical cancer.
- Eat plenty of fresh fruit, vegetables, and whole grains. If unable to do so, a multiple vitamin with B-complex, vitamin C, vitamin E, selenium and zinc may be helpful.
- Eat foods with lots of beta-carotene (orange/yellow vegetables like carrots and sweet potatoes; dark green vegetables; cantaloupe; apricots; and dairy are good dietary sources).
- Make an appointment for a repeat PAP smear or colposcopy when recommended by your doctor. This is very important to see whether cervical dysplasia has healed and to make sure it has not progressed to cervical cancer. ■

Perhaps the best news of all is the recent development of a vaccine that could *prevent* HPV infection. The vaccine is currently in the testing phase. If effective, it could greatly reduce the number of abnormal PAP smears and prevent most cervical cancers.

> *Key point:* Although there is no effective medical treatment for HPV on the cervix, the body's immune system will often fight off the infection and a vaccine may soon be available to prevent HPV infection.

Lowering the risk of abnormal PAPs

Population studies have found that women who don't get HPV infections rarely develop cervical cancer. Groups of nuns, for example, have an extremely low risk of cervical cancer. The biggest risk factors for abnormal PAP smears and cervical cancer include:

- *Multiple sexual partners.* The more partners a woman has, and the more partners her partners have had, the greater her chances of contracting a dangerous strain of HPV.
- *Having sexual intercourse from an early age.* Women who became sexually active before age 17 seem to be especially vulnerable to HPV infection and abnormal PAP smears. A female who has intercourse at age 16 or younger is 3 times as likely to develop severe precancerous changes on her cervix as her peers who don't have intercourse until later.[1]
- *Smoking.* Women who smoke have more trouble fighting off HPV and are more likely to have precancerous changes that need surgical treatments.[1]
- *HIV.* HIV infections weaken the immune system and greatly increase a woman's chance of abnormal PAP smears and cervical cancer.

Understanding risk factors can help women stay healthy and avoid abnormal PAP smears. Abstinence is the only sure way to prevent HIV and HPV, but safe sex is the next-best defense. Condom use reduces, but does not eliminate your chance of getting HPV. You can further reduce your risk by not smoking. An abnormal PAP smear should be a strong motivator for a smoker to quit.

Q *Health tip:* Women should practice safe sex and avoid smoking to reduce their risk of an abnormal PAP smear.

DEALING WITH A PROBLEM PAP SMEAR

Over-treatment of abnormal PAPs

While PAP smears undoubtedly save lives, women should be aware of a tendency in some medical communities toward *overly* aggressive treatment of abnormal PAP smears. When PAP smears were first used, doctors thought that precancerous cells would inevitably progress to cancer. Thus they were very aggressive in treating women with even mildly abnormal cells (called mild or low-grade dysplasia). We have since learned that *most* women with mild abnormalities will heal on their own, and their PAP smears will return to normal with no treatment. In these cases, the best course of action is a repeat PAP test in six months.

Some physicians apparently haven't gotten the message, however, and are still putting women with mild abnormalities through unnecessary procedures to destroy or remove the surface of the cervix. These procedures include freezing, burning with a laser, and removing tissue with a hot wire (loop electrosurgical excision procedure, or LEEP).

For women with mild abnormalities, undergoing immediate, aggressive treatment is usually not warranted, but returning for a follow-up PAP in four to six months is essential to find out whether the abnormality has healed, stayed the same or worsened. Read on to learn more about abnormal PAPs and treatment options.

What to do after an abnormal PAP smear?
When you have a PAP smear, you certainly hope it will be normal. Unfortunately, 5 to 10 percent of PAP results are "abnormal." There are different types of abnormal PAP smears. The most common types are:

- *ASCUS:* Atypical Squamous Cells of Uncertain Significance. Like it sounds, there are some odd-looking cells, but they may or may not be anything to worry about.
- *LSIL:* Low-grade Squamous Intraepithelial Lesion. Mild changes are present in cells from the cervix.
- *HSIL:* High-grade Squamous Intraepithelial Lesion. More significant and worrisome changes are present.

A PAP smear is a *screening* test, not a definitive *diagnostic* test for cervical cancer. The definitive test is a biopsy performed during a procedure called "colposcopy." Colposcopy uses a special magnifying lens to examine the cervix with a 7- to 30-times larger-than-life view. Vinegar is applied to the cervix to turn abnormal areas white. A biopsy can be taken from abnormal areas to more accurately determine the degree of abnormality, and whether any cancer is present. Colposcopy is pretty safe, but can be followed by cramping, bleeding, and—rarely—fainting.

When a PAP smear is abnormal, there are several options to consider. They include repeating the PAP smear after four to six months, performing a test to see whether a high-risk HPV strain is present, or performing a colposcopy. All women with an HSIL result should have a colposcopy for further evaluation, with biopsies of abnormal-appearing areas. Women with a LSIL result can have a repeat PAP smear in four to six months, or opt for a colposcopy. Either decision is reasonable.

Women with an ASCUS result have two choices. A repeat PAP smear in four to six months is the traditional recommendation. A newer option involves HPV typing: When ASCUS is found, the laboratory does an additional test to see whether a worrisome or high-risk strain of HPV is present. If so, colposcopy is recommended. If not, the PAP smear is repeated 12 months later. Women who have several abnormal PAP smears in a row, of any kind, should have a colposcopy for a closer look. The important point is to discuss options with your doctor, form a plan, and follow through.

Key point: There are several options, but an abnormal PAP smear requires a follow-up plan.

Treatment decisions

After a woman has a colposcopy and biopsies, she and her doctor must decide whether to treat, and how to treat, any abnormality that is found. Biopsy results will be labeled "normal," "HPV changes," "precancerous changes," or "cancer." The precancerous (or dysplasia) changes will be rated "mild" (CIN-1), "moderate" (CIN-2), or "severe" (CIN-3). The acronym "CIN" stands for cervical intraepithelial neoplasia.

Treatment options range from simple observation (repeating a PAP smear or colposcopy in four to six months) to more invasive measures to destroy or remove the end of the cervix. The most common invasive treatments include freezing (cryotherapy), burning with a laser, and removing tissue with a hot wire (loop electrosurgical excision procedure or LEEP). These procedures are usually performed in the office. Laser and LEEP procedures require a local anesthetic, but most women recover quickly.

Treatment decisions can be complicated, but a little knowledge can help prevent overly aggressive treatment. Here are some key points:

- HPV changes alone, without precancerous changes (dysplasia), do not require *any* treatment. (Treatment is not effective at eliminating HPV, and it often heals on its own.)
- *Most* low-grade lesions (mild dysplasia or CIN-1) will return to normal within two years, but *a few* will progress to higher-grade lesions and, in rare instances, to cancer. Low-grade lesions do not require any treatment, but do require follow-up every six months until they return to normal or progress (see sidebar on natural therapy).
- Women with higher-grade lesions (moderate [CIN-2] or severe [CIN-3] dysplasia) need treatment. An exception may be teenagers with HSIL. Up to 70 percent of *teens* with HSIL return to normal if they are followed closely.[2] Thus, many teens can avoid surgical treatments that could affect childbearing *if* they are willing to have frequent check-ups. This is not true in older women, who are much less likely to heal high-grade lesions.
- Women with cervical cancer need treatment without delay. Localized, non-invasive cancers can sometimes be cured with laser or LEEP removal of the end of the cervix. More advanced cancers require a hysterectomy and may need chemotherapy or radiation as well.

Q *Health tip:* If faced with a decision on how to treat an abnormal PAP smear or colposcopy result, learn about the various options and have an informed discussion with your health-care provider.

PAP SMEAR GUIDELINES

Too much of a good thing?

PAP smears have been very effective at reducing cervical cancer deaths, but consensus has grown that the same benefit can be achieved with less-frequent screening of lower-risk women. In 2002, the American Cancer Society came out with new recommendations that replaced their 1987 guidelines. The new guidelines aim to reduce the number of PAP smears done in very young and very old women, where abnormal results often lead to non-life-saving, unnecessary procedures.[3]

When to start

When should a young woman have her first PAP smear? Old American Cancer Society guidelines suggested a PAP smear the year a woman became sexually active, or by age 18. However, we now know that cervical cancer will rarely, if ever, develop until a woman is infected with HPV, and that it takes several years for cells to progress from precancerous to cancer. New Cancer Society guidelines are very reasonable in suggesting a PAP smear within *three years* of onset of sexual activity, or at age 21.

> *Key point:* Young women should have a first PAP smear within three years of first sexual intercourse, or by age 21.

How often?

Until recently, most doctors recommended PAP smears once a year throughout a woman's lifetime. For women at high risk of contracting HPV (those with multiple sexual partners) and previous abnormal PAP smears, testing at least once a year is still the recommendation. For monogamous, low-risk women with no previous abnormal PAP smears, however, testing every two to three years is safe. If you're in the latter category and nervous about waiting a few years between tests, it might reassure you to know that most women who are now diagnosed with invasive cervical cancer *never* had a PAP smear or waited more than *five years* between tests.

> ✴ *Key point:* Low-risk women with no abnormal PAP smears in the past can safely wait two to three years between PAP smears.

When to stop

The following women will be glad to learn that they never need another PAP smear:

- *Those who've had a hysterectomy.* You don't need a test for cervical cancer (PAP smear) because you no longer have a cervix. The exceptions are when a hysterectomy was done to treat cervical cancer, or the rare situation in which the cervix was left behind during a hysterectomy (your doctor should have informed you if that was the case).
- *Most women over age 70.* Women who've had a series of normal PAP smears during their 50s and 60s are extremely unlikely to die of cervical cancer. The new American Cancer Society guidelines suggest that you can stop having PAP smears at age 70 if your three previous PAP tests were all normal, and you haven't had any abnormal results for 10 years. An end to PAP smears *does not* mean an end to check-ups, however. Well-woman exams for health counseling and screening for other conditions should continue.

> ○ *Health tip:* If you've had a hysterectomy, or are age 70 and have had normal PAP smears for 10 years, you should not need further PAP smears.

SUMMARY

Cervical cancer occurs when women become infected with a dangerous strain of human papilloma virus (HPV) and their immune system fails to clear the infection. Typically, it takes many years for an HPV infection to bring about cervical cancer. The PAP smear is a life-saving screening test that can detect early cervical cancer and allow curative treatment. PAP smear screening has helped lower death rates from cervical cancer by 80 percent. A current challenge is to develop guidelines for PAP testing and follow-up of abnormal results that will reduce unnecessary treatment of non-cancerous lesions, while protecting women from cervical cancer. An exciting vaccine that could prevent HPV infection and cervical cancer is in the development phase.

CHAPTER FIFTEEN

Lung Cancer: A Long Way to Go, Baby

"Twenty years ago, the tobacco industry began targeting their marketing to the female population. There is a matching curve between their promotional strategies and the increase in lung cancer among women."

—Dr. Joy Johnson,
   Professor of nursing, University of British Columbia

LUNG CANCER—A DEADLY SCOURGE

A sad case

Nick was 64 and looking forward to retirement. He had been in pretty good health all his life, but had never managed to kick his smoking habit. He had cut down a few times, but mostly smoked a pack or two a day since his 20s. Last fall Nick's back started to hurt, even though he didn't remember an injury. The pain kept getting worse until tests finally found cancer. It was in his spine and liver, but had started in his lung. Nick's condition went downhill fast, and he died before Christmas.

The natural history of lung cancer

Sadly, Nick's story is not unique. Lung cancer is by far the deadliest cancer in the United States, killing an estimated 157,000 Americans during 2003. Improvements in treatment help some people with lung cancer live a few months or even a few years following diagnosis, but few people are cured of the disease. The five-year survival rate for all types and stages of lung cancer is a grim 15 percent.[1] (In other words, only 15 of every 100 people diagnosed with lung cancer will be alive five years later.)

Lung cancer used to be a disease mostly affecting men, but cases in women have increased steadily over the past four decades, as more women have taken up smoking. Lung cancer is now the leading cause of cancer deaths among both men and women. In fact, lung cancer kills more Americans than colon, breast, and prostate cancer combined.[1] The average age when people are diagnosed with lung cancer is about 60, and cases are uncommon before age 40.

> *Key point:* Despite advances in treatment, lung cancer remains by far the deadliest type of cancer for both men and women.

What causes lung cancer?

As you probably know, cigarette smoking is the main cause of lung cancer. Smokers are 20 times as likely to develop lung cancer as nonsmokers. This is because cigarette smoke is packed full of cancer-causing chemicals: tar, benzene, arsenic, cadmium, and more. People who smoke develop precancerous changes throughout the lungs, especially in the walls of the bronchi (the air-filled tubes in the lungs). Cells on the outside surface of the bronchi have direct contact with smoke and are most susceptible to damage. These precancerous changes are microscopic and cannot be seen on chest x-rays or CT scans. When a cluster of precancerous cells starts to grow abnormally, a lung cancer can form. Unfortunately, cancerous cells often break off and spread to other parts of the body before the cancer grows large enough to be seen on a chest x-ray or CT scan.

Smoking is directly blamed for 87 percent of all lung-cancer cases.[2] Although most cases occur in smokers, people exposed to second-hand smoke are at increased risk as well. Smaller numbers of lung cancers are caused by exposure to industrial carcinogens like uranium dust or asbestos; naturally-occurring radioactive substances such as radon gas; and tiny-particulate air pollution.

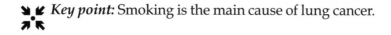 *Key point:* Smoking is the main cause of lung cancer.

CHEST X-RAY—A SCREENING FAILURE

High hopes

Back in the 1950s, medical professionals had high hopes that technology could whip a disease like lung cancer. Recognizing that men who smoked were dying of lung cancer, doctors started recommending yearly chest x-rays for smokers. They assumed that any lung cancer would show up on a chest x-ray, and that an operation would cure the cancer. Early studies suggested that people did live longer if a lung cancer was found on a chest x-ray, before it became so advanced that they started coughing up blood or developed a pain that wouldn't go away. In 1960, the American Cancer Society joined doctors in endorsing annual chest x-rays for smokers.

Reality check

Over time, however, further research revealed that the x-rays were a bust. Three large, randomized, controlled studies all found that there was no change in death rates among smokers who had yearly chest x-rays compared with those who didn't (see sidebar on why screening tests can seem more effective than they really are). We now know that the biology of lung cancer is such that screening with chest x-rays simply does not help. Lung cancers are fast

Why screening tests can seem more effective than they really are

Why did chest x-rays seem so promising as screening tools for lung cancer in early studies? When it comes to cancer screening, we have learned that research studies may be biased in ways that make screening tests seem better than they actually are. Two types of bias come into play.

The first type is called *lead-time bias*. It refers to the fact that people whose cancers are found during screening are by definition diagnosed earlier in time than they would have been without screening. With lung cancer, for example, people screened with chest x-rays were diagnosed about one year earlier than if they had waited until symptoms developed. Thus, people in the screened group lived one year longer with the diagnosis merely because they were diagnosed a year earlier.

The important thing to find out is whether earlier treatment makes any difference for people who are diagnosed during screening. If lung cancer victims live an average of two years after being diagnosed following a screening x-ray, compared with one year after being diagnosed because of symptoms, we have not made any impact at all. Unfortunately, this was the case with lung cancer and chest x-rays.

The other kind of bias is *length bias*. This refers to the fact that not all cancers are alike. Even for a particular kind of lung cancer, for example, some people have slower-growing, less-aggressive tumors while others have faster-growing, more-aggressive tumors. People with slow-growing tumors are going to have lower death rates than people with fast-growing tumors, regardless of screening, just because of the biology of their tumor. But here's the rub—people with slow-growing tumors have a longer phase before they get symptoms. They are more likely to be diagnosed by a screening test than people with a fast-growing tumor. Thus, people who are diagnosed by screening tests may appear to fare better when really it is because they have less-aggressive tumors.

Scientifically, the way to reduce bias is through randomized, controlled trials (RCTs). People in these RCTs are *randomly* (by pure chance) assigned to either a screening group or a control group that will not be screened. Both groups have to be followed for a long time to see whether there is any difference in outcomes, such as death rates or complications. Unfortunately, few cancer screening tests have been studied with RCTs. ∎

growing and tend to spread early, before they show up on chest x-rays. I still have patients who ask about annual chest x-rays. I tell them that the American Cancer Society stopped that recommendation in 1980.

> ⭐ *Key point:* Yearly chest x-rays for smokers do not lower death rates from lung cancer.

CHEST CT SCAN—A SCREENING DILEMMA

High hopes

Fred is a 58-year-old who has smoked for the past 35 years. He knows he should quit and that he is at high risk for lung cancer. Fred came into the office the other day wondering whether a new test—a "lung scan" (actually a CT scan of the chest) being advertised for smokers—could keep him from dying of lung cancer.

Today, some people believe that CT scans (also called "cat" scans) can succeed where chest x-rays failed in the fight against lung cancer. CT, short for "computerized tomography," is indeed a more sophisticated technology than the simple x-ray. A CT scan of the lungs takes multiple x-ray images of the organ in a spiral pattern (imagine photographing slices of a spiral-cut ham), then uses a computer to create cross-sectional views from those images. Some early studies have proved that CT scans can find small cancers that may not be visible on a chest x-ray.

Reality check

Other than a couple-hundred bucks, Fred wanted to know whether there was any downside to having a lung scan. I explained that screening for lung cancer is a complicated matter. Though Fred would like a simple black or white answer to the question, "Am I OK or do I have cancer," a CT scan very likely won't provide it. This is because lung-cancer screening involves a large gray area.

For every 100 people like Fred who get a lung scan, 25 to 50 are not going to like what they hear. They will be told that there is "an indeterminate nodule," meaning a small spot that is probably no big deal but could be cancer. One or two of this group will eventually turn out to have cancer. The other 24 to 48 are going to be worried sick. The only definite way to know whether a given spot is cancerous is to cut it out or stick a needle into it for a biopsy. Most of these spots are going to be too small to find with a needle. To avoid an operation, many doctors will recommend a repeat scan in three months to see whether the spot has changed.

That doesn't sound too bad, but just because it hasn't changed in three months does not mean you are out of the woods. Additional scans are usually recommended at six, 12, and 24 months to be sure that nothing is changing. To make things more complicated, one out of eight smokers will develop a new spot by 12 months, which again may or may not be cancer.[3]

At this time, we simply don't have any long-term research studies to tell us whether screening with CT scans will reduce deaths from lung cancer. We also have no idea how often the test might be needed. So should Fred have a lung scan? I told him there is a small chance it could find an early cancer, but a large chance it would find a benign spot that would be very costly in terms of worry, work-up, and follow-up. In addition, radiation exposure from multiple CT scans to rule out cancer would actually increase his risk of developing a cancer. If Fred is really worried about lung cancer, the best thing he can do is quit smoking.

> *Key point:* CT scans of the lung may find some early lung cancers, but many people will pay the price of worry and extra testing when small spots of unknown significance are found. As yet, there is no scientific evidence that screening with CT scans will save lives.

THE FIGHT AGAINST LUNG CANCER

Three ways to fight cancer

There are three main ways to fight cancer. The first is to take steps to prevent it, called *primary prevention* (see Chapter 13 for healthy habits that can help). The second involves screening programs to find cancer early when it has a higher cure rate, called *secondary prevention*. The third way is treatment, often involving surgery, radiation, and/or chemotherapy.

For some cancers, screening programs and treatments make a big difference. With cervical cancer, for example, a widely used screening program involving PAP smears reduced death rates by 80 percent. When it comes to lung cancer, however, screening and treatment are just not very effective. Primary prevention is absolutely your best defense. Quit smoking, avoid second-hand smoke, and eat antioxidant foods that help combat cancer.

In the future, secondary prevention and treatment of lung cancer are bound to improve. Realistically, given the aggressive nature of lung cancer, screening programs might never be highly effective. I am more optimistic about treatment. With gene therapy, immune-system enhancers, vaccines, and new ways to target cancer cells on the horizon, we may soon have a much better arsenal of weapons to use against lung cancer.

Key point: In the fight against lung cancer, screening will not make much of a dent while we wait for a cure. Preventing this disease is your best line of defense.

Stamp out smoking

Ironically, America's deadliest cancer is also the most preventable. The risk of lung cancer drops steadily after a person quits smoking. Five years after quitting, an ex-smoker's risk drops to half that of a smoker. By 10 years, the risk returns almost to that of a nonsmoker.

Long-term studies (up to 20 years) of groups of people confirm that when smoking rates decline, lung cancer rates soon follow. Take doctors, for example. They led the way in quitting smoking between 1950 and 1980, as the health risks became clear. By the year 2000, the rate of lung cancer deaths among doctors had dropped drastically to match their low smoking rates. American men experienced a similar trend. Their smoking rates have dropped slowly for several decades, and their death rates from lung cancer have dropped 17 percent since 1988. Sadly, for women the trends are reversed. Women's smoking rates increased steadily during the 1970s and 1980s, and they are now paying the price. Their death rates for lung cancer have increased by an alarming 46 percent since 1988.

Personal action plan: If you smoke, quitting is the best way to protect yourself from lung cancer. See Chapter 6 for ideas on how to kick the habit.

Diet can help

People who can't quit smoking may wonder if there is anything else they can do to lower their risk of lung cancer. The answer is yes. Several studies have found that smokers who eat lots of foods containing beta-carotene can reduce their lung-cancer risk.[4,5] Beta-carotene, which is turned into vitamin A in the body, is found in orange, yellow, and dark-green vegetables as well as in some fruits and dairy products. Carrots, sweet potatoes, cantaloupe, and apricots are rich sources of beta-carotene.

Unfortunately, beta-carotene in vitamin-pill form does not help and may even increase the risk of lung cancer. One study to see whether beta-carotene pills could prevent lung cancer among smokers was stopped because *more* lung cancers were being found in the group taking beta-carotene supplements than in the placebo group.[6]

Q *Health tip:* If you smoke or recently quit, eat lots of orange, yellow, and dark-green vegetables. These beta-carotene rich foods may provide some protection against lung cancer.

SUMMARY

Lung cancer is the deadliest type of cancer in the United States, killing more people each year than colon, breast, and prostate cancer combined. The vast majority of lung cancer is caused by smoking. In recent decades, as smoking rates have increased among women, lung cancer has passed breast cancer as the deadliest form of cancer for women. Efforts to screen for lung cancer with chest x-rays failed to lower death rates, and screening with CT scans is unlikely to make much impact. There is hope for better treatments and even a cure in the future, but the key to fighting lung cancer now is to move toward a smoke-free America.

CHAPTER SIXTEEN

Colon Cancer: Of Fiber and Fiber-Optics

"Colon cancer is both preventable and curable."
—Dennis Lee, M.D.

THE PROBLEM WITH POLYPS

A pesky polyp

Tom came in for a check-up when he turned 60 because his wife insisted on it. He was quite healthy and we ended up discussing colon-cancer screening. Tom reluctantly agreed to a screening test called a "sigmoidoscopy," in which a flexible tube with a light and a camera at the end is used to examine part of the colon. About 40 centimeters into Tom's colon, I discovered a polyp. I then referred him to a gastroenterologist for a "colonoscopy," a procedure involving a longer tube to examine the entire colon, during which polyps can be removed. Two polyps were removed from Tom's colon. One was fairly large and had some early cancer cells near the tip. Tom had a repeat colonoscopy two years later and his colon was very healthy.

Tom truly dodged a bullet when he agreed to have a screening test for colon cancer. Undetected, the large polyp in his colon likely would have grown into a full-blown colon cancer. By the time it caused bleeding or other symptoms, Tom would have required major surgery, and the chance for a cure might have slipped away.

Colon cancer and polyps

Colon cancer is the second-deadliest cancer in the United States, trailing only lung cancer. In 2003, an estimated 58,000 Americans died of colon cancer. The disease affects men and women equally, and about 6 out of 100 Americans will develop colon cancer during their lifetime. Most colon cancers are believed to originate in a colon polyp. Polyps are fleshy growths protruding from the wall of the colon. Imagine a small, round mushroom on a stalk growing into the tube that your stool passes through. Most polyps do not cause any symptoms and will never become cancerous. Some polyps will disappear, but a small percentage will grow and transform into cancer over 10 to 15 years.

The larger the polyp, the greater is the risk that it will be cancerous. Tiny polyps are rarely cancerous, but 60 percent of very-large polyps (bigger than 4 cm.) will contain cancer. People with multiple polyps are at highest risk for colon cancer. Removing polyps before they have a chance to turn cancerous is a big part of the strategy to prevent colon cancer. To remove polyps, however, you have to find them. That can only happen if people with certain risk factors (i.e. age over 50 and family history of colon cancer) are willing to undergo the necessary tests.

> *Key point:* Most cases of colon cancer develop from a colon polyp that grows and changes over time. Finding and removing precancerous polyps is one of the keys to fighting colon cancer.

Fiber and other risk factors

Around the world, developed countries have much higher rates of colon cancer than developing nations. Colon cancer is *10 times* more common in Northern Europe and the United States, for example, than it is in Africa and India. Why is our incidence of colon cancer so much higher? Most experts blame the high-fat, low-fiber Western diet. Diets high in saturated fats and red meat are strongly correlated with colon cancer. Obesity, lack of exercise, smoking, and frequent bouts of constipation appear to increase risk as well. On the other hand, the high-fiber, mostly vegetarian diets common in developing countries appear to protect people from colon cancer.

In the United States, the risk of colon cancer increases with age. Ninety percent of all cases occur in people over age 50. Risk increases if a parent or sibling has had either colon cancer or large polyps. The risk is highest for people who have ulcerative colitis, multiple polyps, or many family members with colon cancer.

> *Key point:* The main risk factors for colon cancer are a high-fat, low-fiber diet, age over 50, and a family history of colon cancer or polyps.

PREVENTION PLAN

Diet

Fill up on fiber: In 1971, British missionary surgeon Denis Burkitt hypothesized that high-fiber diets prevent colon cancer after observing that African natives had large, soft, fiber-filled stools and very low colon-cancer rates. Burkitt postulated that high fiber in the stool dilutes carcinogens and causes the stool to travel more quickly through the colon, reducing carcinogen contact with the colon wall. We still don't know whether Burkitt was right about *why* high fiber diets protect against colon cancer, but several studies looking at people who got colon cancer, compared with similar folks who did not, have found lower cancer rates in people who ate more fiber.

In the most impressive study to date, the European Prospective Investigation into Cancer and Nutrition (EPIC), published in 2003, more than 500,000 Europeans were asked about their diets, then followed for five years. Participants who ate the most fiber (30 to 35 grams per day) developed 25 percent fewer colon cancers than those who ate the least fiber (about 12 grams per day).[1] A similar but smaller study in the United States found a 27 percent reduction in colon polyps among high-fiber eaters compared with low-fiber eaters.[2] Based on this research, it appears that one-quarter of colon cancers in the United States could be prevented if Americans simply ate the recommended 25 to 30 grams of fiber each day.

Optimal fiber intake could also help prevent common American colon problems like constipation and diverticulosis. Unfortunately, most Americans have a long way to go to meet the fiber goal. A high-fiber breakfast each day—including foods such as whole-grain cereal, fresh fruit, whole-wheat toast, or oatmeal—is a great way to start a cancer-prevention program. For more ideas on how to increase fiber in your diet, see chapters 2 and 13. Some simple changes, such as incorporating whole-grain foods and beans into your meals and snacks, can improve your colon health and reduce your risk of colon cancer.

Eat your fruits and vegetables: Fruits and vegetables are not only great sources of fiber, but also contain many cancer-fighting nutrients, including the antioxidant vitamins C and E, carotenoids, selenium, and flavenoids. A number of studies have determined that regular consumption of fruit and vegetables helps protect against colon cancer. One large study found that the one-fifth of Americans who ate the most vegetables and grains had a 25 percent lower risk of colon cancer than the one-fifth who ate the least.[3] This and similar research led to the National Cancer Institute's "5-a-day" campaign to encourage Americans to eat five servings of fruit and/or vegetables each day. Five-a-day is a realistic goal for most people and should really help lower colon-cancer risk. For more information on the "5-a-day" plan, including serving sizes, see chapters 2 and 13.

Limit bad fats and red meat: Saturated fat in the diet increases the risk of colon cancer, while monounsaturated fat may help protect against it. Developed countries with high colon-cancer rates have diets that are much higher in harmful fats (saturated fats and trans fats) than the diets of developing countries.

Colon cancer rates also increase in direct proportion to the amount of red meat in the diet. A study in North Carolina found that colon-cancer risk doubled among people who ate the most red meat compared with those who ate the least.[4] Cooking red meat at high temperatures may increase the risk even more by forming carcinogens called heterocyclic amines (HCAs). The North Carolina study found that people who ate a lot of pan-fried or well-done red meat were at highest risk for developing colon cancer.

Monounsaturated fats, the healthiest of all fats, are often credited for the low heart-disease rates in Mediterranean countries. These good fats, especially olive oil, may also help prevent colon cancer. A British study of diet and colon cancer in 28 countries found that Southern European countries where lots of olive oil is consumed had lower than expected rates of colon cancer.[5]

These are all good reasons to reduce the amount of harmful saturated fats and red meat in your diet, while increasing your intake of healthier monounsaturated fats. For more information on "good" and "bad" fats, see the "Fat primer" sidebar in Chapter 2.

> *Personal action plan:* Protect your colon by eating a high-fiber diet with lots of fruits and vegetables while trying to limit red meat and saturated fat.

Exercise

A number of studies have found that people who exercise regularly don't get colon cancer as often as those who are sedentary.[6] Exercisers seem to develop fewer polyps, as well. We don't know how physical activity protects the colon. Exercise does increase muscular contractions of the colon wall, which speeds the passage of stool through the colon. As with fiber, this may reduce the time that any cancer-causing chemicals can stay in contact with the colon wall.

In any case, protecting your colon is another great reason to get off the couch for some physical activity. See Chapter 3 for ideas on how to get started.

Limit alcohol

Alcohol consumption is a definite risk factor for oral and esophageal cancers, and a recent review suggests that heavy alcohol use can cause colon cancer as well.[7] After looking at eight studies of nearly half a million people, researchers concluded that drinking more than three beers, glasses of wine, or shots of hard liquor a day increased the risk of colon cancer by 40 percent. Two drinks a day increased the risk only slightly. Once again, the prescription regarding alcohol is moderation or avoidance.

Consider calcium supplements

Do dairy products and calcium supplements help prevent colon cancer? Research is being done to find out, but we don't yet have conclusive answers. Among people who have had colon polyps removed, studies have found that calcium supplements help prevent the growth of new polyps.[8] A recent Harvard study of nurses and other health professionals found that people who ate two to three servings of calcium-rich dairy products each day had a lower risk of colon cancer than people who rarely ate dairy.[9] The American Cancer Society points out that too much dairy in the diet increases the risk of prostate and ovarian cancer, probably because of the saturated fat. Until more is known, I recommend a modest calcium supplement (500 to 600 mg per day) for people who do not eat much dairy. Those who enjoy several dairy servings a day should look for low-fat or fat-free options.

Aspirin

During the 1990s, several studies raised hopes that regular use of aspirin might prevent colon polyps or colon cancer. Unfortunately, a large long-term study of physicians failed to show any reduction in colon cancer rates from aspirin use.[10] However, a more recent randomized, controlled study to determine whether aspirin could prevent new polyps from forming in people who'd already had polyps removed found that one baby aspirin (81 mg) each day modestly lowered the risk of new polyps compared with a placebo.[11] Of interest, a group that took one regular adult aspirin (325 mg) each day did not have any benefit. The bottom line is that a baby aspirin a day may help prevent colon cancer. If you are considering aspirin to prevent a heart attack (see Chapter 7), this information may help you decide to go ahead.

Key points: To prevent colon cancer, get regular physical activity and eat a high-fiber diet rich in fruits and vegetables. Go easy on red meat and alcohol, stick to low-fat dairy foods, and consider a calcium supplement if you do not eat much dairy.

LOOKING FOR TROUBLE: SCREENING FOR COLON CANCER

Why colon screening can save lives

Similar to cervical cancer, the biology of colon cancer makes it well-suited for screening programs: There is a long phase when people develop precancerous polyps and early colon cancers with no symptoms. There are good screening tests to find these conditions before they become invasive cancers. Finally, removal of these early lesions results in very high cure rates and saves lives. For people at average risk, colon cancer screening should start at age 50.

But whereas cervical-cancer screening via the PAP smear is widely accepted by women and has resulted in an 80 percent reduction in cervical cancer deaths, colon-cancer screening has been slow to gain public acceptance. Colon-cancer deaths have been reduced slightly by limited screening, but widespread screening for this cancer could make a huge impact and save thousands of lives each year.

> ❧ *Key point:* Thousands of lives could be saved each year if more Americans followed recommendations for colon-cancer screening, which should begin at age 50 for average-risk people.

The screening tests

Fecal occult blood testing (FOBT): Fecal occult blood testing (FOBT) is done on your stool to see whether it contains any blood, even trace amounts not visible to the naked eye. This test is useful because large polyps and colon cancers often bleed. Home test kits, available at doctors' offices and pharmacies, have three cards. They require you to collect a small stool sample with a wooden stick on three different days, one sample for each card. Aspirin, vitamin C, red meat, and iron pills should be avoided for a couple of days before collecting samples. The cards are returned to a lab to test the stool for blood.

When FOBT is positive for blood, further tests are needed to examine the entire colon for polyps or tumors. Most people with blood in the stool will end up having a benign reason like hemorrhoids or diverticulosis. Of people over age 50 with blood in the stool, however, about one-fourth will have polyps and up to 10 percent will have colon cancer. Several good studies have shown that people over age 50 who do yearly FOBT lower their risk of dying of colon cancer by as much as one-third.[12]

Sigmoidoscopy: Sigmoidoscopy uses a flexible tube with a light and camera on the end to directly examine the lower part of the colon. Most sigmoidoscopes are 60 cm. (about 2 feet) long. Prior to a sigmoidoscopy, the colon has to be cleaned out with an oral prep of laxatives or an enema. The procedure can cause some cramping, but is usually well tolerated and does not require sedation. Many scopes project the picture onto a monitor so the person having the procedure can watch. Complications of sigmoidoscopy are quite rare. A 60 cm. scope will reach about half of all polyps or colon cancers.

Colonoscopy: Colonoscopy is similar to sigmoidoscopy, but the tube is much longer to enable examination of the entire colon. The procedure requires a bowel-cleaning laxative preparation, and intravenous sedation typically is used to reduce the discomfort. Up to 95 percent of colon polyps or cancers are found by colonoscopy. Polyps can usually be removed with the scope, and biopsies can be taken from suspected cancers. Colonoscopy is generally safe, but serious complications can occur. Perforation of the colon wall may happen one time in every 1,000 to 2,500 tests. Colonoscopy is much more expensive than sigmoidoscopy.

Barium enema: A barium enema is an older test commonly known as the "lower GI." After a laxative prep to clean out the bowels, barium and air are injected into the colon via an enema. A series of x-rays then are taken to examine the lining of the colon. Use of barium enemas for screening is limited because they may miss up to half of smaller polyps. If abnormalities show up on the x-rays, sigmoidoscopy or colonoscopy is recommended for a closer look.

Virtual colonoscopy: This test, sometimes called a "colon scan," uses either a CT scan or a magnetic resonance imaging (MRI) machine to take pictures of the colon. As with the other tests, the colon usually is cleaned out beforehand with a laxative prep. Then either air (for the CT scan) or water (for the MRI) is gently pumped into the colon and pictures are taken. A computer organizes the images so a radiologist can view the inside of the colon much as it appears during an actual colonoscopy. Virtual colonoscopy finds about 90 percent of polyps and cancers larger than 1 cm., but also generates quite a few false-positive results in which something looks worrisome, but turns out to be nothing. If any abnormalities turn up, the patient will need further testing using a scope.

> ⣿ *Key point:* Several screening tests are available for colon cancer, ranging from simple testing of stool for blood (FOBT) to a thorough look at the inside lining of the entire colon (colonoscopy).

SCREENING RECOMMENDATIONS

Screening versus diagnostic tests

Before discussing screening recommendations, it is important to understand the difference between *screening* tests and *diagnostic* tests. *Screening* tests, done on people who feel fine, are designed to catch diseases at an early stage, when treatment is most effective at curing them or slowing their progression. *Diagnostic* tests, on the other hand, are done when people have symptoms or problems to help figure out what's wrong. If you have unexplained blood in your stool, you should see your doctor, who likely will recommend diagnostic testing. People with persistent changes in bowel habits, such as constipation, diarrhea, or pencil-thin stools, likewise should consult with their physician. The screening recommendations discussed below apply to individuals who feel fine and are not having bowel problems.

> $\bigcirc$ *Health tip:* Please consult with your doctor if you have unexplained blood in your stool or a persistent change in your bowel habits.

Are you at high risk?

When contemplating colon-cancer screening, it helps to know whether you have an average risk (see screening recommendations below) or a high risk of developing the disease. High-risk individuals should generally start colon cancer screening at an earlier age, and should be screened more often. Following are some of the factors that place a person at higher than average risk:

- Ulcerative colitis or other inflammatory bowel disease affecting the colon
- Colon cancer in a parent or sibling, especially if younger than age 60
- Close relatives with multiple colon polyps
- Personal history of colon cancer or colon polyps

If you might be at high risk, ask your doctor for advice. For people with a parent or sibling who's had colon cancer, screening should begin at age 40. If the relative was diagnosed at an age younger than 50, screening should start 10 years before the youngest family member was diagnosed.

> ✋ *Personal action plan:* Find out whether colon cancer runs in your family. If so, or if you have other risk factors listed above, be sure to ask your doctor whether you should start colon cancer screening earlier than age 50.

Screening recommendations for "average" Joes and Janes

If you're at average risk for colon cancer, most doctors and cancer-prevention organizations agree that you should start some kind of screening program at age 50. The American Cancer Society recommends yearly FOBT plus a sigmoidoscopy every five years or a colonoscopy every 10 years. At this time, most experts believe that virtual colonoscopy is not quite good enough to recommend as a screening test.

When people ask my opinion on the best way to screen for colon cancer, I say it really depends on personal preference. I strongly recommend yearly FOBT starting at age 50. It's safe and inexpensive, and studies have proven that screening with FOBT saves lives.[12] People who are willing to go a step further should consider a flexible sigmoidoscopy. This procedure is very safe, and can provide an interesting perspective for the patient. People who want the greatest degree of reassurance possible and are willing to accept a small degree of risk should elect to have a colonoscopy.

> 💥 *Key point:* Average-risk individuals should strongly consider colon-cancer screening starting at age 50. Yearly FOBT is a good way to start. A sigmoidoscopy or colonoscopy can provide extra reassurance.

SUMMARY

Colon cancer is most common in developed Western countries, where diets are loaded with red meat and limited in fiber. Colon cancer is the second-deadliest type of cancer in the United States and occurs mostly in people over age 50. High-fiber diets rich in fruits and vegetables, exercise, and calcium supplements all help to prevent colon cancer. Most colon cancers occur as colon polyps grow and transform over several years. Screening tests that identify polyps and early colon cancers have been proven to save lives, but most Americans are not being screened. Average-risk Americans should start colon-cancer screening at age 50. Fecal occult blood testing (FOBT) cards, sigmoidoscopy, and colonoscopy are all good screening options.

....

CHAPTER SEVENTEEN

Breast Cancer: What Women Need to Know

"Women agonize over cancer, we take as a personal threat the lump in every friend's breast."
—Martha Weinman Lear

ONE-IN-EIGHT

Worst fear

Helen was 64 years old and in very good health when she scheduled a routine mammogram, just as she'd done every year since turning 50. This year, however, she got an alarming report: An area in her left breast had some small calcium deposits not present the year before and suspicious for cancer. Helen had a needle biopsy, and her worst fear was confirmed—breast cancer. At first Helen was terrified, but soon she realized that her treatment options and odds of a cure were far better than in the past.

Helen elected to have a "lumpectomy," a procedure in which just the tumor and a small margin around it are removed. In addition, a technique called a "sentinel-node biopsy" allowed her surgeon to find and remove just one lymph node in Helen's armpit. This "sentinel" lymph node is the one cancer cells invade first when breast cancer spreads. Fortunately for Helen, the lymph node was free of cancer. She had radiation treatments to her left breast and now lives a normal life as part of a growing group of breast-cancer survivors.

Breast cancer in the U.S.

Breast cancer is the most common cancer affecting American women, with roughly 213,000 new cases in 2003. Many women have heard that they have a one-in-eight chance of developing breast cancer during their lifetime. The statistic is true, but it's not as grim as it sounds. Because breast cancer becomes more common as women grow older, the risk of developing it before age 50 is relatively low. In fact, 85 percent of cases develop after age 50. A 40-year-old woman has only a 1-in-70 chance of developing an invasive breast cancer by her 50th birthday, and only a 1-in-300 chance of dying of breast cancer by age 50.

Many cases of breast cancer are now diagnosed when the disease is "breast cancer in-situ." In-situ means that cancer cells are present, but they have not yet, and may never, start to invade or spread. The cure rate for in-situ cancer is virtually 100 percent. Treatment has improved for women with "localized" invasive breast cancers as well. Localized breast cancer has started to invade the breast, but has not spread to the lymph nodes. The five-year survival rate for localized breast cancer is 93 percent, compared with 78 percent during the 1940s. Unfortunately, survival rates are lower when breast cancer has spread beyond lymph nodes, and 40,000 women still died of breast cancer in 2003.

> *Key point:* Breast cancer is the most common type of cancer affecting women, but death rates have dropped due to earlier detection and better treatments. Lung cancer, though less common among women than breast cancer, actually takes more women's lives.

Family history and breast cancer

When Helen was diagnosed with breast cancer, her daughter, Sue, was understandably worried about her own risk for breast cancer. A family history of breast cancer, especially affecting a mother or sister, clearly increases a woman's risk. How worried should Sue be? A recent review of 52 breast cancer studies found that a woman whose mother or sister had breast cancer was twice as likely to develop the disease as an average-risk woman.[1] If *two* close relatives had breast cancer, a woman's risk tripled. The risk was greater still if a relative had the disease younger than age 50 or if more than two family members were affected. A small number of breast cancer cases are hereditary, caused by a gene that increases susceptibility. If multiple women in your family have had breast cancer, or if any woman in your family developed breast cancer before age 50 or ovarian cancer at any age, please see the "Hereditary breast cancer" sidebar.

For Sue, her mother's history is nothing to panic about. Ninety percent of women with a positive family history will never develop breast cancer. Unfortunately, lack of family history is not too reassuring because 90 percent of women who get breast cancer have no family history of the disease. There is a great deal, however, that women can do to improve their odds against developing breast cancer.

Key point: A family history of breast cancer *does* increase a woman's chances of getting the disease, but most women with a positive family history will never get breast cancer and most women who get breast cancer have no family history.

Improving your odds

Many women have a fatalistic view when it comes to breast cancer— if it's going to strike, they fear there's nothing they can do about it. In fact, research has dispelled this myth and is painting a far rosier picture. You may not be able to change your genes or family history, but a healthy lifestyle can do a lot to reduce your risk of breast cancer.

Hereditary breast cancer (BRCA 1 or BRCA 2)

About four out of every 1,000 women in North America have an inherited gene—either BRCA 1 or BRCA 2—that makes them highly susceptible to breast cancer and increases their risk for ovarian cancer. These genes are most common in Ashkenazi Jewish women, whose roots are in central or Eastern Europe. The BRCA 1 and BRCA 2 are short for Breast Cancer 1 and 2. Women who have inherited one of these genes from their parents have a 75 percent chance of developing breast cancer by age 70, and a 20–40 percent chance of developing ovarian cancer. Unfortunately, women with one of these genes often will develop breast cancer before they turn 50. Roughly 5 percent of all breast-cancer cases in the United States are caused by one of these abnormal genes.

A test is now available to determine whether a woman has the BRCA 1 or BRCA 2 gene. Health-care providers have differing opinions about who should be tested and what should be done if the gene is present. Close screening, cancer-preventing drugs, and preventive surgeries to remove the breasts and ovaries are all options that may reduce but not eliminate an affected woman's risk of cancer. The following factors increase the chance that a woman may carry the BRCA 1 or BRCA 2 gene:

- More than three women from the same side of the family have had breast or ovarian cancer
- Any woman in the family has had breast or ovarian cancer before age 50
- Any woman in the family has had both breast and ovarian cancer
- Any man in the family has had breast cancer

If any of these factors apply to you, consider genetic counseling to evaluate your family history and discuss your options. ■

Maintain a healthy weight

Though not widely known, obesity has been recognized as a significant risk factor for breast cancer, particularly in post-menopausal women. Obesity is thought to increase breast-cancer risk because fat tissue raises blood levels of estradiol, a form of estrogen. After menopause, fat becomes the main site for estrogen production in a woman's body. The more fat on your body, the greater your levels of estradiol, and the greater the exposure of your breasts to estrogen— which increases your chances of developing breast cancer. The

Nurses' Health Study in Boston found that post-menopausal women who were at least 45 pounds overweight had *twice* the breast cancer risk of their normal-weight peers.[2]

Sadly, obesity is a triple-whammy: Obese women get more breast cancer, the cancers are often found at a more advanced stage, and obesity increases the likelihood of surgical complications. This combination leads to much higher death rates among obese women who get breast cancer.

The bottom line: Maintain a healthy weight if at all possible. Specifically, try not to gain more than 15 to 20 pounds as an adult. A healthy diet and regular physical activity can help keep your weight in check.

Avoid estrogen after menopause

For many years, researchers have debated whether estrogen in pill form causes breast cancer. Estrogen is a main ingredient of birth-control pills as well as hormone-replacement drugs prescribed after menopause. In 1996, a review of 54 studies concluded that there may be a small increased risk of breast cancer among women who currently take birth-control pills or have used them within 10 years.[3] Most of the additional breast cancers were localized, and the risk returned to normal 10 years after stopping the pill. The benefit and convenience of birth-control pills for preventing unwanted pregnancies generally outweighs this small risk of breast cancer.

Looking at hormone replacement, the Women's Health Initiative Study, published in 2002, found that women on estrogen and progesterone after menopause had a 25 percent increase in breast cancer compared with a control group on placebo pills.[4] Of interest, the women on hormones had fewer colon cancers and hip fractures, but an unexpected and dramatic increase in strokes and heart attacks. For the time being, this landmark study has turned the tide of opinion against the routine use of hormone replacement after menopause.

Limit alcohol

Recently, alcohol consumption has been added to the list of risk factors for breast cancer. The more a woman drinks, the higher her risk. Studies estimate that risk increases by about 6 percent for each drink consumed on a daily basis.[5] Thus, a woman who drinks a single glass of wine each day does not have much to worry about. A woman who has four drinks per day, on the other hand, increases her risk by a significant 25 percent. When it comes to preventing breast cancer, moderation regarding alcohol use is advisable and abstinence is best.

Exercise

You can add breast-cancer prevention to the long list of benefits provided by regular physical activity. One study found a 50 percent reduction in rates of breast cancer prior to menopause among women who did moderate exercise four hours per week.[6] Another study found that women who regularly exercised enough to break a sweat as teenagers and during most of their lives likewise had a 50 percent reduction in breast-cancer rates later on.[7] Going out for a walk is great, but more vigorous exertion provides the greatest benefit.

Eat less animal fat

Fat in the diet, like fat around the midsection, may contribute to breast cancer. In 1991, the Nurses' Health Study asked over 90,000 female nurses aged 26 through 46 to describe their diets. Twelve years later, in 2003, the women who reported eating the most red meat and high-fat dairy products had developed one-third more breast cancers than the group who ate the least amount of animal fat.[8] This news contrasts with earlier studies of women after menopause, for whom fat in the diet did not correlate with more breast cancer. Until more is learned, and for other health benefits, women should moderate their consumption of animal fats (meat and cheese). Antioxidant-packed fruits and vegetables, whole grains, and fish are healthy alternatives that may reduce the risk of breast cancer.

Breastfeed your baby

Both child-bearing and breastfeeding appear to protect against breast cancer. A woman who has a pregnancy during her 20s has a greater benefit than a woman who waits until her 30s to start a family. Researchers are not sure of the reason, but one theory is that pregnancy matures breast cells and makes them less susceptible to cancerous changes.

After childbirth, breastfeeding protects the breasts because it lowers estrogen levels. The longer the duration of breastfeeding, the lower the chance of developing breast cancer later on. One study found 15 percent fewer premenopausal breast cancers among women who breastfed for three months compared with women who did not breastfeed at all.[9] Breastfeeding for 13 to 24 months lowered the risk by 34 percent. As an extra benefit, another study found that *daughters* who were breastfed as babies had breast-cancer rates 25 percent lower than those of peers who were never breastfed.

> *Personal action plan:* To improve your odds of avoiding breast cancer, get regular exercise, limit alcohol and animal-fat consumption, control your weight, breastfeed your children, and decline hormone replacement after menopause.

SCREENING FOR BREAST CANCER

The mammogram

Mammograms have been the backbone of breast-cancer screening for many years. They are x-ray pictures of the breasts that look for abnormal patterns of calcium that could indicate cancer. Each breast has to be compressed, or squished, a bit to get the best picture, which can cause some discomfort. Current machines use low doses of radiation, limiting the cancer risk from the test itself. A radiologist studies the pictures and creates a report detailing his findings. Mammogram reports used to vary a great deal depending on the particular radiologist and the region of the U.S. in which he or she practiced. A few years ago, radiologists nationwide agreed to use six standard categories for reporting mammogram results. This system, the "breast imaging reporting and data system," or BIRADS for short, has been widely adopted. The categories are as follows:

- BIRADS 0:   Needs additional images
- BIRADS 1:   Negative
- BIRADS 2:   Benign finding
- BIRADS 3:   Probably benign finding—needs short-term follow-up
- BIRADS 4:   Suspicious abnormality—consider biopsy
- BIRADS 5:   Highly suspicious for cancer

The BIRADS system has helped to reduce confusion, but the mammogram is still a far-from-perfect test. Mammograms find most, but not all, breast cancers (roughly 90 percent). Many mammograms find spots that are questionable—maybe OK, but maybe not—and there is a lot of debate over which of these spots need biopsies and which can be rechecked later.

Do mammograms save lives?

While PAP smears have cut death rates for cervical cancer by 80 percent, mammograms have been much less successful in lowering death rates for breast cancer. The benefit of mammograms is greatest for women aged 50 to 70. For that group, eight randomized, controlled studies found a 25 percent reduction in deaths from breast cancer among women who had a mammogram every one to two years compared with women who did not.[10]

For younger women, it is less clear whether mammograms provide any benefit. Unfortunately, younger women have denser breasts that reduce the ability of a mammogram to find small cancers. Some studies show a small reduction in death rates among women aged 40–49 who have mammograms versus those who don't, but other studies show no difference at all. One interesting analysis of the data concluded that for every 10,000 women aged 40–49 who are screened with a mammogram, there would be:

- 600 abnormal mammograms
- 300 biopsies
- 4 breast cancers detected
- 1 life saved

Women in the 40–49 age range should be aware that there is less benefit from mammograms for them than for older women. They should take their personal risk factors and family history into account when deciding whether to have mammograms.

> *Health tip:* If you are a woman aged 50–70, you stand to gain the most from a mammogram and should have one every one to two years. If you are 40–49, you might benefit from a mammogram, but there's an even greater chance that you might have a falsely positive test, which can only be proved wrong by more tests accompanied by lots of worry.

Mary's choice

Mary just turned 40 and asked me whether she should have a mammogram. I replied that it would be reasonable, but shared with her the controversy about the benefits for women her age. Mary decided to go ahead and have the test. A few days later, the report came back saying that her right breast had one little area that was not normal, but "probably benign," a BIRADS 3. The radiologist recommended that Mary have a repeat mammogram in six months to recheck the area. Mary wanted to know if the spot could be cancer. I honestly answered that it could be, but the chances were quite small, probably only 1 percent. The only way to be more certain would be to have a biopsy. Unfortunately, Mary was experiencing first-hand the imperfect and often murky nature of breast-cancer screening. She opted to wait, and was very relieved when her next mammogram showed no change in the area of concern.

When to stop

Although breast cancer gets more common as women get older, at a certain point the benefit of finding a very early cancer actually goes down. This is because breast cancers often behave less aggressively in elderly women than they do in young women. In addition, the older a woman gets, the more likely she is to die of another cause, such as heart disease or a stroke.

So when should you stop having mammograms? To date, breast-cancer screening studies have not included women over age 75, so we don't really have a scientific answer. Until better information is available, I tell healthy women patients that mammograms after age 75 are optional. For elderly women with multiple medical problems or poor functional status, there is not likely to be much benefit. According to the American Geriatric Society, women over age 75 with an estimated life expectancy of more than five years should get a mammogram every three years.

> *Key point:* A mammogram every three years is a reasonable choice for healthy women over age 75.

Other tests

Breast ultrasound is often used in younger women with breast lumps to help distinguish benign cysts and tumors from cancers. Ultrasound uses no radiation and can be quite helpful as a diagnostic tool. *Breast MRI* is a newer test being advocated by some for breast-cancer screening. It is much more expensive than mammography and requires intravenous injection of dye to get the best pictures. MRI uses a magnet, but no harmful radiation. Breast MRI can find some very small cancers that don't show up on mammograms. It also finds a lot more small spots of questionable significance that lead to worry and unnecessary biopsies. MRI is not currently recommended for screening, but that may change when studies are done to compare MRI with mammography.

> ❦ *Key point:* Although not perfect, mammograms remain the mainstay of breast-cancer screening. The greatest benefit in terms of lives saved is for women in the 50–75 age range.

CONTROVERSIES IN BREAST CANCER

Breast self-examination

Breast self-examination (BSE) long has been promoted as an important way for women to find breast cancer early. I personally spent a lot of time teaching women to do breast self-exams, handing out shower reminders, and making women patients feel guilty about not doing self-examination. Until recently, scientific data to support the value of BSE was very limited.

In 2002, however, the results of three large studies from China, Russia, and Canada all found no difference in breast cancer death rates in women who did BSE compared with those who did not.[11] The main difference, in fact, was that women doing BSE found more benign breast lumps, and therefore had more unnecessary biopsies and operations. I now believe that women who feel more secure doing BSE should continue, but that those who don't want to should not worry about it. Any woman who notices a new breast lump or change in a breast should, of course, see her health-care provider.

> ℚ *Health tip:* See your doctor if you notice a change or lump in your breast, but stop feeling guilty if you don't check your breasts every month.

Drugs to prevent breast cancer

"Chemoprevention," the use of anti-estrogen drugs such as tamoxifen and raloxifene to try to prevent breast cancer, has generated a lot of excitement in the past several years. Studies during the 1990s found that women diagnosed with breast cancer who took tamoxifen cut in half their risk of a second breast cancer compared with women who took a placebo. Other studies have confirmed that tamoxifen decreases the risk of developing invasive breast cancer in women who have precancerous results on biopsies. These findings have led researchers to wonder whether high-risk women or those with a family history of breast cancer should consider tamoxifen or the related drug, raloxifene, to lower their risk.

Some studies since have shown that tamoxifen and raloxifene can lower breast-cancer risk as much as 50 percent in women at high risk for the disease. Unfortunately, there is no free lunch: The anti-estrogen drugs have some very serious side effects, including blood clots in the legs and lungs, strokes, and uterus cancer. The risk of experiencing these side effects generally increases with age and when other risk factors like obesity or smoking are present. Women in their 40s and those without a uterus have a lower risk of complications from anti-estrogen drugs. Because of the side effects, women at low or average risk of developing breast cancer should forget about chemoprevention.[12] Women at high risk should discuss the pros and cons of this therapy with their doctor.

> *Key point:* Due to serious side effects, women at low or average risk of developing breast cancer should not take tamoxifen or raloxifene to prevent breast cancer. Women at high risk for the disease should discuss the pros and cons of these anti-estrogen drugs with their doctor.

Treatment of ductal carcinoma in-situ (DCIS)

Ductal carcinoma in-situ (DCIS) is a condition in which cancer cells are present in the milk ducts, but the cancer is completely localized and has not begun to invade the surrounding breast. While this condition may never spread or become invasive, sometimes it will. Up to one-third of women who die of other causes will have DCIS on autopsy. Unfortunately, there is currently no good way to predict which cases will stay dormant and which will grow.

Because of increasing use of mammograms, a lot of young women are being diagnosed with DCIS. Up to half of all breast cancers now diagnosed in 40- to 49-year-old women are DCIS. Doctors have differing opinions about how to treat DCIS. Recommendations range from a simple lumpectomy (removing just the affected area) or a lumpectomy with radiation treatment, to a mastectomy (removing the entire breast), or a protocol of anti-estrogen drugs and close follow-up. Some people have likened a mastectomy for DCIS to killing an ant with a sledge hammer, but up to half of American women hear the words "cancer cells" and elect the sledge-hammer approach. Further research is needed to help doctors and patients make more informed decisions regarding DCIS treatment.

> *Key point:* At present, there is no solid research to tell us the best way to treat localized breast-cancer cells known as ductal carcinoma in-situ (DCIS). Women diagnosed with DCIS should consult with their physician to determine the most reasonable treatment option for them.

SUMMARY

Breast cancer is the most common cancer affecting American women. Earlier detection and better treatments have improved survival rates for women who develop the disease. Women can take an active role in preventing breast cancer by exercising, limiting alcohol consumption, breastfeeding their babies, and avoiding obesity. In recent studies, breast self-examination, once a cornerstone of prevention efforts, did not appear to prevent deaths from breast cancer. Hormone replacement after menopause does increase breast cancer risk. Use of anti-estrogen drugs to prevent breast cancer is promising for high-risk women, but serious side effects make them too hazardous for low- or average-risk women. Screening for breast cancer with mammograms is recommended for women over age 40. Women age 50 to 70 have the greatest benefit, with a 25 percent reduction in breast cancer death rates.

CHAPTER EIGHTEEN

Prostate Cancer: Is Ignorance Bliss?

"To do nothing is sometimes a good remedy."
—Hippocrates

ONE-IN-TWO

Will you die *with* prostate cancer or *from* it?
Joe was in my office the other day and asked whether he should have
a PSA test, the blood test used to screen for prostate cancer. Joe was
pretty healthy, and had just celebrated his 85th birthday. He was surprised and a bit alarmed when I told him there was a *50 percent* chance
that he had cancer in his prostate gland just based on his age. He felt
a lot better, however, when I reassured him that the chance of prostate
cancer causing him any problems was very, very small. We both agreed
that new glasses and some physical therapy to strengthen his injured
leg were far more important than a PSA test. Joe, like most American
men, is far more likely to die *with* prostate cancer than *from* it.

What is the prostate gland?
The prostate gland is a walnut-sized organ found in men below the
bladder and in front of the rectum. The tube that carries urine from

the bladder and out through the penis, the urethra, passes right through the prostate gland. The prostate makes fluid and enzymes that help carry sperm when a man ejaculates. The prostate gland tends to grow slowly as men get older, often to the size of a golf ball or larger. During a rectal exam, an examiner's finger can feel the back surface and sides of the prostate gland.

The nature of prostate cancer

Prostate cancer is the most common cancer affecting American men, with roughly 220,000 cases diagnosed in 2003. Though one-in-two, or half, of all men in this country will get prostate cancer at some time during their life, it is much less deadly than some other common cancers, such as lung cancer. Even with new treatments, most men diagnosed with lung cancer die of the disease within a year. Prostate cancer is much more forgiving. With no treatment at all, 80 percent of men diagnosed with prostate cancer still will be living 15 years later.

Prostate cancer occurs when a group of cells in the gland grow abnormally, forming a nodule or tumor. The tendency to get prostate cancer runs in families, and the disease becomes more common as men get older. Prostate cancer is very rare in men under 40, affects up to 2 percent of men in their 50s, and up to 15 percent of men in their 70s.

Many prostate cancers are diagnosed in elderly men like Joe. In these cases, the men usually die of other problems like heart attacks or strokes before their prostate cancer spreads. Though some prostate cancers diagnosed in elderly men spread more quickly and do cause death, it's uncommon. Death from prostate cancer is more likely among men diagnosed when in their 50s or 60s, because they are less likely to die of something else before the cancer spreads. In 2003, roughly 29,000 American men died of prostate cancer—about one death for every seven cases diagnosed.

> *Key point:* Prostate cancer is the most common cancer affecting American men—one-in-two will get it during their lifetime—but the majority of those who have the disease will die of other causes.

PROSTATE-CANCER PREVENTION

An American blight

As you can see from table 18.1 (below), prostate cancer is much more common in the United States than anywhere else in the world. African-American men have the highest rates of any group in the world, with an incidence about 50 percent higher than that of Caucasian-American men. The prostate-cancer rate in the United States is more than 10 times as high as in Japan and the rest of Asia.

Although no one knows for sure why American men get so much prostate cancer, their high consumption of red meat and dairy products likely contributes.[1] When Japanese men move to the United States and start eating American food, their rates of prostate cancer skyrocket. Among Americans, the major risk factors for the disease include African-American ethnicity, obesity, inactivity, advancing age, and a family history of prostate cancer.

Table 18.1: Prostate cancer rates around the world

Country or region	Incidence per 100,000 men
United States	92.4
Australia	49.7
Caribbean	42.4
Western Europe	39.6
Southern Africa	31.0
Tropical South America	28.1
Central America	24.8
Southern Europe	16.9
Japan	8.5
Western Asia	7.1
China	1.1

Source: Global cancer statistics, 1999

> ❧❧ *Key point:* Prostate cancer is far more common in
> the United States than in the rest of the world. Risk
> factors include family history, African-American ethnic-
> ity, obesity, lack of exercise, and advancing age.

Tomatoes to the rescue

The statistics above should be scary to any American man, but you don't have to be a sitting duck to prostate cancer. You can take steps to lower your risk of getting the disease. Start by incorporating tomatoes and tomato products into your diet.

Tomatoes are a rich source of lycopene, a potent antioxidant that is 100 times stronger than vitamin E in counteracting cancer-causing free radicals. Lycopene is red in color and also found in watermelon, pink grapefruit, guava, and rosehip. In men, lycopene collects in the prostate gland. Researchers have noticed that prostate cancer is much less common in Southern Europe, where people eat a lot more tomatoes than in the United States.

A 12-year study of 47,365 male health professionals done by the Harvard School of Public Health found that men who ate tomatoes and tomato-based foods like tomato sauce had fewer prostate cancers than those who did not.[2] Men who ate tomato sauce two or more times per week had 23 percent fewer prostate cancers than men who ate less than one serving per month. The message for men is clear: Eat more tomatoes and tomato products to protect your prostate.

> ⊙ *Health tip:* Eating tomatoes may prevent prostate
> cancer. Look for ways to add tomatoes to your diet—
> such as tomato slices in sandwiches, tomato wedges in
> salads, tomato-based sauces for pasta, cherry tomatoes as
> hors d' oeuvres, and fresh or canned tomatoes in soups
> and stews.

Again, eat those fruits and vegetables

Although tomatoes may be the best food for the prostate, other fruits and vegetables are loaded with a variety of vitamins, minerals, and cancer-fighting antioxidants that likely benefit the prostate. What's more, men who eat more fruits and vegetables almost certainly will eat less of the red meat and dairy products that may contribute to prostate cancer. A study of 14,000 male Seventh-day Adventists helped confirm the benefit of fruits and vegetables. The men completed detailed diet questionnaires, and then were observed for six years. In addition to tomatoes, consumption of beans, lentils, peas, raisins, dates and other dried fruit all appeared to reduce the risk of prostate cancer.[3] For both cancer prevention and a healthier heart, try to eat five servings of fruits or vegetables each day. See chapters 2 and 13 for ideas and serving sizes.

Healthy lifestyle

Howard is in his 70s and has several friends who have been diagnosed with prostate cancer. Howard has been fortunate—his PSA tests have been quite normal and his prostate gland is healthy. Howard attributes his good fortune to an active sex life. He jokingly asked for a doctor's note recommending sex twice a week that he could give to his wife if the need arose. Indeed, some experts have theorized that regular ejaculation could "clean out" the prostate gland and prevent problems. Although research has failed to prove that ejaculation prevents prostate cancer,[4] I told Howard that it certainly wouldn't hurt to try.

Lifestyle-related factors that have been proven to *increase* the risk of prostate cancer include lack of exercise and obesity. Regular physical activity and reduction of fatty foods in the diet could go a long way toward improving overall health and preventing prostate cancer. Please review Chapter 3 for suggestions on exercise and Chapter 8 if you are overweight.

> ❄❄ *Key point:* A diet loaded with fruits and vegetables, ❄❄ especially tomatoes, combined with regular physical activity should lower a man's risk of developing prostate cancer.

TO CHECK OR NOT TO CHECK—THE PSA DEBATE

What is a PSA test?

When Fred came in for a physical at age 62, I asked if he knew about the PSA test and whether he wanted to have one. Fred admitted he didn't know much about it, and I explained that PSA is short for Prostate-Specific Antigen. The "PSA test" is a blood test that has been widely used during the past decade to screen men for prostate cancer. Normal prostate tissue makes a little bit of PSA, which gets into the blood stream. Prostate cancers tend to make more PSA, which causes higher levels in the blood. The higher the PSA level in your blood, the more likely that you might have prostate cancer.

Unfortunately, the PSA is not a perfect test. Several benign conditions can also raise PSA levels. These include infection or inflammation of the prostate gland and benign enlargement of the prostate, which is very common. In addition, men can have prostate cancer with a normal PSA level. Despite its imperfections, the PSA test often helps find prostate cancer early.

> ❄❄ *Key point:* The PSA is a blood test used to screen ❄❄ men for prostate cancer.

Does early diagnosis make a difference?

Hearing that PSA tests help find prostate cancers early, Fred assumed that the test is beneficial. Though early detection is helpful if you have cervical, colon, or breast cancer, it can be a mixed blessing for men with prostate cancer. The key to whether PSA screening is beneficial is whether early diagnosis leads to treatment that improves health and prolongs life.

Prostate cancer is a disease mostly found in older men. Without *any* treatment, 80 percent of men still will be living 15 years after the cancer is diagnosed.[5] Indeed, most men with prostate cancer will die of something else. In addition, diagnosing and treating prostate cancer is not at all benign. Two out of three men with high PSA tests don't end up having prostate cancer, but do end up with needle biopsies that can cause infections and lots of worry. Those who are diagnosed with prostate cancer experience a great deal of stress and anxiety. Both surgery and radiation treatments often cause impotency and loss of bladder control (incontinence).

All this would be worthwhile if we knew that prostate-cancer screening saves lives. Currently, however, there are no scientific studies proving that men who have PSA tests live any longer on average than men who do not. Large, well-designed studies are currently underway in the United States, Canada, and Europe to find out whether PSA screening makes a difference. Until the answer is known, men should consult with their doctors, consider their risk factors, and make an informed decision about whether to have a PSA test.

Key point: At present, there are pros and cons to screening for prostate cancer, but studies have not proven a benefit in terms of saving lives.

Understanding your PSA test result

The "normal" range for a PSA is often listed as 0 to 4 ng/ml. Mild elevations of PSA in the 5 to 10 range can be caused by cancer, infection, or benign enlargement of the prostate. Levels greater than 10 can be caused by benign disease, but are more likely to be due to prostate cancer. To confuse things more, PSA levels can fluctuate up and down,[7] and cancer can be present when a PSA level is less than 4.

Anywhere from 10 to 25 percent of PSA tests will yield an abnormal result. Men with abnormal results usually end up having an ultrasound of the prostate using a probe inserted into the rectum, then several biopsies done with a needle through the wall of the rectum and into the prostate gland. Roughly one-third of men with an elevated PSA will be diagnosed with prostate cancer, while two-thirds will not. Screening with PSA tests definitely leads to the diagnosis of prostate cancer earlier than not doing screening.

To improve the accuracy of the PSA test, some doctors look at the "PSA velocity," or how fast the level is changing. If a man's PSA is less than 4, but his PSA level has increased by one full point compared to a year ago, it increases the odds that cancer could be present. If, for example, Joe's PSA increased from 1.7 ng/ml last year to 3.4 ng/ml this year, he could have a problem.

At this time, there is no consensus among health-care providers about what to make of this situation (a normal PSA that has gone up more than expected). A repeat test in a few weeks is a reasonable option, since PSA values can fluctuate up or down over time. In general, the trend of several PSA tests is a better indicator of whether cancer is present than just two points in time. Many doctors would recommend a biopsy if Joe's repeat PSA was still higher than expected. ∎

What do the experts recommend?

Given the uncertainty about whether PSA tests save lives, it's not surprising that medical agencies offer differing screening recommendations. The U.S. Preventive Services Task Force reviewed all the available scientific evidence and concluded that there's not enough evidence to recommend for or against prostate-cancer screening. Other groups believe PSA screening may save lives, and that future studies will prove it. Both the American Cancer Society and the American Urological Society recommend yearly PSA tests for men over age 50 who are likely to live another 10 years. Some studies suggest that screening every other year will reduce the number of unnecessary biopsies while still finding most prostate cancers early.[6]

Should you get a PSA?

After hearing all of this, Fred asked whether I thought he should get a PSA test. I told him that it really is a personal choice. I definitely recommend PSA tests for high-risk men between ages 50 and 70, even if they seem perfectly well. The high-risk group includes African-American men and those with a family history of prostate cancer (father, brother, or uncles). PSA tests also are reasonable for healthy, low-risk men between ages 50 and 70, as long as they understand that screening is imperfect and could lead to further procedures without a proven benefit. I discourage PSA tests for men over age 70 because the risks of treatment increase, and older men are more likely to die of something else. If you decide to get a PSA test, see the sidebar on "Understanding your PSA test result."

Personal action plan: Learn about the pros and cons of PSA screening for prostate cancer. If you are a man aged 50–70, consider a PSA test every one to two years, especially if you are African-American or have a family history of prostate cancer.

PROSTATE CANCER TREATMENT—OPTIONS AND CONTROVERSY

Localized disease

Because of PSA screening, more and more men are being diagnosed with early-stage prostate cancer—"localized disease" that has not spread beyond the prostate. When prostate cancer is diagnosed, additional tests are performed to see whether the cancer has spread to the lymph nodes or bones. Currently, about 60 percent of men with a new diagnosis of prostate cancer will have localized disease (no apparent spread). At present, there is much controversy over how best to treat localized disease. The main treatment options include surgery, radiation, or watchful waiting.

Surgery, in the form of a radical prostatectomy, offers the best chance for cure. The operation, usually done by a urologist, involves removal of the entire prostate gland, a little surrounding tissue, and some lymph nodes. Older techniques always caused impotency because nerves needed for erections were cut. Newer techniques try to save these nerves, but many men still have erectile dysfunction after the surgery. They often find medication or devices helpful. Loss of bladder control can occur, but often improves over time. Radical prostatectomy is major surgery. Death is a rare complication of the operation, but the risk of death increases with age. National data shows that 8 percent of men over age 75 have a coronary event within 30 days of a radical prostatectomy.

Radiation offers similar short-term cure rates to those provided by surgery. Radiation can be delivered in one of two ways: via beams of radiation during a series of outpatient treatments, or via radioactive-seed implants placed directly into the prostate gland. These procedures are safer than surgery, but impotency and incontinence complications still occur. Radiation can cause damage to the rectum, resulting in pain and problems with bowel movements. Some experts believe prostate cancer is more likely to recur after radiation treatment than after surgery.

Watchful waiting means doing nothing. This may sound radical to American men who want to take care of business, but it's probably appropriate for many men over age 75. Watchful waiting avoids all the complications of treatment, allows for hormonal treatment if symptoms develop, and recognizes that most men in this age range will die of something other than prostate cancer.

Deciding how to treat prostate cancer can be complicated. Both age and type of tumor (see "Gleason score" sidebar) influence the decision. For otherwise healthy younger men (aged 50–69) with prostate cancer, many experts believe that radical prostatectomy is the treatment of choice. Older men and men who want to avoid the risks and complications of surgery often choose radiation therapy.

The Gleason score: Giving your prostate cancer a grade

Under the microscope, prostate tumors can be graded to help predict how slowly or quickly they might grow. The Gleason score, developed in 1974, is most commonly used. The pathologist examines two different areas of the prostate tumor, and gives the cells in each area a grade from 1 through 5. The more abnormal the cells look, the higher the grade. The two grades are added together to give a Gleason score (ranging from 2 through 10). The Gleason score is a fairly good predictor of how aggressively the tumor will behave. Gleason scores can be interpreted as follows:

- *Gleason 2–4:* Mildly abnormal cells. Very slow growing, unlikely to spread.
- *Gleason 5–6:* Moderately abnormal cells. Slow growing.
- *Gleason 7:* Mix of moderately and highly abnormal cells. In between.
- *Gleason 8–10:* Highly abnormal cells. Rapid growth, likely to spread.

As a rule, a lower Gleason score means a better prognosis. A score of 6 or lower is considered favorable, and is one factor that may support more conservative treatment. Unfortunately, lots of men have Gleason 7 scores, which are "in between" in prognosis. Some experts say that a Gleason 7 that has *mostly* moderately abnormal cells is better than a Gleason 7 that has *mostly* highly abnormal cells. In medicine, however, no rules are perfect. Some men with high Gleason scores do very well and some men with low scores fare poorly. ■

Interestingly, geographic location in the United States strongly influences type of treatment. For example, rates of radical prostatectomy are much higher on the West Coast compared with the East Coast, where radiation treatment is more popular.

> *Key point:* There are several good options for treating localized prostate cancer. Men should discuss the pros and cons of surgery, radiation, or watchful waiting with their health-care providers to make an informed decision.

Metastatic disease

If prostate cancer has already spread to lymph nodes or bones at the time of diagnosis, or if it spreads after an attempted cure (surgery or radiation), then it is considered "metastatic." At this point, cure is out of the question. The best shot at prolonging life is to minimize production of male hormones, which promote this type of cancer. The most effective way to halt production of male hormones is surgical removal of the testicles. Another effective option is to take "anti-male hormone" pills or shots. About 80 percent of men with metastatic prostate cancer will respond to these treatments and have several more good-quality years of life, though sexual function will be lost.

SUMMARY

Prostate cancer is the most common cancer affecting American men. The disease affects mostly older men, who typically die of another cause before their prostate cancer spreads. Obesity, sedentary lifestyle, family history of the disease, and African-American ethnicity are risk factors for prostate cancer. Regular physical activity and a diet full of tomatoes and other fruits and vegetables may lower a man's risk of getting prostate cancer. The PSA blood test can help to diagnose prostate cancer early, but there are many falsely positive tests and it is unknown whether early detection saves lives. Healthy men between the ages of 50 and 70, especially those with risk factors for prostate cancer, are most likely to benefit from PSA tests every one to two years. If prostate cancer is diagnosed, treatment options include surgery, radiation therapy, or watchful waiting.

PART IV

Active Aging

CHAPTER NINETEEN
....

The Golden Years:
How to Age Gracefully

"The things that should accompany old age:
fairly good health to the end, an unceasing
interest in life, and the affectionate esteem
of a large circle of friends."
—William Osler, M.D.

LIVING LONGER AND LONGER

Americans are living longer than ever. Upon reaching age 65, a woman will live on average until age 84 and a man until age 81. By the year 2020, when most baby boomers will have reached retirement age, there will be *four times* as many Americans over age 65 as there were during the peak of the baby boom back in the 1950s.

While most people would agree that living longer is a good thing, it does have a down side. Between aging baby boomers and their parents, more and more people will be facing health problems that often go hand in hand with getting older. The rest of this chapter focuses on how to live longer and healthier by preventing or managing common aging-related health concerns. These include vision and hearing loss, incontinence, infections, multiple medications, and safety both on the road and in the home.

Subsequent chapters address three more serious problems—osteoporosis, arthritis, and memory loss—with an emphasis on prevention and reducing suffering. The book's final chapter deals with end-of-life medical decisions, and tools such as living wills that can help clarify your wishes.

How long can you live?

My patient Ruth was the oldest person I have known. She was as sharp as a tack, had a delightful sense of humor, and lived independently when she turned 100. Ruth started to decline at 105, and needed help with bathing, dressing, and eating. She was still very bright, but did not want to be a burden. She said she was ready to join her friends who had died many years ago, and she passed away in her sleep after her 106th birthday.

I often wonder why Ruth lived so long. Researchers in a relatively new field called "anti-aging medicine" are trying to answer similar questions: Why do some people live well past 100? If free from illness and degenerative disease, how long *can* humans live? How can we extend the human lifespan and improve the quality of life along the way? At present, there are no certain answers, but anti-aging proponents believe that most aging-related illness can be prevented, or at least slowed. Currently, researchers are studying nutritional supplements, vitamins, herbs, natural hormones, and even single-gene mutations for potential anti-aging affects.

With anti-aging medicine in its infancy, no one really knows how much the human lifespan can be extended. According to the *Guinness Book of Records*, the world's longest-lived person with an authenticated birth record was Frenchwoman Jeanne Calment, who died in 1997 at the age of 122. If anti-aging research eventually pans out, humans might be living even longer in the future.

How to live longer and better

So far, no treatments or supplements have been able to slow aging. In animal studies, only one strategy has actually extended lifespan: restricting calories. With both mice and rats, thin animals fed limited amounts of food lived longer than overweight animals that ate as much as they desired. Similar studies are underway on monkeys, and initial results are promising. It is unknown whether simple calorie restriction will extend the lives of people. Even if it does, polls show that most people would not be willing to limit calories to live longer.

Until more is learned, the common-sense advice for a long, healthy life boils down to the lifestyle lessons learned throughout this book:

- Eat a healthy breakfast and take a once-a-day multiple vitamin
- Stay physically active—walking and yoga are great activities most older people can enjoy
- Get a good night's sleep to improve mood and energy level
- Drink alcohol in moderation or not at all
- Do not smoke
- Wear a seatbelt, and don't drive if your skills have slipped
- Have a positive attitude—negative thoughts are bad for your health as well as your mood, so let them go
- Keep on learning to keep your brain healthy
- Make time for family, friends, and pets

Of course, despite the healthiest lifestyle, aging often brings health challenges that affect people's ability to carry on with daily activities and enjoy life. Read on to learn more about how to prevent and treat common aging-related health problems. For a little good news, look at the sidebar "Not just older, but in many ways better," which discusses some medical conditions that actually improve with age.

Not just older, but in many ways better

Fine wines, Scotch whiskey, and rare coins all improve with age. The same cannot always be said of people. Many medical conditions worsen with aging. Fortunately, there are some nice exceptions: *Migraine headaches*, most bothersome during midlife, tend to get less frequent and less severe as people age. *Allergies*, which are very annoying to young and middle-aged adults, sometimes improve as people get older. *Breast cancer*, which tends to be much more aggressive and likely to spread when it affects young women, is often slower growing when it occurs in older women.

For many people, another benefit of getting older is that they have learned, through wisdom and experience, to enjoy life more. A friend told me that he has enjoyed simple pleasures in life more since turning 50 than he ever did before. With age, many people actually do take the time to smell the roses. A patient in his 60s once told me, "I allow more time now, but I'm not in a hurry like I used to be, so it all works out." ■

COMMON ISSUES OF AGING

Vision loss

Maureen is 85 years old and suffers from *macular degeneration*, a condition in which the vision cells in the back of the eye deteriorate. She has blurred vision and can no longer read. Maureen is very fearful that she may lose her sight completely. Unfortunately, Maureen is not alone. Up to one-fourth of people over the age of 75 have some degree of macular degeneration. Until recently, treatment of macular degeneration has not been very successful. That changed in 2001 when exciting results from the Age-related Eye Disease Study (AREDS) offered hope for people like Maureen.

In the study, individuals with moderately severe macular degeneration or severe disease in just one eye who took antioxidant vitamins and zinc supplements lowered their risk of vision loss by 25 percent compared with similar people who took a placebo.[1] The antioxidant vitamins included 500 mg of vitamin C, 400 units of vitamin E, and 15 mg of beta-carotene. This combination of nutrients, found in supplements like Ocuvite and VisiVite, is now widely recommended for people with moderate or severe macular degeneration. Current or former smokers may be better off with VisiVite's smoker's formula, which leaves out the beta-carotene (beta-carotene supplements may increase the risk of lung cancer in smokers).

Despite the great news regarding *treatment*, the AREDS study was disappointing with regard to *prevention* of macular degeneration. The participants with no macular degeneration or only mild disease did not appear to benefit from supplements during the seven-year-long study. A healthy lifestyle might be the best bet for prevention. The Nurses' Health Study found that a healthy body weight, not smoking,[2] and a diet full of fruits and vegetables all seemed to protect against macular degeneration. Some interesting preliminary studies suggest that the cholesterol-lowering statin drugs may also reduce the risk of macular degeneration. Stay tuned for further research on whether cholesterol reduction might help protect vision.

Cataracts are the other major cause of vision loss in older eyes. Cataracts are cloudy areas in the normally clear lens of the eye. Almost half of all people will have cataracts by age 75. Years of exposure to sunlight and smoking both contribute to cataracts. Wearing sunglasses or ultraviolet-blocking prescription glasses and avoiding smoking can help to prevent or slow cataracts. Fortunately, surgical removal of cataracts has become very safe and almost routine in the United States, with excellent results at restoring vision.

> *Health tip:* If you are over age 65, get your vision checked every one to two years. Vision loss from cataracts is easy to cure via surgery, and vision loss from macular degeneration may be slowed by antioxidant vitamin and zinc supplements.

Hearing loss

Fred is my typical older patient with hearing loss. He is 72 years old, and was dragged into the office by his wife because he sets the volume on the TV too high and ignores her when she talks to him. Fred claims he is simply not paying attention, but a hearing test confirms that he has significant hearing loss, especially in the higher frequencies. He has trouble hearing his wife's high-pitched voice, especially with the television blaring, but he can hear his low-pitched buddies out in the neighborhood quite well. Fred is not alone. More than one-third of adults, men more often than women, have trouble hearing by age 65. By age 85, 30 percent of people are totally deaf in one ear.

Loud-noise exposure is the major preventable risk factor for hearing loss. Noise-caused hearing loss is the most common injury among workers in the United States—from machines in factories and shops, loud engines, hammering, or sirens. Noise from guns, lawn mowers, trimmers, loud music, and motors contributes as well. The key to hearing-loss prevention is to use ear protection during exposure to loud noise. Inexpensive foam earplugs are a great way to protect your hearing when involved in noisy activities like mowing the lawn.

Older adults should have their hearing checked if anyone notices or suspects a hearing problem. Hearing aids have gotten better at amplifying the frequencies that need to be louder so that there is less distortion of sound. They are also smaller than ever, with most units fitting right in the ear canal. Even though sounds will not be perfect, most people with age-related hearing loss will notice a big improvement with hearing aids.

Personal action plan: If you or someone you care about is having trouble hearing, arrange for a hearing test and find out whether a hearing aid will help.

Urine incontinence

When 66-year-old Karen came in for a well-woman examination, I asked my routine question about bladder problems. She said she was embarrassed to admit it, but she did occasionally lose control of her bladder. Sometimes she would lose a little urine during a cough or sneeze. Other times she would feel a strong urge to go, and if she didn't get to a bathroom quickly, she might leak some urine. She had started to wear a pad and thought nothing would help.

I reassured Karen that her problem is quite common. Up to one out of three people over age 65 experiences at least occasional problems with urine incontinence (accidental loss of urine). Karen has experienced the two most common kinds of incontinence, known as "stress" and "urge." Stress incontinence involves loss of small amounts of urine during coughing or sneezing. Urge incontinence occurs with a sense of urgency, where a person has got to go right away "or else," and the or else can involve losing a fair amount of urine.

Although there is no cure for incontinence, some simple exercises and behavioral modification can help. See the "Bladder training for better control" sidebar for some exercises that may improve matters. If incontinence persists, see your physician for an evaluation or referral to someone with expertise in treating urine incontinence.

Tests may be recommended to be sure the bladder is emptying properly and that there is no infection in the urine. Medications like oxybutinin (Ditropan) or tolerodine (Detrol) may help in some situations, especially with nighttime incontinence. The medications can cause side effects such as dry mouth or constipation. Surgery may be an option when the bladder has "dropped" due to childbearing or following a hysterectomy.

Key point: Urinary incontinence is a very common problem affecting older adults. Bladder-training exercises can help control it.

Bladder training for better control

Kegel exercises: The urinary sphincter is a small muscle that normally prevents urine from leaking out of the bladder. It is part of the pelvic-floor muscles that surround your rectum and anus. Imagine that you are pinching off a bowel movement. Squeeze these pelvic floor muscles, and count to four. Do not tighten your buttocks or abdominal muscles. Relax, and then squeeze again.

Try to do this 25 times, twice a day. Some people do a couple squeezes each time they stop at a red light while driving. As the muscle gets stronger, bladder control should improve. Once you have practiced, try to do a squeeze *before* you cough or sneeze, and it should prevent urine from leaking. When you have a strong urge to empty your bladder, three quick squeezes can prevent a bladder contraction and decrease leakage.

Bladder training: A normal bladder should be able to hold at least 12 ounces of urine. Due to both nerves and habit, many people get the urge to go long before their bladder is full. To train your bladder, collect and measure the amount of urine present when you first get the urge to go. If it measures less than 6 ounces, bladder training may help your bladder control. The next time you have to go, try to "hold it" an extra 10 or 15 minutes (do this at home). Hold it a little longer each day until your capacity has increased, and you can manage the urge better. If you are out and get a strong urge to go, stop, squeeze your pelvic floor muscles until the urge eases, then calmly walk to the bathroom. ∎

PREVENTING PROBLEMS

Infections

The immune system slows down a bit as people age, causing older individuals to have more problems with infections. That's why the West Nile virus that sweeps through the country each summer is much more likely to cause serious illness in people over age 65 than in younger adults. More common infections, including influenza and pneumonia, likewise take a much greater toll on the elderly. In fact, the combination of influenza and pneumonia is the seventh-leading cause of death in the United States. Fortunately, vaccines can prevent the majority of influenza cases and some of the most serious cases of pneumonia.

The "flu" (influenza) vaccine is recommended each fall for all adults over the age of 50. The pneumonia shot, called "Pneumovax," protects against several strains of strep pneumonia, a nasty bacteria that can cause pneumonia and bloodstream infections. The pneumonia vaccine is recommended once at age 65 or earlier for people with emphysema, diabetes, or other medical conditions that increase their risk of pneumonia.

People who get their first Pneumovax before age 65 should get a booster shot after they turn 65, at least five years after their first shot. Although not an official recommendation, I advise people who got their first pneumonia shot after age 65 to get a single booster seven to 10 years later.

Personal action plan: If you are older than 50, or have a chronic medical condition, get a flu shot every year. If you are 65 or have any chronic medical condition, get a pneumonia vaccine.

Multiple medications

June came in as a new patient with dizziness, upset stomach, headaches, and a list of eight medications and several over-the-counter supplements that she took on a regular basis. It was very hard to figure out whether June's symptoms were due to an illness or some of the medicines. After I carefully pared her list down to three essential medications, June felt much better and was very grateful for a simpler and less-expensive lifestyle.

Today's longer lives are often accompanied by chronic medical conditions and multiple well-intentioned medications. Unfortunately, whenever people take more than one medication, each additional medicine dramatically increases the risk of adverse reactions, harmful drug interactions, and mix-ups in dosing. People taking five daily medications have a 50 percent chance of a harmful reaction or drug interaction, and the odds approach 100 percent when eight medications are used each day.

The best bet for preventing problems from multiple medications (also called "polypharmacy") is to make sure that there's a good reason to take each recommended medicine, and to stop medications that are not doing the job or are no longer necessary. If you take more than one medication daily, here are some pointers to help prevent a polypharmacy problem:

- Keep an up-to-date list of all the medications you take, including both prescription and over-the-counter medicines and supplements.
- Indicate on your list why you take each pill (i.e. blood pressure) and how often.
- Bring your list of medicines (or the actual bottles) to each doctor's visit.
- At least once per year, ask whether any of the medications on your list can be stopped.
- If a medicine was prescribed for a symptom (such as pain or upset stomach), and the symptom has stopped, ask whether you can stop the medicine or use it only as needed.
- Get a weekly pill organizer with a compartment for each day of the week. Fill it the same day each week and use it to be sure you take medicines when needed, without skipping or taking extra doses by mistake.

Safety on the road

When an 86-year-old man careened through a crowded farmer's market near Los Angeles in 2003, 10 people died and national attention was focused on the safety of elderly drivers. Accident statistics confirm that drivers over the age of 75 have the highest death rates per mile driven of any age group. Injury rates are highest for drivers aged 18 to 24, but drivers over age 75 are a close second. The overall death and injury toll is limited because older drivers drive far fewer miles compared with younger drivers. Older drivers also tend to avoid riskier driving times like rush hour and after dark. Still, one of the toughest decisions faced by elderly drivers (and their families) is when to hang up the keys for good.

There are no clear guidelines or absolute criteria that say when it is unsafe to continue to drive. Some people drive safely throughout their lives, and others drive poorly from the start. In most families, however, adult children or a spouse know when an older driver's skills have slipped enough to create a danger. The key is for someone to speak up and tell the person that it's no longer safe for him or her to drive. If the driver refuses to listen, a personal physician can be very helpful as an "authority figure" to make a formal recommendation.

Safety at home
Like motor-vehicle accidents, home accidents and falls that cause injury or even death are more common among the elderly. Poor vision, slower reflexes, weaker muscles, and medication side effects all contribute. A safer home environment can do a great deal to reduce the risk of injuries. Remove clutter, throw rugs, loose cords, and furniture that people can trip on. Add night lights in the bedroom and bathroom, grab bars in showers and tubs, and padding for sharp corners and edges.

Older adults should get their vision checked on a regular basis, so they can see as well as possible in their home. Walking and other physical activity keeps muscles strong and reduces the risk of a fall. With a little effort, many accidents can be prevented.

Older adults who live alone face some special problems. Can they safely do all the needed activities of daily living, like cooking, cleaning, shopping, and managing finances? When do they need extra help in the home or even an assisted-living environment? Is someone checking each day to be sure they are doing okay? These can be difficult questions to answer.

With friends and family to help, many people can live safely at home despite significant health problems. There are no absolute criteria for determining when people can no longer live independently. This is another area in which common sense, family involvement, and advice from health-care professionals can all help balance a desire for independence with safety.

Q *Health tip:* The daily newspaper can be a good safety check for an older person who lives alone. A friend in the neighborhood can look each day, and check on the person if the newspaper is left out on the driveway.

SUMMARY

Americans are living longer, healthier lives than ever. As scientists look for ways to extend the human lifespan even further, more people are facing health issues related to aging. Vision loss from cataracts can be cured with surgery, and vitamin and zinc supplements may slow down macular degeneration. Although age-related hearing loss is very common, many cases can be helped with hearing aids. Urinary incontinence is also very common, but can often improve with exercises, bladder training, or medication. Annual flu shots and a pneumonia shot at age 65 can prevent a lot of infections among the elderly. Awareness and careful attention to the need for medications can help prevent problems related to too many medications (polypharmacy). Finally, some simple, common-sense measures can help to reduce accidents among the elderly both on the road and in the home.

CHAPTER TWENTY

Osteoporosis: Give Your Bones a Break... So They Won't

"Osteoporosis is a silent disease process that takes an enormous medical and economic toll on an aging population."
—National Osteoporosis Foundation

BRITTLE BONES

A bad break

At age 72, Lois had always considered herself a healthy person. She was trim and had never been to a hospital except to give birth to her children. That changed suddenly one Saturday when Lois slipped on some water in her bathroom. She fell and broke her right hip. Lois ended up with a hip replacement and an unexpected couple of weeks in a nursing home to recover. A bone-density test (a DEXA scan) done afterwards found that Lois has severe osteoporosis, or thinning of her bones, that she had been completely unaware of. Lois is fortunate to be back home and in fairly good shape. Many people who break a hip do not fare as well. Some end up in a nursing home long term, or have to cope with a permanent disability.

What is osteoporosis?

Osteoporosis literally means "porous bones." Imagine a light chunk of cement filled with lots of big air bubbles, compared with a heavy piece that has only tiny pockets of air. Bone with osteoporosis, like the air-filled cement, is much more likely to break than denser bone or the heavier cement. An estimated 8 million women and 2 million men in the United States have osteoporosis, or bones that are much thinner or less dense than they should be. Another 18 million Americans have bones that are thinner than normal, but not thin enough to meet the medical definition of osteoporosis.

Osteo*porosis* is NOT the same as osteo*arthritis*. Osteo*porosis*, or bone thinning, causes no pain unless or until a bone actually breaks. Osteo*arthritis* is the most common kind of arthritis. It occurs when the knees, hips, joints in the hands, or other joints start to wear out, causing pain and stiffness. Read Chapter 21 to learn more about osteo*arthritis*, but stay tuned here to find out about preventing and treating osteo*porosis*.

Silent epidemic

Osteoporosis is usually a silent condition. Like Lois, most affected people have no symptoms at all until a thin bone breaks. Unfortunately, broken bones or fractures happen much too often in people with osteoporosis. Hip fractures are the most serious, and 300,000 occur each year in the United States. Painful and disabling fractures of spine vertebrae, the wrist, and other bones happen as well. Overall, osteoporosis is blamed for 1.5 million broken bones each year in the United States. In fact, one out of every two American women will have a fracture due to bone thinning at some point in her life. This is unsettling news, but women will be glad to hear that osteoporosis often can be prevented, or treated if it has already developed.

> ❱❰ *Key point:* Osteoporosis is a painless thinning of
> ❰❱ bones very common among older Americans, espe-
> cially women. People with osteoporosis are much more
> likely to suffer a hip fracture or other broken bone. A lot
> can be done to prevent and treat osteoporosis.

WHO IS AT RISK FOR OSTEOPOROSIS?

Bones change as you age

The thickness or density of bones increases throughout childhood
and adolescence. As children and teens grow, their bones get longer,
but also thicker, denser, and stronger. Bones get increasingly dense
until they peak between ages 25 and 35. The bones are like a storage
bank for calcium. The more that is stored up during the first three
decades of life, the more that will be available to draw upon during
old age. Young people can maximize their bone strength and fill
their bone banks by eating lots of calcium-rich foods (mostly dairy)
and getting plenty of exercise.

Bone density is usually stable during the 30s and 40s, but
decreases after age 50. If bones start out strong and lose mass slowly
and gradually, they will stay strong enough that they are not likely
to break. If bones start out thinner, or lose mass too quickly, osteoporosis develops and breaks are much more likely.

> Q *Health tip:* Children and teens should eat plenty of
> calcium-rich dairy products and get regular exercise
> to build strong bones that will last a lifetime.

The gender gap

Women are much more likely than men to develop osteoporosis for
two reasons. First, women generally have smaller bones and lower
bone density at their peak than men. Second, bone mass tends to

drop quickly in women during the first five to 10 years after menopause, as levels of estrogen decrease. This double whammy puts women at much greater risk than men for osteoporosis and broken bones.

Men are not immune, however. My father was a sad example. Many years ago, he suffered from several painful fractures in the vertebrae of his mid-back. At the time, I did not realize that men got osteoporosis. Despite bigger bones and greater bone density, however, men still lose bone mass after age 50. If they live long enough, and especially if they have other risk factors for bone loss (see table 20.1), they do develop osteoporosis. My father smoked, drank more than he should have, and took oral steroids for asthma—all of which robbed calcium from his bones.

Like my father, roughly one in three men will have osteoporosis by age 75. Unfortunately, men tend to fare worse with the disease than women, experiencing higher rates of death and disability following hip fractures compared with women the same age.

> ✹ ✹ *Key point:* Women develop osteoporosis more often than men due to smaller peak bone density and rapid bone loss after menopause. Men get osteoporosis more often than people think, especially when in their 70s and 80s.

Risk factors for thin bones

Bone is a much more active structure than most people realize. Living cells inside our bones are constantly remodeling and rebuilding the structure of the bone. Some cells dissolve and take away damaged areas, while other cells rebuild and strengthen the bone. When this system is in balance, bones remain strong and healthy. When the system is out of whack, bones get thinner and the structure of the bone itself is weaker and more likely to break. A variety of factors can disturb this balance of bone breakdown and rebuilding and lead to osteoporosis.

Table 20.1 lists some of the common risk factors for developing osteoporosis. Some of these risk factors cannot be changed, including gender, race, family history, and frame size. People with these inherited risk factors should be especially conscientious about taking steps to prevent osteoporosis and being screened for the disease. Several medications and medical conditions also increase the risk of osteoporosis. Some of the common ones are listed in Table 20.1. People who take oral steroids (like prednisone) on a long-term basis are at extremely high risk for osteoporosis and fractures. Finally, a number of unhealthy lifestyle choices negatively impact bone health. Smoking, excess alcohol, lack of exercise, and inadequate calcium intake each contribute to bone thinning.

Table 20.1: Risk factors for osteoporosis

Things beyond your control

Female sex

Runs in your family (especially parent or sibling)

Caucasian or Asian race

Slender frame

Early menopause or removal of ovaries

Medical conditions / medications

Overactive thyroid or excess thyroid-replacement medication

Bulimia or anorexia

Long-term steroid use (oral or injected)

Anti-estrogen medication (i.e., tamoxifen)

Choices you can control

Smoking

Excess alcohol

Physical inactivity

Lack of calcium and vitamin D in diet

✋ *Personal action plan:* If you have taken an oral-steroid medication like prednisone or cortisone on a long-term basis, you are at very high risk and should ask your doctor about preventing and screening for osteoporosis.

❧ *Key point:* When it comes to osteoporosis, some risk factors are beyond a person's control, but healthy lifestyle choices can do a great deal to prevent a problem.

LIFESTYLE FOR HEALTHY BONES

Don't smoke

Many people are surprised to hear that smoking contributes to osteoporosis. Smoking is thought to decrease the body's ability to absorb calcium, and has some anti-estrogen effect (estrogen is the female hormone that helps to keep women's bones strong). The Framingham Study found that women who took estrogen after menopause had fewer hip fractures than those who didn't. Women who took estrogen but smoked, however, lost the protective effect and had as many hip fractures as the women who did not take estrogen.[1] For smokers, osteoporosis is yet another reason to kick the habit.

Be active

Everyone knows that exercise makes muscles stronger, but exercise also makes bones stronger. By simply supporting the weight of a person's body, the cells that build bone are stimulated and bone strength improves. When bones stop supporting weight, they lose strength quickly. When astronauts are weightless in space, for example, loss of bone mass occurs rapidly and poses a threat upon return to Earth. Confining a person to bed has a similar harmful affect on bone density. Fortunately, an opposite, bone-strengthening effect occurs when bones are stressed with "weight-bearing" exercise.

Weight-bearing exercise refers to pretty much any physical activity done outside of a swimming pool. Walking, jogging, bicycling, dancing, tai chi, aerobics, and weight training are all examples of weight-bearing exercises. The more active you are, the stronger your bones are likely to be. Inactive people who start to walk even a few blocks a day will benefit.

Limit alcohol intake

Excess alcohol is toxic to cells in the bone marrow that remodel and rebuild bones. Too much alcohol also flushes calcium from the body, reduces absorption of calcium from foods, and often displaces healthier foods that contain calcium from the diet. Heavy alcohol consumption is clearly a risk factor for developing osteoporosis. To add insult to injury (literally), people who drink are more likely to fall or get into other accidents in which their already thin bones are likely to break.

Studies confirm that men who abuse alcohol have more osteoporosis and higher rates of fractures compared with non-drinkers. Women who drink moderately, on the other hand, appear to have bones that are as healthy as tee-totaling women.[2] For healthy bones, limit alcohol consumption to one drink daily for women and two per day for men.

> *Key point:* People can help prevent osteoporosis by doing plenty of weight-bearing physical activity, avoiding tobacco, and limiting or avoiding alcohol.

CALCIUM AND VITAMIN D

Calcium needs

The mineral calcium is the main building block of our bones. Though most of the body's calcium is stored in bones, the mineral is used by cells throughout the body. If you don't eat enough calcium, your body steals it from your bones to meet its needs. Over time, this process will thin the bones and possibly lead to osteoporosis.

Calcium requirements vary during a person's life. Although experts offer differing recommendations, most agree that growing teens need more calcium to fuel fast-growing bones, and people over age 50 need extra calcium to slow the loss of bone. Following are the recommended amounts of calcium people should consume each day to build and keep healthy bones:

- Ages 11 to 24:   1,200–1,500 mg per day
- Ages 25 to 50:   1,000 mg per day
- After age 50:   1,200–1,500 mg per day

Unfortunately, the typical American diet contains less than 600 mg of calcium, not enough for optimal bone health.

> *Key point:* Most Americans eat far less calcium than the amount recommended for building and maintaining healthy bones.

Calcium—sources and supplements

Table 20.2 lists some good sources of dietary calcium. The richest and most available calcium sources are dairy products—such as milk, yogurt, or cheese. In general, three to four servings a day of dairy will supply most people's calcium needs. People who don't get enough calcium in their diet should take a supplement. If you eat one to two servings of dairy each day, I recommend 500 mg of *elemental* calcium in a supplement once a day. If you rarely or never eat dairy, I recommend 500 mg of elemental calcium in a supplement twice a day.

Each of the various calcium supplements on the market contains one of three types of calcium salts or compounds:

- *Calcium carbonate*, the most commonly used form of calcium, is found in Os-cal, Tums, Rolaids, and Viactive Soft Calcium Chews, to name a few. Calcium carbonate is best absorbed when taken with food, and it can cause constipation.
- *Calcium citrate*, found in Citrical, can be taken with or without food. It may be absorbed better than calcium carbonate in elderly people who have less stomach acid.
- *Calcium phosphate* is found in Posture and calcium-fortified orange juice and soy milk. It is well absorbed with or without food, and may cause less constipation than other types of calcium.

Read the label to see how much elemental calcium your supplement contains. For example, 1,250 mg of calcium carbonate contains 500 mg of elemental calcium. The body does not absorb more than 500 mg at a time very well, so it is better to take 500 mg twice a day than 1,000 mg all at once. The bottom line is to find an affordable supplement that you can take without experiencing unwanted side effects.

Table 20.2: Calcium-rich foods

Dairy group	Calcium
Yogurt, plain nonfat (1 cup)	400 mg
Yogurt, plain low fat (1 cup)	350 mg
Yogurt, fruit flavored (1 cup)	320 mg
Milk—whole, 1%, 2%, skim (1 cup)	300 mg
Swiss cheese (1 oz)	280 mg
Cheddar cheese (1 oz)	200 mg
Ice cream or ice milk (1 cup)	190 mg
Mozzarella cheese (1 oz)	180 mg
American cheese (1 oz)	175 mg
Cottage cheese, 2% (1 cup)	160 mg

Other foods

Sardines with bones (3 oz)	350 mg
Tofu, calcium-set (½ cup)	270 mg
Orange juice, calcium fortified (1 cup)	260 mg
Spinach, cooked (1 cup)	245 mg
Salmon, canned with bones (3 oz)	215 mg
Kale, cooked (1 cup)	180 mg
Okra, cooked (1 cup)	170 mg
Bread, calcium fortified (2 slices)	160 mg
Almonds (⅓ cup)	120 mg
Broccoli (1 cup)	100 mg

Key point: Milk, yogurt, and cheese are rich sources of calcium. People who do not eat three or four servings of dairy or other calcium-rich foods each day should take a calcium supplement.

Vitamin D

Vitamin D, also called calciferol, is a fat-soluble vitamin needed to help the body absorb calcium from food and use it to build stronger bones. The major food source of vitamin D is milk. Milk has been fortified with vitamin D for many years to prevent rickets—a bone disease in children caused by vitamin D deficiency. One cup of milk contains 100 international units (IU) of vitamin D.

Vitamin D is also found in fish and fish oil, with large amounts in cod-liver oil. In addition, people produce their own vitamin D when they are exposed to the ultraviolet rays in sunshine. On a clear day, 30–60 minutes of sun exposure may be enough to help the body meet most of its vitamin D needs.

For younger adults, the recommended daily requirement of vitamin D is 400 IU. For those over age 50—who can't absorb the vitamin as well from foods or make as much when exposed to sunlight—many experts recommend 800 IU of vitamin D per day. Because we don't always get enough sunshine or eat the right foods to meet the recommended amounts of vitamin D, supplements are a good idea.

Studies have found that older people who take vitamin D supplements have fewer broken bones[3] and even fall less often[4] than similar people who do not take vitamin D. Taking vitamin D plus calcium appears to build bone and prevent fractures better than taking calcium alone. I recommend that people who take calcium supplements also take 400 IU of vitamin D each day (unless your calcium supplement already contains 400 IU of vitamin D). Frail elderly people, especially if they are confined indoors, should take 800 IU per day of vitamin D in supplement form.

Like other fat-soluble vitamins, too much vitamin D can be harmful to the kidneys and heart. How much is too much depends on the person, but more than 1,800–2,000 IU is considered unsafe. To be prudent, don't take vitamin D supplements exceeding 800 IU per day.

Q *Health tip:* If you eat two or fewer servings of dairy each day, consider taking a 500 mg supplement of calcium along with a 400 IU supplement of vitamin D daily. (You won't need the extra vitamin D if your calcium supplement already contains 400 IU of vitamin D.)

SCREENING FOR OSTEOPOROSIS

Screening tests

Several good tests are available to check your bones for thinning or osteoporosis.

- The *DEXA scan* (short for Dual-Energy X-ray Absorptiometry) uses low-dose x-rays to measure the density of the hip, lower spine, and sometimes the wrist bones. It is fairly quick, reliable, and affordable.

Understanding your DEXA scan results

A DEXA scan measures bone density in the lower spine, hips, and sometimes wrists. Two scores are reported for each bone, a Z-score and a T-score. The Z-score compares your bones to those of other people your age of the same sex. The T-score compares your bones to those of a "normal" 30-year-old, when bones are the densest. Although Z-scores are interesting to see how you compare with your peers, T-scores are used medically to define osteoporosis. A T-score of 0 means your bones are as dense as those of a 30-year-old. The lower, or more minus, the T-score, the thinner your bones are compared to that ideal. A T-score of minus one (–1) means that your bone is about 10 percent less dense than that of the normal young person. Based on T-scores, each bone (your hip, spine, or wrist) falls into one of the following categories:

- *Super strong:* T-score greater than zero (any positive number)
- *Normal:* T-score zero to –1
- *Low bone mass or "osteopenia":* T-score –1 to –2.5
- *Osteoporosis:* T-score below –2.5

For example, if your spine has a T-score of –1.8 and your hip has a T-score of –3.1, then you have low bone mass in your spine and osteoporosis in your hip. Since hip fractures are the most serious consequence of osteoporosis, treatment decisions are often based on the T-score of the hip bone. For the mathematically minded, Z-scores and T-scores are actually standard deviations. Thus, a T-score of minus two (–2) is two standard deviations below the mean or average bone density of a normal young adult. ∎

- The *CT scan*, technically called a Quantitative Computed Tomography (QCT), can also measure bone density of the spine accurately. However, QCT uses more radiation and is more expensive than a DEXA scan.
- *Ultrasound* scans of the heel bone can detect whether the bone is normal or too thin. Ultrasound uses only sound waves, so there's no radiation. It's inexpensive, but not accurate enough to monitor small changes in bone density that may occur with medications used to treat osteoporosis.

The DEXA scan currently is the test most commonly recommended by medical professionals to screen for and monitor osteoporosis. (If you have one of these tests, see the sidebar on "Understanding DEXA scan results" to learn more about the findings.)

Ultrasound screening often is used for awareness raising and screening large groups of people at community events like health fairs.

> ❧❧ *Key point:* The DEXA scan is a very accurate and ❧❧ fairly affordable way to screen for osteoporosis and measure bone density. Ultrasound of the heel bone is an inexpensive, but less accurate test often used for osteoporosis screening.

Who should be screened?

Now that accurate tests can diagnose osteoporosis, and treatments are available that lower fracture risk in affected people, national efforts are underway to encourage screening of individuals at high risk for the disease. The highest risk group includes women over 65 years old. Since 2002, the U.S. Preventive Services Task Force (USPSTF) has recommended that all women over age 65 undergo routine screening for osteoporosis.[5] The USPSTF also recommends screening women age 60 to 64 if they weigh less than 150 pounds or did not undergo hormone replacement therapy following menopause. In addition, I recommend a DEXA scan for any postmenopausal woman who breaks a bone.

Unfortunately for men, current screening guidelines focus only on women. Older men who have several of the risk factors listed in Table 20.1 or an unexpected fracture should ask their doctor about osteoporosis screening.

> ❧❧ *Key point:* Osteoporosis screening is now recom-❧❧ mended for all women over age 65 and for high-risk women over age 60 (including women who weigh less than 150 pounds or never took hormones after menopause).

PREVENTING FRACTURES

Avoid a fall

Once osteoporosis is diagnosed, the goal of treatment is to prevent painful and disabling fractures. An often overlooked strategy is to prevent falls that lead to broken hips and wrists. The following steps can reduce the chance of a fall for you or a loved one:

- Have an eye check-up—new glasses or cataract treatment may improve vision
- Install a grab bar in the bathroom near the shower or bathtub
- Begin walking and doing leg exercises to build strong legs (and bones)
- Take up tai chi. The ancient Chinese martial art improves balance and strength and has been shown to reduce falls.[6]
- If unsteady, get a physical-therapy evaluation for a cane or walker
- Make sure your home has good lighting and a night light in the bathroom
- Remove throw rugs, loose cords, and furniture that someone could trip over
- If you're a frail woman prone to falls, consider hip pads in the undergarments

Calcium and vitamin D

People with osteoporosis should get at least 1,200 mg of calcium daily between their diet and supplements, as well as 400–800 IU of vitamin D. The combination of calcium and vitamin D is better than either one alone for preventing fractures. Please review the section on calcium and vitamin D for information on sources and supplements of these important nutrients.

Bisphosphonates

The bisphosphonate drugs alendronate (Fosamax) and risedronate (Actonel) slow the breakdown and absorption of bone, allowing the body to build stronger and denser bones. These are the most potent medications used to treat osteoporosis, reducing the risk of spine, hip, and other fractures.[7] Both drugs can be taken daily or just once a week, but they can cause serious inflammation or ulcers of the esophagus or stomach. To reduce the risk of this complication and to improve absorption of these drugs, they must be taken with a glass of water in the morning 30 minutes before eating or taking other medications. Patients should remain upright during the 30 minutes.

Calcitonin

Calcitonin is a hormone that also slows the breakdown of bone and helps treat osteoporosis. Calcitonin is not as potent as a bisphosphonate, but has some advantages. It comes as a nose spray—nasal calcitonin (Miacalcin)—and one spray daily helps to prevent spinal fractures. Since there are no pills to swallow, people with heartburn or a sensitive stomach do well with calcitonin. If a painful spinal fracture occurs, calcitonin helps relieve the pain as the fracture heals. The nasal spray can cause irritation or running of the nose, but calcitonin is well-tolerated by most people.

Estrogen

Estrogen treatment after menopause, also called hormone-replacement therapy (HRT), has a very healthy effect on women's bones. Women on HRT have far fewer spinal and hip fractures than women who do not take hormones. Unfortunately, the Women's Health Initiative Study in 2002 found that women on combination HRT (estrogen and progesterone) had more heart attacks, strokes, blood clots, and breast cancer than women taking a placebo.[8] This landmark study turned the tide against the routine use of HRT. Estrogen is still an option for women with osteoporosis, but the risks, benefits, and alternatives should be considered carefully.

Selective estrogen receptor modulators

A class of drugs called selective estrogen receptor modulators (SERMs) provide some of the benefits of estrogen without some of the harmful effects. SERMs protect bone like estrogen does, but do not increase the risk of breast cancer. (In fact, the SERM tamoxifen is used to treat and prevent breast cancer.) The SERM raloxifene (Evista) has been shown to reduce the risk of spinal fractures by 36 percent. Unfortunately, there's a down side: Like estrogen, raloxifene increases the risk of blood clots and heart disease; but unlike estrogen, it does not prevent hot flashes. Raloxifene may be a good choice for women who can't tolerate bisphoshonates or are at high risk for breast cancer.

> *Key point:* Exercise, a safe home environment, and adequate intake of calcium and vitamin D are important for all people with osteoporosis. Several effective medicines are available to strengthen bones and help prevent fractures.

SUMMARY

Osteoporosis is a painless thinning of the bones that affects millions of older Americans and causes over 1 million hip, spine, or wrist fractures each year. Thin, Caucasian or Asian women have the greatest risk. Smoking, alcohol consumption, and lack of weight-bearing exercise all contribute to bone thinning. Good calcium and vitamin D intake will help maintain strong bones. Screening for osteoporosis is now recommended for all women over age 65. Several effective medications are available to treat osteoporosis and prevent osteoporosis-related fractures.

CHAPTER TWENTY-ONE

Arthritis: Coping with Creaky Joints

"Arthritis is the leading cause of disability among Americans over age 15."
—Arthritis Foundation

UNDERSTANDING ARTHRITIS

Wear and tear

Fred, who had just turned 64, came to see me because he feared he had arthritis. Fred's knees were bothering him and he was thinking of quitting his bowling league. I knew it was serious because Fred had bowled for 30 years. A set of x-rays confirmed that Fred had mild to moderate osteoarthritis of his knees. I explained to him that the cartilage in his knees, the shock-absorbing tissue between his upper and lower legs, was thinning and wearing out. The good news was that it was not gone completely.

Fred agreed to try leg-strengthening exercises, glucosamine (a supplement that may protect and heal cartilage), and ibuprofen before bowling. Fred continues to bowl and says his knees feel better now than they have for years. Fred does have arthritis, but he is coping quite well for the time being.

What is arthritis?

Arthritis, a word that combines the Greek words *arthron* (joint) and *–itis* (inflammation), is a disease characterized by painful and inflamed joints in the body. There are more than 100 different types of arthritis affecting people of all ages, but arthritis is more common as people get older. Because arthritis is one of the leading causes of disability in the United States, efforts to prevent and treat the disease are increasing nationwide.

Osteoarthritis, also known as degenerative joint disease (DJD), is the most common kind of arthritis. It occurs when the cartilage in a joint breaks down and wears out, causing pain and stiffness. The cause of osteoarthritis is not known, but we do know that it runs in families and is more common in people who are obese and in joints that have been injured. Osteoarthritis affects more than 20 million Americans. Women are afflicted more often than men, and the disease usually occurs after age 45.

Osteoarthritis typically affects the knees, hips, low back, neck, base of the thumb, and fingers. It usually develops gradually over months to years, as a nagging pain in the joint, sometimes with stiffness or swelling. Middle-aged men sometimes develop osteoarthritis in one hip or knee, especially a knee with a prior injury. Middle-aged and older women are more likely to get osteoarthritis in both knees and hands, and sometimes in the hips, feet, or shoulders. Osteoarthritis has a broad range of severity—from mildly annoying to so severe that it's hard to walk. Simple x-rays can help make the diagnosis.

> *Key point:* Osteoarthritis, or wear and tear of the joints, is the most common type of arthritis and often affects the knees, hips, back, or hands.

What are some other common types of arthritis?

Rheumatoid arthritis affects roughly 2 million Americans, mostly women. The cause or trigger of rheumatoid arthritis is unknown, but we do know that it is an "auto-immune" disease in which the body's own immune system attacks the tissue lining the inside of joints, causing inflammation. The joint lining, called "snyovial tissue," becomes thickened and inflamed and damages the nearby cartilage and ends of the bones. The disease often starts in middle age, but can affect children or the elderly. It can start gradually or suddenly, but usually involves small joints in the hands or wrists. The elbows, shoulders, neck, hips, knees, ankles, or feet can be involved as well.

Rheumatoid arthritis is usually symmetric, meaning similar joints are affected on both sides of the body. The involved joints become swollen, warm, and stiff. Stiffness in the morning often lasts more than an hour. People with rheumatoid arthritis often feel sick, complaining of fatigue, loss of appetite, or fever. An experienced physician can usually make the diagnosis with some help from x-rays and blood tests. Early diagnosis is important because drug treatments often are effective in slowing or stopping the progression of the disease. Without treatment, rheumatoid arthritis can cause deformities and disability.

Gout also affects as many as 2 million Americans, but mostly men instead of women. The first sign of gout usually is the sudden onset of swelling, pain, redness, and warmth in the joint at the base of a big toe. The area is quite painful, even to a light touch. The first gout attack resolves in a few days, but the same joint or other joints in the feet, ankles, or even hands can flare up later on. Gout is one type of arthritis whose cause is well understood: Too much uric acid in the blood, which leads to uric acid crystals (imagine salt crystals) forming in the affected joint. High uric-acid levels and gout can run in families, but are most common in overweight men and heavy drinkers. England's King Henry VIII, with his portly build and penchant for mead, is perhaps the best-known gout sufferer in history. Fortunately, lifestyle changes and medication can be very effective in controlling gout.

Fibromyalgia is not a type of arthritis, but it has some similar symptoms and is often mistaken for arthritis. Fibromyalgia mostly affects women, causing muscle pain, fatigue, and insomnia. Pain is common in the neck, shoulders, and back where muscles attach to bones. The pain can be widespread and has been described as stiffness, aching, or burning. People with fibromyalgia often have trouble falling asleep, wake up frequently, or awake without feeling refreshed. X-rays and blood tests are normal with fibromyalgia, and its cause is unknown. Though the disease can be chronic, exercise often helps and there's no long-term damage to the muscles or joints.

Several medical conditions (including psoriasis, lupus, Lyme disease, ulcerative colitis, and Crohn's disease) can include arthritis as part of the affliction. In addition, joints can be directly infected by bacteria like staph or gonorrhea, causing a sudden, very painful arthritis called septic arthritis. An infected joint needs emergency treatment with antibiotics and sometimes surgical drainage. People with any unexpected or unexplained joint pains should get an opinion from their doctor.

Personal action plan: If you have persistent pain in any joint, see your personal physician for an evaluation. Any hot, red, or extremely painful joint needs to be checked urgently.

PREVENTING ARTHRITIS

Maintain a healthy weight

Many people fear that arthritis is an inevitable part of aging. This is simply not true. The biggest single thing you can do to protect your joints is maintain a healthy weight. If you're overweight or obese and doubtful that you'll ever be able to get down to your "ideal" weight, don't despair. Even a modest weight loss of 10 to 20 pounds will significantly reduce the strain on your joints. Research suggests that as little as 11 pounds of weight loss can reduce the risk of osteoarthritis of the knees by *50 percent*.[1] This is because each pound of weight carried around the waist exerts 4 pounds of extra force on the knees. If you find this hard to believe, place 20 pounds of weights or canned food in a backpack or shoulder bag. Carry it around for half an hour,

Does running or other sports cause arthritis?

For years, experts have debated whether the wear and tear of running and other high-impact sports causes arthritis, especially of the knees and hips. The latest evidence indicates that the answer is no—at least when it comes to running. Studies comparing long-time runners with non-runners have generally found no increase in arthritis among the runners. A classic study of college varsity athletes found that former runners were no more likely than former swimmers to develop arthritis.[7]

The connection between osteoarthritis and sports seems to occur only when a joint is seriously injured. Serious knee injuries are the biggest culprit—the later development of osteoarthritis in the injured knee is almost guaranteed. Here's why: Ligament injuries can cause a knee to be unstable, which increases wear and tear. Cartilage injury causes abnormal wear and circulation to the remaining cartilage.

Unfortunately, a lot of sports place high twisting loads on the joints. Such sports include basketball, football, baseball/softball, volleyball, soccer, and racket sports. The key to preventing arthritis down the road is injury prevention, and good treatment and rehabilitation of injuries that will inevitably occur. For athletes, good physical conditioning, stretching, and safety equipment will help prevent injuries. ∎

then feel the sense of relief and ease on your joints when you take it off. Now try to imagine how much better you would feel carrying 10 or 20 fewer pounds on your frame all the time.

> *Health tip:* If you are overweight, as little as 10 pounds of weight loss can greatly reduce your chances of getting arthritis in your knees.

Be active, but sensible

At one time, experts worried that too much exercise could cause arthritis and recommended rest for arthritis sufferers. We have since learned that strong muscles help support joints and may prevent joint damage. With activity, circulation to cartilage improves and joints get stronger and more flexible. Sensible exercise is now a mainstay of arthritis treatment, but patients often wonder how much exercise is too much. For some answers, see the sidebar "Does running or other sports cause arthritis?"

For arthritis prevention, a program of regular physical activity is the key. Exercise helps you maintain a healthy weight, strengthen muscles, and improve stamina and mobility. Low-impact sports such as walking, swimming, and cycling are easy on the joints but great for fitness. If you like to jog, keep it up, but consider lower-impact exercises if your joints start to complain.

If you're currently inactive, find something you enjoy and start doing it three days a week for 20 minutes or more. Garden, dance, mow the lawn, walk the dog—just do it. Start gradually and pay attention to your body. If a joint is sore, try an activity that uses other joints. If you get injured, allow time to heal and resume activity gradually. If a joint continues to hurt, or is very painful, seek a medical opinion.

> *Key point:* Regular physical activity is your best bet for maintaining healthy joints and preventing osteoarthritis. Use common sense to avoid joint injuries.

Consider glucosamine

Though lots of drugs are promoted for treating the pain and stiffness of osteoarthritis, none has been shown to prevent the development or progression of the disease. However, the popular food supplement glucosamine may prove to be the magic bullet for arthritis prevention. Glucosamine is a chemical that occurs naturally in our joints and is thought to promote the growth and repair of cartilage. The glucosamine in supplements is extracted from crab, shrimp, or lobster shells. It was used for years to prevent sore joints in racehorses and dogs before someone decided to try it on people.

Studies in humans have found that taking glucosamine supplements daily for several weeks provides arthritis pain relief similar to that provided by ibuprofen-type medications.[2] An exciting Belgian study found that people with osteoarthritis of the knees who took glucosamine regularly for three years had no worsening of the disease, while those who took a placebo did experience worsening.[3] Currently, the National Institutes of Health (NIH) has a large research study underway to assess whether glucosamine, and another supplement, chondroitin, really do slow the progression of osteoarthritis.

Chondroitin, a substance found in cartilage, may also help to repair damaged joints. Chondroitin in supplements comes from shark cartilage or cartilage from the tracheas of other animals. In recent studies to determine whether chondroitin provides any benefit for arthritis sufferers, findings have been mixed.

Glucosamine supplements come as either glucosamine *sulfate* or glucosamine *HCl*, and often contain chondroitin as well. The glucosamine sulfate form is better absorbed and is used in most research studies.

While awaiting the NIH study results, I recommend plain glucosamine sulfate for my patients with osteoarthritis and for those who have some sore joints plus a family history of the disease. Glucosamine is more likely to protect big, weight-bearing joints like the knees and hips than the smaller joints in the hands and spine. The usual dose is 1,500 mg per day.

> *Personal action plan:* If your hips or knees hurt from time to time, or you have early osteoarthritis, try glucosamine for a couple of months to see whether it helps.

Other tips to prevent arthritis:
- Eat plenty of fruits and vegetables. They contain vitamin C and other antioxidants that may protect your joints.

- Eat more fish. Fish oil has a natural anti-inflammatory effect, and some studies suggest that people who eat more fish are less likely to develop rheumatoid arthritis (the disease is much less common in Japan, where lots of fish is consumed, compared with the United States).
- If you have flat feet, get supportive walking or running shoes designed for "pronators." They should have a good arch support. You can also try orthotics or insoles like "SuperFeet" with a well-formed and well-fitting arch. Proper arch support will help keep the ankle, knee, and hip joints in balance and pain free.
- If you have high-arched feet, get walking or running shoes with plenty of cushioning to reduce the pounding on your joints.
- Avoid high-heeled shoes (a three-inch heel puts seven times as much force on your foot joints as a one-inch heel).
- Arrange a comfortable work space. Use a wrist pad at your computer keyboard, get a chair with good back support that lets your feet rest comfortably on the floor, and place your computer monitor at eye level to avoid neck strain.
- Prevent tick bites to reduce your chance of getting Lyme disease arthritis. When hiking or camping in wooded areas, use insect repellent, wear long sleeves and pants, and check for ticks after your outing.

COPING WITH ARTHRITIS

The medical team

If you have arthritis, find a good family physician or internist to oversee your medical care. A rheumatologist (specialist in arthritis) will likely play a key role in your care if you have an inflammatory condition such as rheumatoid arthritis or lupus. Orthopedic surgeons often are involved in treating severe arthritis, mainly if joint-replacement surgery becomes necessary. Physical therapists, massage therapists, nutrition counselors, and other providers can help arthritis sufferers as well. Learn as much as you can about your particular condition, because informed patients make better decisions about treatment options. Organizations like the Arthritis Foundation are great information sources.

Healthy living with osteoarthritis

As with most medical conditions, a healthy lifestyle is a key component of the treatment plan for osteoarthritis. Adopting the arthritis prevention strategies discussed above may be even more important if you have already developed osteoarthritis. Here are some of the main recommendations:

- Maintain as healthy a weight as possible. If overweight, try to lose 10 pounds to reduce the stress on your joints.
- Stay active: Walk, cycle, or swim at least three days a week, but don't push too hard if the activity makes your joints hurt. Studies confirm that people with osteoarthritis who get regular exercise have fewer symptoms than those who are inactive.
- Use a walking stick or cane to take some stress off a sore knee or hip. Hold the stick on the non-painful side for a better-balanced gait.
- Consider yoga, tai chi, or low-impact aerobics.
- Make time during each day for periods of rest, and try to get a good night's sleep.
- Laugh, play, relax, and soak in a warm tub or spa from time to time.

Medications for osteoarthritis

Acetaminophen, the pain-relieving ingredient in Tylenol, has become a mainstay of osteoarthritis treatment. Acetaminophen is generally safe, inexpensive, and has few side effects. It is a good pain reliever with a mild anti-inflammatory effect. Doses up to 4,000 mg per day are usually safe (eight 500 mg tablets), but people who weigh less than 110 pounds and those with liver or kidney problems should limit their daily dose to 3,000 mg or less. Many people with mild osteoarthritis manage very well with a couple of acetaminophen per day. High doses of acetaminophen can thin the blood further in people taking the blood thinner warfarin (Coumadin).

Glucosamine, with or without chondroitin, can also benefit some people with osteoarthritis. As noted above, this supplement may help prevent arthritis, and also appears to help reduce pain and worsening in individuals with mild or moderate osteoporosis. However, it won't help severely arthritic joints in which the cartilage layer is completely gone and bone is rubbing on bone. Glucosamine is quite safe, but must be taken for several weeks before its anti-inflammatory effect kicks in. Large, weight-bearing joints like the hips and knees get the most benefit from glucosamine.

Non-steroidal anti-inflammatory drugs (NSAIDs) are a large class of drugs that are very effective in relieving both pain and inflammation. Aspirin was the first of this group, called "non-steroidals" because they do not contain steroids such as prednisone. Table 21.1 lists some of the commonly used NSAIDs. Although generally safe, NSAIDs can have serious side effects that lead to a number of hospitalizations and even deaths each year. These include stomach or duodenal ulcers with possible bleeding, kidney failure, high blood pressure, and swelling of the feet, to name a few. Smaller people (less than 110 pounds) and those over age 65 should use lower than typically recommended doses.

> Q *Health tip:* Take non-steroidal anti-inflammatory drugs with food to reduce stomach upset.

Table 21.1: Partial list of Non-steroidal anti-inflammatory drugs (NSAIDs)

Generic name (brand names)
Aspirin
Diclofenac (Cataflam, Voltaren)
Diflunisal (Dolobid)
Etodolac (Lodine)
Fenoprofen (Nalfon)*
Flurbiprofen (Ansiad)*
Ibuprofen (Advil, Motrin)
Indomethacin (Indocin)*
Kertoralac (Toradol injection)*
Ketoprofen (Orudis, Oruvail)
Nabumetone (Relafen)
Naproxen (Aleve, Anaprox, Naprelan, Naprosyn)
Oxaprosin (Daypro)
Piroxicam (Feldene)*
Salsalate (Disalcid)
Sulindac (Clinoril)
Tolmetin (Tolectin)

may have higher risk of side effects per the FDA

COX-2 inhibitors are a newer generation of NSAIDs that, until recently, were being promoted as a safer alternative to traditional NSAIDs. This new class includes roficoxib (Vioxx), celecoxib (Celebrex), and valdecoxib (Bextra). The COX-2 drugs block pain and inflammation the same as traditional NSAIDs, but with less tendency to cause stomach irritation and bleeding. Stomach bleeding still occurs, but the rates are about half that of traditional NSAIDs. On the downside, the COX-2 inhibitors are expensive and have the same potential for kidney damage, increased blood pressure, and swelling of the feet as NSAIDs. Unfortunately, roficoxib (Vioxx) was removed from the market in 2004, after studies found an increased risk of heart attacks with prolonged use. Similar concerns have been raised regarding other COX-2 inhibitors. Until more is known, I advise caution with these drugs.

Fish oil, which is loaded with omega-3 fatty acids, is a natural anti-inflammatory that has been proven to reduce inflammation in people with rheumatoid arthritis. This is because the omega-3 fatty acids in fish oil lower the production of chemicals that cause inflammation in our bodies. In a number of studies, 3 grams per day of fish oil reduced inflammation from rheumatoid arthritis about as much as a daily dose of most NSAIDs.[4] (People with rheumatoid arthritis usually need treatment with disease-modifying drugs in addition to an anti-inflammatory.) Though helpful for rheumatoid arthritis, fish oil does not appear to benefit those afflicted with the more common osteoarthritis.

> *Key point:* Acetaminophen is a safe, first-line pain medication for osteoarthritis. Glucosamine relieves pain and may prove to protect joints from further damage.

Injections

Cortisone injections are one of the best ways to quickly reduce inflammation in a joint. When rheumatoid arthritis flares up in one or two joints, a cortisone shot can be very effective. Cortisone shots are more controversial when it comes to osteoarthritis. They may provide temporary relief, but they do not prevent worsening of the disease. Many experts believe that joints might wear out faster if cortisone shots are overused because they reduce the ability of cartilage to repair itself.

In recent years, its become popular to inject lubricating medication into arthritic knees. The main ingredient is hyaluronic acid, a chemical normally found in joint fluid. Researchers have theorized that injecting additional hyaluronic acid would act as both a lubricant and a shock absorber, reducing pain as well as wear and tear. The product is injected into the painful joint weekly for several weeks, and may give relief for up to six months.

Several slightly different forms of hyaluronic acid are available (brand names include Synvisc, OrthoVisc, Hyalgan, and BioHy).

Unfortunately, results of studies on hyaluronic acid injections have been mixed. A recent review concluded that such injections, compared with placebo shots, provided minimal benefit.[5] Clinical studies in the next few years should help clarify whether they truly help and who is most likely to benefit.

🌟🌟 *Key point:* Cortisone shots can help an acutely painful joint. Time will tell whether "lube jobs" (hyaluronic acid injections) offer any long-term benefit for osteoarthritis.

Surgery—the miracles: The development of the artificial hip joint in 1962 was a true miracle of modern medicine. In cases of severe osteoarthritis, when the cartilage wears out and bone painfully rubs on bone, replacing a joint can relieve pain and return people to activities they never dreamed they would do again. In the decades since the first artificial joints were implanted, stronger materials and better surgical techniques have made the devices more durable, allowing patients to do more.

Hip replacement is the most common joint-replacement surgery, with more than 150,000 performed each year in the United States. Years ago, cement was routinely used to keep the artificial hip in place. With time or too much activity, the cement could crack and the metal joint could loosen and fail. Today, most implants are done without cement. The surface of the artificial hip is rough and porous where it contacts the thigh bone, so that the bone can actually grow into the metal surface, forming a tighter, more durable bond than cement. New artificial hips last much longer than the old ones, around 20 years, and allow activities like hiking, swimming, cycling, bowling, golf, and cross-country skiing. Higher impact activities like jogging, basketball, or handball are discouraged. Hips most often are replaced due to severe osteoarthritis, but also when other types of arthritis or injuries have damaged the hip joint.

Knee replacement is the next-most-popular joint surgery. Like artificial hips, knee replacements have improved over time and often last for 20 years. In knees, the worn out joint is not actually removed, but the upper and lower parts of the bones are resurfaced with smooth metal-and-plastic linings. Good pain relief is achieved, and most people can resume an active lifestyle. Newer techniques also are being used to replace finger joints (in people with severe or deforming rheumatoid arthritis), ankles, wrists, and even shoulders.

The big question with joint replacement is when to bite the bullet and do it. There are no exact guidelines. Younger, more active people are more likely to wear out an artificial joint and require a difficult second joint-replacement operation. People who are too frail or have multiple medical problems are at higher risk for complications from the surgery. Ultimately, long-time arthritis sufferers will know when they are ready to proceed. If you currently have mild arthritis, it should be comforting to know that joint replacement will be an option if you need it down the road.

> ❧❧ *Key point:* Hip- and knee-joint replacements are
> ❧❧ highly successful in the treatment of severe
> osteoarthritis.

Surgery—the bust: People with mild or moderate osteoarthritis of the knees are often offered *arthroscopy* to "clean out" and smooth the cartilage in a knee that is not bad enough to need a replacement. Arthroscopy uses pencil-sized instruments to look inside the knee and do the necessary trimming and smoothing. Only small incisions are needed. Until recently, more than 300,000 Americans per year had arthroscopy to treat their osteoarthritis.

Unfortunately, a 2002 study at the Houston Veterans Administration Hospital suggested that the procedure could be doing more harm than good.[6] The study compared three groups of individuals with osteoarthritis of the knee. One group underwent an arthroscopy technique called "rinsing," the second group underwent a different type of arthroscopy known as "trimming," and the third group had a fake or placebo surgery that involved anesthesia and small incisions but no actual arthroscopy. The study followed the participants for more than a year after the procedure (or fake procedure) and came up with some surprising results: There was no benefit from *either* of the arthroscopy techniques. In fact, patients who had the real operations had more knee pain and stiffness during the next year than patients who did not have arthroscopy. Although arthroscopy has an important role in treating knee injuries, it appears to offer no benefit for osteoarthritis.

Q *Health tip:* Steer clear of arthroscopy if it is recommended purely to treat osteoarthritis in your knee.

SUMMARY

Many different types of arthritis can cause painful and stiff joints. The most common by far is osteoarthritis, associated with wear and tear on the joint cartilage. Osteoarthritis affects the knees, hips, spine, and hands of millions of older Americans. A healthy body weight and regular, sensible physical activity help prevent osteoarthritis. The supplement glucosamine, with or without chondroitin, may slow the worsening of osteoarthritis and offer some pain relief. Acetaminophen and non-steroidal anti-inflammatory medications like ibuprofen also provide some relief. People with osteoarthritis fare best if they choose low-impact, rather than high-impact physical activities. For severe osteoarthritis, knee or hip replacement surgery can work miracles.

CHAPTER TWENTY-TWO

Memory Problems: How to Keep from Forgetting

"The charm, one might say the genius of memory, is that it is choosy, chancy, and temperamental."
—Elizabeth Bowen

THE BANE OF DEMENTIA

Worried about your memory?

Sue came in one day worrying that she was losing her memory. Sue had always been very sharp with numbers. She had retired from the banking business a year earlier at age 62. She was worried because she sometimes had trouble remembering someone's name when she ran into them after not seeing them for a while. In addition, she occasionally forgot to buy an item or two at the store, whereas she used to remember the whole grocery list. Sue feared that she had early Alzheimer's disease. She remembered her grandmother declining with Alzheimer's, and was terrified that she might follow suit.

In my office, Sue got a perfect score on a simple memory test. She said she had no problems balancing her checkbook or finishing crossword puzzles. I reassured Sue that it's usually a good sign when a person is worried about her own memory. It's much more worrisome when only her family realizes there's a problem. Fortunately, Sue appears to have a little benign forgetfulness, not early Alzheimer's disease. Sue's fears are understandable, however. Anybody who sees a family member decline with Alzheimer's mourns the loss, struggles with care decisions, and naturally fears a similar fate.

> Q *Health tip:* If you're worried about being forgetful, but are reading this chapter, it's very unlikely that you have a serious problem.

Defining dementia and Alzheimer's disease

When non-medical people hear the word *dementia*, or *demented*, they often imagine a crazed person like Dr. Jekyll's alter-ego, Mr. Hyde. In medicine, however, dementia simply refers to mental deterioration that has lasted for a while. A person with mild dementia may have a poor memory and a decreased ability to do simple tasks like arithmetic. With severe dementia, judgment and reasoning ability is lost. People become increasingly confused and disoriented, and often will not know the date, their location, or even their name. An estimated 2–4 million Americans suffer from aging-related dementia.

Dementia has many causes, but *Alzheimer's disease* is by far the most common cause and accounts for about two-thirds of dementia cases. Alzheimer's can start gradually with poor recall of recent events, but progresses with a steady and relentless decline of memory, judgment, speech, and reasoning. Agitation, paranoid behavior, and confusion often worsen in the evening. Affected people eventually lose the ability to interact socially and to care for themselves.

Diagnosing and treating dementia

Unfortunately, there is no simple test to diagnose Alzheimer's disease. Positron emission tomography (PET) scans of the brain can be helpful, but are not yet reliable enough to recommend as a definitive diagnostic tool. The only way to confirm Alzheimer's with certainty is to examine the affected person's brain under a microscope after he or she has passed away.

Vascular dementia is the second-most-common type of dementia. Thought to be caused by lots of small strokes that damage the brain and impair thinking, it's also called "multi-infarct" dementia. It is suspected when people have evidence of strokes on brain scans and risk factors for stroke like high blood pressure. To prevent further brain damage in patients thought to have vascular dementia, physicians often prescribe aspirin or medications that lower blood pressure or cholesterol. Despite such efforts, people with vascular dementia often fare poorly.

When someone develops dementia, the main medical strategy is to rule out some of the less common, but possibly curable causes (see table 22.1). To do so, a health care provider might recommend that a patient do the following:

- Have a brain scan and blood tests to look for problems such as brain tumors, bleeding into the brain, hydrocephalus, vitamin B-12 deficiency, syphilis, and AIDS.
- Stop (if possible) taking any medications that could impair mental function, such as sedatives and pain pills.
- Be screened for depression, which can impair mental function and mimic dementia, and also occurs frequently in individuals with Alzheimer's and other forms of dementia. When depression plays a role, antidepressant medications can be a big help.

Though it's worth investigating, finding a truly fixable cause of dementia is uncommon. Observation over time often confirms the suspicion that a person with dementia has Alzheimer's disease.

Table 22.1: Causes of dementia (memory impairment)

65 %	Alzheimer's disease
15 %	Vascular (Multi-infarct, or many small strokes)
10 %	Parkinson's disease (and other degenerative brain diseases)
10 %	Potentially curable causes: depression, multiple medications, alcoholism, brain tumors, bleeding into the brain (subdural hematoma), hydrocephalus, vitamin B-12 deficiency, thyroid problem, syphilis, and AIDS

Key point: The most common cause of dementia is Alzheimer's disease, a progressive condition with no known cure. Some causes of dementia may be curable (see table 22.1).

What causes Alzheimer's disease?

Alzheimer's is a degenerative brain disease in which abnormally high numbers of cells in the gray matter die off. Tangled clusters of cells and plaques form in other parts of the brain. The tangles look like a hairball stuck on a comb, and are full of a chemical called tau. The plaques are full of sticky chemicals called beta-amyloid proteins. Some plaques and tangles form in a normally aging brain, but the process goes haywire in people with Alzheimer's disease. No one knows exactly why. Theories have ranged from poor circulation to aluminum toxicity. Though we are still unraveling the mystery of Alzheimer's, we have been able to identify the following risk factors for the disease:

- *Advancing age.* This is the strongest risk factor for Alzheimer's disease, which mostly afflicts the elderly. The incidence of Alzheimer's doubles every five years after age 65. Experts estimate that 1 percent of people are affected with Alzheimer's by age 60, but rates increase to 25 percent or more by age 85.

- *Genetics.* A gene known as ApoE affects the likelihood of Alzheimer's disease. One form of ApoE makes people more susceptible to Alzheimer's, while a different form seems to protect against the disease. A rare, inherited type of Alzheimer's disease affects people during their 40s or 50s. Several genes responsible for early Alzheimer's have been discovered, but families prone to the disease account for only 20 percent of all cases.
- *Down's syndrome.* For unknown reasons, some people with Down's syndrome develop the plaques and tangles of Alzheimer's disease very early, usually in their 30s or 40s.
- *Lack of education.* Studies have found that people who achieve higher education levels (i.e., college and post-graduate studies) have lower rates of Alzheimer's disease.
- *Female gender.* Sorry ladies, but women are a little more prone to Alzheimer's disease than men.
- *Obesity (in women only).* Weight may play a role in development of Alzheimer's disease in women, but not in men. A group of 70-year-old Swedish adults from Goteborg were weighed, measured and then observed for 18 years. The women who were overweight were much more likely to develop Alzheimer's compared with the normal weight women.[1] For the men, overweight did not increase the risk.
- *Homocysteine.* Data from the Framingham Heart Study revealed that older people with high homocysteine levels in their blood had twice the risk of developing Alzheimer's disease compared with their peers who had low levels.[2] Homocysteine is an amino acid that has been recognized as a risk factor for heart disease (see Chapter 7).
- *Hormone replacement after menopause.* Once hoped to protect against dementia, hormone replacement therapy after menopause now appears to actually increase the risk.[3]
- *Smoking.* New studies suggest that smoking may increase a person's risk of Alzheimer's disease.[4]

❄❀ *Key point:* Alzheimer's disease can run in families,
❀❄ but advancing age is the main risk factor in 80 percent of cases.

PRESERVE YOUR MEMORY

After I had reassured Sue that she didn't yet have Alzheimer's, she
asked me how likely she was to get the disease later on and what
she could do to prevent it. I admitted to her that the statistics are
scary: If you reach age 65, you have a one-in-three chance of developing dementia during your lifetime if you are a woman, and a one-
in-five chance if you are a man. I also pointed out, however, that the
vast majority of elderly individuals will stay sharp as a tack. And I
told Sue that there was plenty she could do to help preserve her
mind and memory. This section explores some of the Alzheimer's
prevention strategies Sue and I discussed.

Brain exercises—they'll keep you mentally fit

As strange as it sounds, "using your head" may be the best way to
keep your brain in working order. Activities that stimulate the
brain, like reading, playing musical instruments, and playing cards
or board games, seem to protect the brain from dementia. Retro-
spective studies of people who developed Alzheimer's disease in
their old age found that they had done comparatively fewer of these
brain-stimulating activities during middle age than peers who
didn't get Alzheimer's. As noted above, there is also an inverse relationship between education level and Alzheimer's disease; in other
words, the *more* years of education, the *less* likely you are to develop
Alzheimer's disease.

Researchers have debated whether mental activity really protects the brain, or if people destined to develop Alzheimer's have
subtle brain problems earlier in life that decrease the amount of
brain-intensive activities they do. Two new studies support the
notion that an active mind actually protects against dementia.

The Religious Orders Study followed 800 older nuns and priests with initially normal mental function for about five years. Results published in 2002 found that participants who did more mental activity (reading, playing games, going to museums, watching television, or listening to the radio) were less likely to develop dementia.[5]

The Bronx Aging Study enrolled 488 mentally sharp people between the ages of 75 and 85 in the early 1980s, and tested the survivors every 12 to 18 months. Results published in 2003 found that participants who frequently played board games, read, or played musical instruments were much less likely to develop dementia of any kind.[6] Of interest, physical activity did not appear to protect the brains of people in the Bronx study.

> Q *Health tip:* During leisure time, exercise your brain with enjoyable activities like games, reading, playing a musical instrument, or working on a puzzle.

Diet—antioxidants are good for your brain

Damage to brain cells caused by oxidation and free radicals likely contributes to the development of Alzheimer's disease. Thus, antioxidant foods and vitamins may help to protect the brain from damage. Two studies published in 2002 give some evidence that diets rich in antioxidant vitamins C and E do indeed protect against Alzheimer's disease.

The Rotterdam Study gathered dietary information from 5,395 Netherlanders over the age of 55 with normal initial mental function and followed them for an average of six years.[7] The Chicago Health and Aging Project followed a group of 815 people over the age of 65 for an average of four years.[8] Both studies found much lower rates of Alzheimer's disease in the people who ate the most vitamin E-rich foods, compared with those who ate the least. The Rotterdam Study also noticed protection against Alzheimer's in people who ate a lot of vitamin C-rich foods. Importantly, in these studies the Alzheimer's prevention benefit came from eating antioxidant-rich *foods*, but not from taking vitamin *supplements*. Vitamin E-rich foods include whole grains, nuts, milk, and egg yolks. Foods rich in vitamin C include citrus fruits, broccoli, cabbage, sprouts, and kiwi.

Researchers at Case Western Reserve University suggest that a high-antioxidant, low-fat diet may prevent a significant number of Alzheimer's cases. This healthy diet includes lots of fruit, vegetables, tomatoes, whole grains, fish, and poultry. The Case Western researchers compared the diet histories of people suffering from Alzheimer's with those of a control group. They found that people who ate a low-antioxidant, high-fat diet (lots of red and processed meats, fried foods, sweets, and high-fat dairy products) during midlife had about one-third higher rates of dementia than individuals who consumed a healthy diet.[9]

> ❧ *Key point:* A diet loaded with antioxidant vitamins may help to prevent Alzheimer's disease. For good brain health, eat plenty of fruits, vegetables, whole grains, and nuts.

Alcohol—easy does it

Does alcohol use contribute to dementia (by damaging the brain and increasing the odds of a brain injury) or can it help protect the brain (by reducing arteriosclerosis)? Experts have debated this question for some time. Data from the Cardiovascular Health Study, published in 2003, should help settle the argument. In this study, the lowest rates of Alzheimer's disease and all causes of dementia were found in people who drank between one and six drinks per week (one drink was a 12 ounce beer, 6 ounces of wine, or one shot of liquor).[10] Abstainers and heavy drinkers both had higher rates of dementia. Based on this data, moderate alcohol use appears to prevent Alzheimer's disease.

> ❧ *Personal action plan:* Try one drink a day to lower your risk of Alzheimer's disease, *if* you are not prone to drinking in excess.

Cholesterol-lowering statin drugs might help prevent Alzheimer's

Some exciting current research on Alzheimer's disease focuses on the cholesterol-lowering drugs known as "statins." These drugs include lovastatin (Mevacor), simvistatin (Zocor), atorvastatin (Lipitor), and others. In preliminary, non-randomized studies, people who took statins for cholesterol treatment seemed a lot less likely to develop Alzheimer's disease.

Interestingly, non-statin cholesterol-lowering drugs did not appear to offer the same protection. Researchers theorize that in addition to their cholesterol-lowering properties, statins have an anti-inflammatory effect that may help protect brain arteries as well as heart arteries. Before statins can be recommended solely for the prevention or treatment of Alzheimer's disease, however, randomized, controlled studies are needed to confirm both benefit and safety. Meanwhile, people who need statins to lower cholesterol will be happy to know that their brain may benefit as well.

> ❧ *Key point:* To prevent Alzheimer's disease, put your brain to good use, follow a healthy diet packed with antioxidant vitamins, drink alcohol in moderation or not at all, avoid tobacco, and take a statin drug if you have high cholesterol.

MEMORY SAVERS THAT HAVE NOT PANNED OUT (SO FAR)

Hormone hopes dashed

Not long ago, researchers had high hopes that hormone replacement therapy (estrogen) after menopause might reduce a woman's odds of developing dementia. Unfortunately, the Women's Health

Initiative Memory Study (WHIMS), published in 2003, has dashed those hopes. In the WHIMS study, 4,500 women over the age of 65 were assigned randomly to either hormone replacement (estrogen and progesterone) or a placebo. After four years, the hormone-replacement group had twice the rates of dementia as the placebo group.[3]

The reason for more dementia with hormones is unknown, but one factor may be circulation. The hormone-treated group also had 30 percent more strokes than the placebo group. Some older studies of hormone replacement suggested a protective effect on the brain. Those studies were not randomized, however, and the women who chose to take hormones were a healthier group in general than the women who did not or could not take hormones. For now, older women should avoid hormone replacement to reduce the risk of dementia.

> Q *Health tip:* Forget about hormone replacement as a way to preserve your mental well-being; hormones actually appear to increase a woman's risk of dementia.

Non-steroidal anti-inflammatories (NSAIDs)

For a while, another class of drugs, the non-steroidal anti-inflammatory drugs (NSAIDs), also seemed promising for Alzheimer's prevention. The NSAIDs, which include ibuprofen and naproxen, are often used to treat arthritis. Dementia researchers got excited about NSAIDs when several non-randomized studies suggested that folks who took them on a regular basis had a slightly lower risk of developing Alzheimer's disease. They theorized that by blocking inflammation in the brain, these drugs could help ward off dementia.

Unfortunately, the first randomized, controlled study to try to prove the benefit of NSAIDs for Alzheimer's disease was a big disappointment. The Alzheimer's Disease Cooperative Study tested two NSAIDs against a placebo for a year in 350 people with mild to moderate Alzheimer's disease. The two NSAIDs were naproxen (found in Aleve and Naprosyn) and rofecobix (a newer NSAID found in Vioxx that is a little easier on the stomach). In results published in 2003, the NSAIDs failed to slow the decline in memory and thinking ability that occurred during the year. In fact, the rofecoxib group did a little worse than the placebo group.[11] Pending further research, NSAIDs remain good drugs for arthritis and aches and pains, but I don't recommend them for prevention or treatment of Alzheimer's disease.

Alzheimer's vaccine—hope on hold

Scientists currently are working on a vaccine to prevent Alzheimer's disease. Recognizing that plaques full of beta-amyloid protein are found in the brains of people with Alzheimer's, the scientists theorized that giving small amounts of beta-amyloid protein as a vaccine could trigger the immune system to destroy beta-amyloid in various parts of the body, including in the brain. Tests of the vaccine in mice prone to Alzheimer's were very encouraging—the vaccinated mice performed better in mazes and developed fewer plaques in their brains.

When vaccine testing was started on people with early Alzheimer's in 2000, however, severe brain swelling occurred in about 6 percent of the vaccinated group. Testing was suspended in 2002. Scientists think the side effects were due to an over-reaction of the immune system, and are trying to develop a safer form of the vaccine. We might have to wait a while, but a safe, effective vaccine to prevent Alzheimer's is still a possibility and provides hope for the future.

Ginkgo biloba

Ginkgo biloba leaf extract, an herbal product made from maidenhair-tree leaves, has been used for years to *treat* dementia (see ginkgo biloba listing below, under "Treatment of Alzheimer's disease). Many people also take ginkgo to try to *prevent* Alzheimer's or to improve their ability to concentrate. Unfortunately, there are no good studies proving that ginkgo prevents dementia, and a recent study at Williams College in Massachusetts casts doubt on ginkgo's ability to improve mental function. The randomized, controlled study, published in 2002, looked at whether ginkgo could improve memory and concentration. A group of people over age 60 with normal mental function were placed on either ginkgo biloba or a placebo. After six weeks, there was no difference in memory, learning, concentration, or attention between people who took ginkgo versus the placebo.[12]

> *Key point:* When it comes to preventing Alzheimer's disease, don't count on hormone replacement after menopause, non-steroidal anti-inflammatory medication, ginkgo biloba, or a vaccine.

TREATMENT OF ALZHEIMER'S DISEASE

At age 87, Mildred was brought into my office by her daughter, Ellen, because of a failing memory and an inability to care for herself. For the past year, Ellen had been doing all of Mildred's grocery shopping, and had become concerned when Mildred left the stove on overnight a few times. The final straw came when Mildred got lost in her own neighborhood.

Tests confirmed significant problems with Mildred's short-term memory and judgment, and failed to find any fixable cause. Mildred was diagnosed with dementia—most likely Alzheimer's disease. Ellen decided to take Mildred into her own home, and wanted to know whether treatment was available. I explained that the care and treatment of people with Alzheimer's disease is challenging, complex, and evolving. Caregivers like Ellen need to find an understanding medical team and good social support to help manage the physical and emotional needs of both the patient and themselves. The following section discusses some key issues in treating people with Alzheimer's disease.

Caregiver support

At present, there is no cure for Alzheimer's disease. Affected individuals steadily decline to the point where they require constant care and attention. The stress placed on family members and loved ones can be enormous. A real key for the caregivers is adequate support and education on how to be a good caregiver. The Alzheimer's Association is a great resource for needed information. Local chapters can help answer questions and connect caregivers to support services. Volunteers are often available to relieve some of the burden. If you are a caregiver, please get help and be sure to arrange for personal time away from your care-giving role.

Managing disruptive behaviors

One of the most difficult issues for caregivers of Alzheimer's patients is how to manage behavioral disturbances like hallucinations, paranoid fears, agitation, or aggressive actions. Patience, common sense, and old-fashioned parenting techniques can all help. Because of poor short-term memory, people with dementia need to be re-oriented to their surroundings frequently, and may need to be redirected often to safer activities or locations. Familiar objects and pictures can be comforting and help with orientation. Maintaining regular sleep-wake cycles and toilet routines are also important. Medications may be needed if these measures fail.

Medications

To date, no medications are proven to alter the inevitable decline in a person with Alzheimer's. Medications may, however, relieve symptoms or offer temporary and modest improvement in mental function.

Antidepressants are often prescribed for people with Alzheimer's disease. Testing for depression is more difficult when people have dementia because their judgment and reasoning are impaired, but depression often occurs in people with Alzheimer's. It may take some trial and error to find the right drug and dose, but antidepressants sometimes improve the mood and even mental function of individuals with dementia.

Cholinesterase inhibitors—including donepezel (Aricept), tacrine (Cognex), galantamine (Reminyl), and rivastigmine (Exelon)—are widely used to try to improve mental function in Alzheimer's patients by improving the chemical balance in their brain. Several studies of cholinesterase inhibitors have found that the different drugs appear to be equally effective. Overall, they help mental function a little bit, especially in early or moderately severe Alzheimer's disease. Unfortunately, they do not appear to slow the progression of the disease or to prolong life.

Realistically, these drugs may improve function enough that the person with Alzheimer's can remain at home a little bit longer and be slightly less of a burden to caregivers. Further research is needed to determine whether quality of life is truly improved by these drugs. On the down side, these drugs are expensive and can cause side effects such as nausea or headache that are hard to evaluate in a person with poor mental function.

Ginkgo biloba leaf extract has been used for years to treat dementia, especially in Europe. It is thought to improve blood flow to the brain. Several randomized, controlled trials have shown modest improvements in mental function in people with dementia treated with ginkgo biloba.[13] Even though ginkgo does not improve memory in *normal* people, it has about the same benefit as cholinesterase inhibitors in people with dementia. Ginkgo has some blood-thinning effect, and people on the blood thinner warfarin should have a blood test to make sure that adding ginkgo does not thin their blood too much. A common dose is 60 mg twice a day, and the most common side effect is an upset stomach.

Anti-psychotic medications have been tried in Alzheimer's patients who develop frightening hallucinations, agitation, or aggressive behavior, and for whom behavioral interventions have failed. Older anti-psychotics like haloperidol (Haldol) and thioridazine (Mellaril) are inexpensive but have lots of side effects. The most serious are involuntary movements that can become permanent. The newer anti-psychotics risperdone (Risperdal) and olanzipine (Zyprexa) have gained favor because of fewer side effects. Both are expensive and can cause weight gain and diabetes. Any anti-psychotics pre-scribed for Alzheimer's patients should be used in the lowest effec-tive dose and stopped whenever possible.

End-of-life decisions

Despite the best of care, people with Alzheimer's disease inevitably worsen. Near the end of life, they often need round-the-clock care, and family members must make some difficult decisions. In particu-lar, they often struggle with three decisions: whether to resuscitate if the Alzheimer's patient stops breathing or their heart stops, whether to insert a feeding tube if they are unable to eat, and whether to con-sider "comfort care only" (no further medical interventions).

When available, advanced directives—completed by the person with Alzheimer's when he or she could still make decisions about his or her own care (see Chapter 23)—can be very helpful to family members. Otherwise, they'll have to consult with health-care providers, search their hearts, and make the best decisions they can. Following are brief summaries of what each decision means:

Resuscitation Orders: When a person with dementia enters a nurs-ing home, the first decision is whether to perform cardio-pul-monary resuscitation (CPR) if the person's heart stops or they stop breathing. Most family members are comfortable with a do not resuscitate (DNR) order for a severely demented relative. It basi-cally means that if the person dies naturally, no heroic attempts will be made to restore life.

Feeding tube: When demented people can no longer feed them-selves, next-of-kin must decide whether a feeding tube (a plastic tube placed directly into the stomach) should be used to supply nutrition. In U.S. nursing homes in 1999, one in three severely demented Alzheimer's patients were being fed through a tube.[14] Family members often believe it is kinder to use a feeding tube, but research suggests otherwise. Contrary to what people often think, feeding tubes do *not* prolong life or improve comfort in people with dementia.[15] In fact, there may be higher infection rates and worse quality of life with a feeding tube. Once a feeding tube is in place, demented people tend to get less human contact and simply fail to thrive.

Comfort care only: When people can no longer get out of bed, bathe, dress, eat, or communicate, it is reasonable to consider comfort care only. Comfort care means that every effort will be made to keep a person comfortable, but that medical treatments like antibiotics, blood transfusions, intravenous fluids, and surgeries will not be used. Comfort includes good skin and mouth care, medication for pain and anxiety, and human contact. Hospice organizations can be very helpful resources for families who are considering the comfort-care approach.

SUMMARY

Alzheimer's disease is the most common kind of dementia, or deterioration of mental functioning, and affects roughly one out of every four people by age 85. It causes a steadily progressive loss of memory, judgment, reasoning, and ability to care for oneself. Alzheimer's disease is more common in some families, but the main risk factor is advancing age. For women, both obesity and hormone replacement after menopause may increase the risk. People may lower their risk by exercising their brains (reading and playing games or musical instruments), eating antioxidant rich foods (fruits, vegetables, whole grains, and nuts), drinking alcohol in moderation or not at all, avoiding smoking, and taking statin drugs if they have high cholesterol levels. Once Alzheimer's disease develops, caregivers assume a tremendous burden. Medications can help control symptoms like depression or agitation, and may improve mental functioning a little, but they do not alter the inevitable decline of the affected person. For people with severe, end-stage Alzheimer's disease, there is a trend toward care to maintain comfort and dignity without heroic measures to prolong life.

CHAPTER TWENTY-THREE

Advance Medical Directives: How to Guide Your Final Scene

"Dying can be a peaceful event or a great agony when it is inappropriately sustained by life support."
—Dr. Roger Bone in *Reflections*

END-OF-LIFE DECISIONS

It may seem strange to end a prevention book with a chapter on dying, but death is an inevitable part of the amazing cycle of life. With a healthy lifestyle, you can hope to live long and feel well most of the time. Eventually, however, everyone faces a final scene. Though you might hope to drift off during the night at a ripe old age, the final scene often doesn't play out that way. Dying can be a slow process in which, toward the end, you become unable to communicate your wishes about whether to stop medical interventions. You can prevent unwanted prolongation of your life in such a situation by creating an "advance directive," a legal document that puts your preferences into writing. Read on for a better understanding of end-of-life decisions and how to assure that *your* wishes are honored if you become unable to call the shots.

A sad ending

Sir William Osler, considered the father of modern medicine, said many years ago that "pneumonia is an old man's best friend." I remember the sad case of a patient I'll call Joe, whose "friend" was held at bay by modern medical interventions. Joe was admitted to my hospital one night during the 1980s from a nursing home because he had a fever and trouble breathing. Poor Joe was 85 years old and had end-stage Alzheimer's disease. He could no longer talk to or even recognize his wife or children. He had stopped eating months ago, and his well-meaning family had decided on a feeding tube to provide nutrition. Joe had no control over his bladder or bowels, so he had a catheter to collect his urine. He had severe arthritis and could no longer walk or even sit in a chair. He spent his days curled up in bed, softly moaning. A chest x-ray showed that Joe had pneumonia.

I discussed the options with Joe's wife. She said Joe had lived through pneumonia before, and wanted us to do what we could. At that time, few people had advance directives or living wills, so we followed the wishes of the family. We started Joe on antibiotics and breathing treatments. His condition stabilized after a few days and he returned to the nursing home. I never saw Joe again, but was haunted by the feeling that we'd been unkind to prolong his life. I told my wife that if I ever had an irreversible condition that took away my ability to think and care for myself, I would not want a feeding tube or any other treatments to prolong my life. Unfortunately, when he still could, Joe had never talked about what he would have wanted in such a situation. The rest of this chapter discusses measures you can take to avoid a fate like Joe's.

Final chapters

Ben Franklin said that nothing is certain except death and taxes. Despite its inevitability, many Americans are reluctant to talk about death. Nonetheless, some preferences are known. In polls, most people say they would prefer to die at home, free of pain, and surrounded by loved ones. When asked what they would want done if they were suffering from a terminal disease, or were in a permanent coma, most people say they would *not* want heroic, life-prolonging interventions. Despite this, many people find it hard to decide to withhold treatments for loved ones in these situations. Advance directives such as living wills are a good way to take the burden off family members. These legal documents clarify for everyone what interventions you would want, or not want, if you were dying and no longer able to communicate.

The history of advance directives

Americans have not always had the right to refuse medical treatments. Prior to World War II, nature generally took its course and most people died at home. Subsequently, however, improvements in medicine and technology brought about the ability to prolong life, and some brand-new ethical dilemmas. Perhaps you remember the Karen Quinlan case, which riveted the nation in 1976. The unfortunate 21-year-old had suffered brain damage and lapsed into a coma the year before after drinking alcohol and taking tranquilizers at a party. After she'd been on a ventilator for a year with no sign of brain activity, her father asked to have the ventilator removed. Permission was denied and he went to court.

The case went to the New Jersey Supreme Court, which made two wise and important rulings: First, people have the right to refuse medical treatment, even if the refusal will lead to their death. Second, decisions that could lead to the death of a mentally incompetent person are best made by the patient's family, with input from physicians, rather than by the courts. Karen Quinlan's ventilator was removed, and the movement for advance directives gained momentum.

In 1990, a case involving a feeding tube reached the U.S. Supreme Court. Nancy Cruzan had been in a coma in Missouri since an automobile accident in 1983. She had been kept alive with a feeding tube, but her family wanted it removed. The Supreme Court concluded that individuals do have a constitutionally protected right to refuse unwanted medical treatment, then returned the case to the Missouri courts to determine Nancy Cruzan's wishes regarding the feeding tube. The state court, convinced by testimony from Nancy's family and friends, finally decided that she would not want a feeding tube and allowed it to be removed.

Soon after, in 1991, the U.S. Congress passed the Patient Self-determination Act, which requires hospitals to ask whether patients have or want to have an advance directive. By 1992, all 50 states had passed laws to legalize advance directives. The specifics vary from state to state, but the laws generally say that people can have living wills to state their end-of-life wishes, and that they are legally binding. The laws also specify who can make medical decisions if a person is unable to do so and does not have a living will.

> *Key point:* You have the right to refuse medical care—including feeding tubes, ventilators, and fluids—that might prolong your life against your wishes. Advance directives allow you to put your end-of-life preferences into writing now so that they will be known and honored in the future, if you are dying and unable to communicate.

PROTECTING YOURSELF—THE OPTIONS

Living wills

A living will states what medical care you would want if you were unable to make your own decisions. Most living wills address terminal illness, irreversible coma, and persistent vegetative state. Terminal illness is defined as "having an incurable disease or condition that will inevitably lead to death, usually within six months." A coma is a state of unconsciousness in which a person cannot respond to others in any meaningful way. A coma is considered irreversible when there has been significant brain damage and there is virtually no chance of recovery. People who have been unconscious for months to years are considered to be in a "persistent vegetative state." People in this state can often breathe on their own, and may respond to pain, but they cannot eat, talk, or communicate.

Only one in five American adults currently has a living will to clarify their wishes should they develop a terminal illness, an irreversible coma, or a persistent vegetative state. Those who do have living wills usually say that they *do not* want life-prolonging medical interventions in these situations.

Health-care power of attorney

If you get sick, you probably will be presented with more than one treatment option. To make the right choice for you, you'll need to understand the risks and benefits of each option. If you're suffering from anemia due to blood loss, for example, would you rather have a blood transfusion that will give you more energy right away or take iron supplements and wait for your body to generate its own blood cells? If you are unable to make such decisions, whom do you want to decide?

Most states have laws that designate who will decide if you can't. In Arizona, for instance, a spouse is the first choice, followed by adult children, then parents, domestic partners, siblings, and close friends who have shown special care and concern. You can, however, pick someone in advance and designate him or her as your "health-care power of attorney." This gives you the advantage of making sure that person understands your philosophy and wishes when it comes to end-of-life medical care.

When left to the law, difficult situations can arise that pit family members against one another. I remember such a case with a widow I'll call Mildred. Mildred suffered a severe stroke that paralyzed one-half of her body and left her unable to eat, talk, or communicate in any way. She had no living will and had not designated a health-care power of attorney. Mildred had two adult daughters who, by law, became her decision makers. The problem was that they disagreed on whether to use a feeding tube to keep Mildred alive after it was clear that she was not improving. Mary said her mother would not want to be kept alive in her current condition, but Sue said she was not ready to let her mom die. In Mildred's case nature intervened, but all involved would have benefited from some advance planning.

Pre-hospital directives

A "pre-hospital directive" is an advance directive used by terminally ill people still living at home to specify that they do not want *any* emergency medical treatments or resuscitation in the event of their collapse. A pre-hospital directive often is posted on the terminally ill person's refrigerator, along with their picture. It is intended to allow the sick person to die peacefully at home, without being subjected to cardiopulmonary resuscitation (CPR) or rushed off to the hospital. Pre-hospital directives are *only* appropriate for people who clearly are terminal and want no intervention.

A similar, but less-restrictive directive is a "do not hospitalize" order that merely clarifies a person's wish not to return to a hospital setting for treatment. I have had a number of older, but otherwise well people ask about those "forms for the refrigerator." I am quick to explain that they are not the same as a living will. The refrigerator form means you will get no treatment at all, whereas the living will applies only if and when you are deemed terminal and are unable to communicate further wishes.

Do not resuscitate order

The final commonly used advance directive is the "do not resuscitate" (DNR) order. A DNR directive is used both in hospitals and nursing homes to indicate a person's preference not to be resuscitated if their heart stops or they stop breathing. A DNR order is not the same as refusing medical treatments like tube feeding, antibiotics, or even surgery. It merely states that, if, despite ongoing treatment, a person should pass away, he or she does not want CPR in an attempt to restore life. Importantly, a DNR order should not affect the level of nursing care and compassion that a person receives.

🖐 *Personal action plan:* Talk to a loved one about your wishes for medical interventions in the event that you become comatose or terminally ill and unable to communicate. Complete a living will to clarify your wishes, and choose a health-care power of attorney to make medical decisions if you cannot.

COMMON DILEMMAS FOR DECISION-MAKERS

A living will is a valuable tool for expressing your general philosophy regarding end-of-life interventions. In real life, however, it is often hard to decide when the living will applies, or exactly what a person would choose in a given situation. A health-care power of attorney who knows a patient's wishes well can play a crucial role in many situations. Decision makers do best when they focus on what the *patient* would want if he or she could be in the room to discuss the options. Below are some of the common dilemmas faced by families and decision makers.

When is a situation hopeless?

Living wills usually do not apply until a person is determined to have a terminal illness. Sometimes this is clear cut, as with end-stage, widespread cancer. Many times, however, it is not so clear. A patient I'll call Fred is a good example. Fred suffered from severe emphysema and had made out a living will. He had quit smoking, but required an oxygen tank to get by. Fred told me he did not want to be kept alive on a ventilator if his situation ever became hopeless.

Fred ended up in the hospital one winter with pneumonia. Because of his bad lungs, he needed the help of a ventilator to keep him alive while we tried to treat the pneumonia. Sadly, Fred did not improve. He was quite ill and unable to communicate, and his family wanted to know if the situation was hopeless. The honest answer was, I did not know. The specialists and I agreed that Fred could pull through, but the odds did not look good and even if he survived it would not be long before he was back in the same boat.

I knew Fred would not want to linger for weeks on the ventilator, but should we stop life support? Fortunately, Fred's wife was very familiar with Fred's wishes. She said he knew the end was near, and that he did not want to be kept alive by machines. When his condition continued to worsen, the family agreed to stop the ventilator, and Fred passed away peacefully.

Should a feeding tube be used?

When people are critically ill and unable to eat, feeding tubes can be an important part of treatment to help supply the nutrition needed to heal and recover. When recovery is not likely, however, it can be very difficult to decide whether a feeding tube should be used to try to prolong life. Is a feeding tube appropriate for someone who's had a severe stroke like Mildred's; for an Alzheimer's patient who has lost all memory and can no longer perform basic functions; or for someone with Lou Gehrig's disease whose mind is fine but whose body is completely paralyzed? There are no easy answers, but a living will and a designated decision-maker who knows the patient's wishes can be invaluable.

As discussed in Chapter 22, feeding tubes generally are not a good idea for Alzheimer's patients. Studies show that survival may be *shortened* by feeding tubes and medical complications increased, possibly because patients get less human contact once a feeding tube is placed.[1] In other situations, decision makers must consider the patient's quality of life, personal preferences (if known), and chances for recovery before making a feeding tube decision. When it is unclear whether a patient is going to recover—from a stroke or coma, for example—family members might decide to try a feeding tube for a while. The tube can always be removed if the loved one fails to improve.

Should fluids be stopped?

When a person is clearly dying and can no longer eat or drink, family members often ask whether intravenous fluids should be used to reduce thirst. The answer from many researchers and hospice-care experts is a definite *no*. Intravenous fluids at the end of life serve to prolong the dying process, but do not appear to provide any additional comfort.[2] People who have survived near-death experiences during which they became dehydrated uniformly describe a sense of calm and peacefulness as the end approached. The main source of discomfort with dehydration is dry mouth and chapped lips. Good care of the dying includes regular moistening of the mouth and ointment for dry lips. Terminally ill people who stop taking all fluids usually lapse into unconsciousness within a day or so.

Is it time for hospice?

Another common dilemma families face is whether and when to ask for hospice services. Hospice programs are designed to help terminally ill people and their families through the dying process. Hospice services include education, caring and comforting nursing support, and medications to relieve suffering and anxiety. Many people have the misconception that hospice is needed only for the final few days of life. The reality is that hospice can help for weeks or even months, providing the support needed for the particular stage of an illness. Medicare will cover hospice care once an attending physician estimates that a patient has fewer than six months to live. Since no one has a crystal ball, some patients start with hospice, but then stabilize and no longer need services. That is perfectly OK, as hospice can get involved again when needed.

As a doctor, I face the challenge of figuring out when and how to suggest hospice services for a dying patient. It can be awkward to mention the word hospice, because many times a patient and his or her family have not yet faced the reality that death is near. My patient Rob was a good example. Rob had a particularly aggressive form of prostate cancer that had spread to his bones. I got reports from a radiation therapist managing radiation treatments, an oncologist prescribing chemotherapy, and a urologist prescribing hormone treatments. When I saw Rob, he was thin and gaunt and it was clear to me that he was dying. I asked Rob and his wife if anyone had mentioned hospice. They looked surprised and said no.

The other doctors meant well, however none had explained that the treatments were meant to buy some time, but would not cure Rob's cancer. Rob's wife was reluctant at first, but finally agreed to talk to the hospice caregivers. The next week, she called to thank me, saying a tremendous burden had been lifted from her shoulders. Rob wanted to die at home, and with hospice support he passed away peacefully several weeks later. Rob's wife had only one regret—that she hadn't gotten hospice involved earlier.

SUMMARY

By putting your preferences into writing now, you can prevent life-prolonging interventions such as feeding tubes and ventilators should you become permanently comatose or terminally ill and unable to communicate. A living will is a legally binding way to state your wishes in advance in case such a situation arises. You can also designate a health-care power of attorney to make medical-care decisions for you if you become unable to do so. This person should know your philosophy, and may have to make hard choices regarding feeding tubes or when to stop life support. For people who are terminally ill and likely to live less than six months, hospice can provide tremendous support to both the patient and family members.

Appendix A:
List of Tables and Figures

Figure 1.1   Estimated causes of premature deaths in America

Table 2.1   Good sources of fiber

Figure 2.1   Mediterranean diet food pyramid

Table 4.1   Major life events and illness

Table 5.1   Alcohol impairment chart for men

Table 5.2   Alcohol impairment chart for women

Table 7.1   Heart risk assessment table

Table 8.1   Body mass index (BMI) table

Table 9.1   High blood pressure classifications for adults

Table 10.1   Lipid levels: where do you stand?

Table 10.2   Risk factors for heart disease

Table 10.3   LDL cholesterol goals based on cardiac risk factors and 10-yr. risk

Table 11.1   Blood-sugar (a.k.a. glucose) screening

Table 11.2   Hemoglobin A1c (HgbA1c) results

Table 13.1   Estimates of new cancer cases and deaths in the Unites States in 2003

Table 18.1   Prostate cancer rates around the world

Table 20.1   Risk factors for osteoporosis

Table 20.2   Calcium-rich foods

Table 21.1   Partial list of non-steroidal anti-inflammatory drugs (NSAIDs)

Table 22.1   Causes of dementia (memory impairment)

Appendix B:
List of Sidebars

Chapter 1   Improving indoor air quality 8
Chapter 2   Fiber's health benefits 18
             Fat primer 22
             Iron: Too much can kill 28
Chapter 3   Does physical fitness really
             make you live longer? 34
             Exercise for the overweight....................36
             Should you worry about your
             target heart rate? 46
Chapter 4   Depression; Panic attacks 50
             Self-relaxation technique 57
Chapter 5   Women and alcohol....................................66
             Drinking and driving: Is it ever safe? 69
Chapter 6   Safer tobacco? I don't think so!..............77
Chapter 8   Eating disorders 111
             Sensible diet tips 118
Chapter 9   Dietary approaches to stop
             hypertension (DASH) 132
             Number needed to treat (NNT)............136
             Home blood pressure cuffs 137
Chapter 10   Apolipoproteins...146
Chapter 11   Alcohol and diabetes................................168
             The glycemic index:
             How sweet are your carbs? 169

Chapter 12   Stroke and Woodrow Wilson 179
             Atrial fibrillation..180
             Transient ischemic attack (TIA) 183
Chapter 13   Cancer-prevention Tips..194
             Cancer warning signs...199
Chapter 14   Biology and cancer screening 203
             Natural therapy for cervical dysplasia
             and HPV 205
Chapter 15   Why screening tests can seem more effective
             than they really are...216
Chapter 17   Hereditary breast cancer (BRCA 1 or BRCA 2)....238
Chapter 18   Understanding your PSA test result 256
             The Gleason score: Giving your prostate
             cancer a grade..259
Chapter 19   Not just older, but in some ways better................264
             Bladder training for better control 268
Chapter 20   Understanding your DEXA scan results 284
Chapter 21   Does running or other sports cause arthritis? 293

References

Chapter 1 – Good health
1. Healthy People: The Surgeon General's Report on Health Promotion and Disease Prevention, Government Printing Office, Stock Number 017-001-00146-2.
2. Vinck W, Fagard R, Loos R, Vlietinck R. The impact of genetic and environmental influences on blood pressure variance across age-groups. J Hypertens. 2001;19(6):1007–13.
3. Doll R, Peto R. The causes of cancer: quantitative estimates of avoidable risks of cancer in the United States today. J Natl Cancer Instit. 1981;66:1193–1308.

Chapter 2 – Diet
1. van Dam R, Rimm E, Willett W, et al. Dietary patterns and risk for type 2 diabetes mellitus in U.S. men. Ann Intern Med. 2002;136:201–9.
2. Linseisen J, Kesse E, Slimani N. Meat consumption in Europe—results from the EPIC study. IARC Sci Publ. 2002;156:211–2.
3. Bazzano L, Serdula M, Liu S. Dietary intake of fruits and vegetables and risk of cardiovascular disease. Curr Atheroscler Rep. 2003;5:492–9.
4. Rimm E, Ascherio A, Giovannucci E, et al. Vegetable, fruit, and cereal fiber intake and risk of coronary heart disease among men. JAMA. 1996;275:447–51.

5. Czeizel A, Dudas I. Prevention of the first occurrence of neural-tube defects by periconceptional vitamin supplements. N Engl J. Med. 1992; 327:1832–5.
6. Schnyder G, Roffi M, Pin R, et al. Decreased rate of coronary restenosis after lowering of plasma homocysteine levels. N Engl J Med. 2001;345:1593–600.
7. Liem A, Reynierse-Buitenwerf G, Zwinderman A, et al. Secondary prevention with folic acid: effects on clinical outcomes. J Am Coll Cardiol. 2003;41:2105–13.
8. Vivekananthan D, Penn M, Sapp S, et al. Use of antioxidant vitamins for the prevention of cardiovascular disease: meta-analysis of randomised trials. Lancet. 2003;361:2017–23.
9. HOPE Study: Vitamin E supplementation and cardiovascular events in high-risk patients. N Engl J Med. 2000;342:154–60.

Chapter 3 – Exercise

1. Paffenbarger R Jr, Hyde R, Wing A, et al. The association of changes in physical-activity level and other lifestyle characteristics with mortality among men. N Engl J Med. 1993; 328:538–45.
2. Fiatarone M, O'Neill E, Ryan N, et al. Exercise training and nutritional supplementation for physical frailty in very elderly people. N Engl J Med. 1994;330:1769–75.
3. State-specific prevalence of selected chronic disease-related characteristics—behavioral risk factor surveillance system, 2001. MMWR Surveill Summ. 2003;52:1–80.
4. Blair S, Kohl H, Paffenbarger R, et al. Physical fitness and all-cause mortality. A prospective study of healthy men and women. JAMA. 1989;262:2395–401.
5. Lee I, Hsieh C, Paffenbarger R. Exercise intensity and longevity in men. The Harvard Alumni Health Study. JAMA. 1995;273:1179–84.
6. Kujala U, Kaprio J, Sarna S, Koskenvuo M. Relationship of leisure-time physical activity and mortality: the Finnish twin cohort. JAMA. 1998;279:440–4.

Chapter 4 — Stress

1. Peters R, Brooks M, Zoble R, et al. Chronobiology of acute myocardial infarction: cardiac arrhythmia suppression trial (CAST) experience. Am J Cardiol. 1996;78:1198–201.
2. Holmes T, Rahe R. The social readjustment rating scale. J Psychosom Res. 1967;11:213–8.
3. Wagner U, Gais S, Haider H, et al. Sleep inspires insight. Nature 2004;427:352–5.

Chapter 5 — Alcohol

1. Gaziano J, Gaziano T, Glynn R, et al. Light-to-moderate alcohol consumption and mortality in the Physicians' Health Study enrollment cohort. J Am Coll Cardiol. 2000;35:96–105.
2. Ajani U, Hennekens C, Spelsberg A, Manson J. Alcohol consumption and risk of type 2 diabetes mellitus among U.S. male physicians. Arch Intern Med. 2000;160:1025–30.
3. Walsh C, Larson M, Evans J, et al. Alcohol consumption and risk for congestive heart failure in the Framingham Heart Study. Ann Intern Med. 2002;136:181–91.
4. Ruitenberg A, van Swieten J, Witteman J, et al. Alcohol consumption and risk of dementia: the Rotterdam Study. Lancet. 2002;359:281–6.
5. Richman A, Warren R. Alcohol consumption and morbidity in the Canada health survey: inter-beverage differences. Drug Alcohol Depend. 1985;15:255–82.
6. Wannamethee S, Shaper A. Taking up regular drinking in middle age: effect on major coronary heart disease events and mortality. Heart. 2002;87:32–6.
7. A guide to substance abuse services for primary care clinicians. Treatment Improvement Protocol (TIP) Series 24. DHHS Publication No. 98-3257;1998.
8. Mokdad A, Marks J, Stroup D, Gerberding J. Actual causes of death in the United States, 2000. JAMA. 2004;291:1238–45.
9. Morse R, Flavin D. The definition of alcoholism. JAMA. 1992; 268:1012–14.

Chapter 6 — Smoking

1. Mokdad A, Marks J, Stroup D, Gerberding J. Actual causes of death in the United States, 2000. JAMA. 2004;291:1238–45.
2. Centers for Disease Control and Prevention. Cigarette smoking—attributable mortality and years of potential life loss—United States, 1990. MMWR. 1993;42:645–9.
3. Stockwell H, Goldman A, Lyman G, et al. Environmental tobacco smoke and lung cancer risk in nonsmoking women. J Natl Cancer Instit. 1992;84:1417–22.
4. Li J, Peat J, Xuan W, Berry G. Meta-analysis on the association between environmental tobacco smoke (ETS) exposure and the prevalence of lower respiratory tract infection in early childhood. Pediatric Pulmonology. 1999;27:5–13.
5. Enstrom J. Trends in mortality among California physicians after giving up smoking: 1950–1979. Br Med J. 1983;286:1101–05.
6. Slovic P. Smoking: Risk, Perception, and Policy. Sage Publications, 2001.
7. Sargent J, Dalton M. Does parental disapproval of smoking prevent adolescents from becoming established smokers? Pediatrics. 2001;108:1256–61.
8. Silagy C, Lancaster T, Stead L, et al. Nicotine replacement therapy for smoking cessation. Cochrane Database Syst Rev. 2002;(4):CD000146.
9. National Cancer Institute. Smoking and Tobacco Control Monograph 13: Risks Associated with Smoking Cigarettes with Low Machine-Measured Yields of Tar and Nicotine. 2001.

Chapter 7 — Heart disease

1. Mokdad A, Marks J, Stroup D, Gerberding J. Actual causes of death in the United States, 2000. JAMA. 2004;291:1238–45.
2. Centers for Disease Control and Prevention. Cigarette smoking—attributable mortality and years of potential life loss—United States, 1990. MMWR. 1993;42:645–9.
3. Ayas N, White D, Manson J, et al. A prospective study of sleep duration and coronary heart disease in women. Arch Intern Med. 2003;163:205–9.

4. Collaborative Group of the Primary Prevention Project (PPP). Low-dose aspirin and vitamin E in people at cardiovascular risk: a randomised trial in general practice. Lancet. 2001; 357: 89–95.

5. Hayden M, Pignone M, Phillips C, Mulrow C. Aspirin for the primary prevention of cardiovascular events: a summary of the evidence for the U.S. Preventive Services Task Force. Ann Intern Med. 2002;136:161–72.

6. Homocysteine Studies Collaboration. Homocysteine and risk of ischemic heart disease and stroke: a meta-analysis. JAMA. 2002;288:2015–22.

7. Dietary supplementation with n-3 polyunsaturated fatty acids and vitamin E after myocardial infarction: results of the GISSI-prevenzione trial. Lancet. 1999;354:447–55.

8. Hackam D, Anand S. Emerging risk factors for atherosclerotic vascular disease. JAMA. 2003;290:932–40.

9. Miller G, Rejeski W, Williamson J. The arthritis, diet and activity promotion trial (ADAPT): design, rationale, and baseline results. Control Clin Trials. 2003;24:462–80.

10. Randomized trial of intravenous streptokinase, oral aspirin, both, or neither among 17,187 cases of suspected acute myocardial infarction: ISIS-2 (Second International Study of Infarct Survival) Collaborative Group. J Am Coll Cardiol. 1988;12:3A-13A.

11. Ahmed M, Griffiths P. Statins and the secondary prevention of coronary heart disease. Br J Community Nurs. 2004;9:160–5.

Chapter 8 – Overweight

1. Flegal K, Carroll M, Ogden C, Johnson C. Prevalence and trends in obesity among U.S. adults, 1999–2000. JAMA. 2002; 288:1723–7.

2. Hu F, Li T, Colditz G, et al. Television watching and other sedentary behaviors in relation to risk of obesity and type 2 diabetes mellitus in women. JAMA. 2003;289:1785–91.

3. Peeters A, Barendregt J, Willekens F. Obesity in adulthood and its consequences for life expectancy: a life-table analysis. Ann Intern Med. 2003;138:24–32.

4. Calle E, Rodriguez C, Walker-Thurmond K, Thun M. Overweight, obesity, and mortality from cancer in a prospectively studied cohort of U.S. adults. N Engl J Med. 2003;348:1625–38.

5. Huang Z, Hankinson S, Colditz G, et al. Dual effects of weight and weight gain on breast cancer risk. JAMA. 1997;278:1407–11.

6. Padwal R, Li S, Lau D. Long-term pharmacotherapy for obesity and overweight. Cochrane Database Syst Rev. 2003; (4):CD004094.

7. Clinical guidelines on the identification, evaluation, and treatment of overweight and obesity in adults. National Institutes of Health Publication No. 98-4083. September 1998.

8. Streit K, Stevens N, Stevens V, Rossner J. Food records: a predictor and modifier of weight change in a long-term weight loss program. J Am Diet Assoc. 1991;91:213–6.

Chapter 9 — High blood pressure

1. Your Guide to Lowering Blood Pressure. National Institutes of Health; National Heart, Lung, and Blood Institute. NIH Publication No. 03-5232, May 2003.

2. Vasav S, Beiser A, Seshadri S, et al. Residual lifetime risk for developing hypertension in middle-aged women and men: The Framingham Heart Study. JAMA. 2002;287:1003–10.

3. Benetos A, Thomas F, Bean K, et al. Prognostic value of systolic and diastolic blood pressure in treated hypertensive men. Arch Intern Med. 2002;162:577–81.

4. Himmelman A, Hedner T, Hansson L. The growing importance of systolic blood pressure. Blood Press. 1998;7:131–2.

5. John J, Ziebland S, Yudkin P, et al. Effects of fruit and vegetable consumption on plasma antioxidant concentrations and blood pressure: a randomised controlled trial. Lancet. 2002;359:1969–74.

6. Whelton S, Chin A, Xin X, et al. Effect of aerobic exercise on blood pressure: a meta-analysis of randomized, controlled trials. Ann Intern Med. 2002;136:493–503.

7. Dahlof B, Devereux R, Kjeldsen S, et al. Cardiovascular morbidity and mortality in the losartan intervention for endpoint reduction in hypertension study (LIFE): a randomised trial against atenolol. Lancet. 2002;359:995–1003.

Chapter 10 — Cholesterol

1. Pignone M, Phillips C, Mulrow C. Use of lipid lowering drugs for primary prevention of coronary heart disease: meta-analysis of randomised trials. BMJ. 2000;321:983–6.
2. Executive summary of the third report of the National Cholesterol Education Program (NCEP) expert panel on detection, evaluation, and treatment of high blood cholesterol in adults (Adult Treatment Panel III). JAMA. 2001;285:2486–97.
3. Randomised trial of cholesterol lowering in 4,444 patients with coronary heart disease: the Scandinavian simvastatin survival study (4S) Lancet. 1994;344:1383–9.
4. Prevention of cardiovascular events and death with pravastatin in patients with coronary heart disease and a broad range of initial cholesterol levels. The Long-Term Intervention with Pravastatin in Ischaemic Disease (LIPID) Study Group. N Engl J Med. 1998;339:1349–57.
5. Serruys P, Feyter P, Macaya C, et al. Fluvastatin for prevention of cardiac events following successful first percutaneous coronary intervention: a randomized controlled trial. JAMA. 2002;287:3215–22.
6. Henley E, Chang L, Hollander S. Treatment of hyperlipidemia. J Fam Pract. 2002;51:370–6.

Chapter 11 — Diabetes

1. Astrup P, Finer N. Redefining type 2 diabetes: 'diabesity' or 'obesity dependent diabetes mellitus'? Obes Rev. 2000;1:57–9.
2. Cho E, Rimm E, Stampfer M, et al. The impact of diabetes mellitus and prior myocardial infarction on mortality from all causes and from coronary heart disease in men. J Am Coll Cardiol. 2002;40:954–60.

3. Hu F, Manson M. Walking, the best medicine for diabetes? Arch Intern Med. 2003;163:1397–98.

4. Knowler W, Barrett-Connor E, Fowler S. Reduction in the incidence of type 2 diabetes with lifestyle intervention or metformin. N Engl J Med. 2002;346:393–403.

5. Lindstrom J, Eriksson J, Valle T, et al. Prevention of diabetes mellitus in subjects with impaired glucose tolerance in the Finnish diabetes prevention study: results from a randomized clinical trial. J Am Soc Nephrol. 2003;14:S108–13.

6. Manson J, Nathan D, Krolewski A, et al. A prospective study of exercise and incidence of diabetes among U.S. male physicians. JAMA. 1992;268:63–7.

7. van Dam R, Rimm E, Willett W, et al. Dietary patterns and risk for type 2 diabetes mellitus in U.S. men. Ann Intern Med. 2002;136:201–9.

8. Gregg E, Gerzoff R, Caspersen C, et al. Relationship of walking to mortality among U.S. adults with diabetes. Arch Intern Med. 2003;163:1440–47.

Chapter 12 – Stroke

1. Reynolds K, Lewis L, Nolen J, et al. Alcohol consumption and risk of stroke: a meta-analysis. JAMA. 2003;289:579–88.

2. Benavente O, Moher D. Carotid endarterectomy for asymptomatic carotid stenosis: a meta-analysis. BMJ. 1998;317:1477–80.

3. Cina C, Clase C, Haynes R. Carotid endarterectomy for symptomatic carotid stenosis. Cochrane Database Syst Rev. 2000; (2):CD001081.

4. Scott R, Wilson N, Ashton H, Kay D. Influence of screening on the incidence of ruptured abdominal aortic aneurysm: 5-year results of a randomized controlled study. British J of Surg. 1995;82:1068–70.

5. Camargo C, Stampfer M, Glynn R, et al. Prospective study of moderate alcohol consumption and risk of peripheral vascular disease in U.S. male physicians. Circulation. 1997;95:577–80.

6. Guide to Clinical preventive services, Second edition, Report of the U.S. Preventive Services Task Force. 1996;63–7.

Chapter 13 – Controlling cancer

1. Cancer facts and figures 2003. American Cancer Society, Inc. Surveillance research, 2003; p 4.
2. Doll R, Peto R, The causes of cancer: quantitative estimates of avoidable risks of cancer in the United States today, J Natl Cancer Inst. 1981;66:1191–308.
3. Potter J, Finnegan J, Guinard J, et al. Five a day for better health program evaluation report. National Cancer Institute. NIH Publication No. 01-4904. p 11–12.
4. Bingham S, Day N, Luben R, et al. Dietary fibre in food and protection against colorectal cancer in the European prospective investigation into cancer and nutrition (EPIC): an observational study. Lancet. 2003;361:1496–501.
5. Peters U, Sinha R, Chatterjee N, et al. Dietary fibre and colorectal adenoma in a colorectal cancer early detection programme. Lancet. 2003;361:1491–5.
6. Lee I, Paffenbarger R, Hsieh C. Physical activity and risk of developing colorectal cancer among college alumni. JNCI. 1991; 83:1324–9.
7. Giovannucci E, Ascherio A, Rimm E, et al. Physical activity, obesity and risk for colon cancer and adenoma in men. Ann Intern Med. 1995;122:327–34.
8. Michaud D, Giovannucci E, Willett W, et al. Physical activity, obesity, height, and the risk of pancreatic cancer. JAMA. 2001;286:921–9.
9. Vachon C, Cerhan J, Vierkant R, Sellers T. Investigation of an interaction of alcohol intake and family history on breast cancer risk in the Minnesota breast cancer family study. Cancer. 2001;92:240–8.

Chapter 14 – Cervical Cancer

1. Deacon J, Evans C, Yule R, et al. Sexual behavior and smoking as determinants of cervical HPV infection and of CIN-3 among those infected: a case-control study nested within the Manchester cohort. Br J Cancer. 2000;83:1565–72.

2. Wright T, Cox J, Massad S, et al. 2001 Consensus Guidelines for the Management of Women With Cervical Cytological Abnormalities. JAMA. 2002;287:2120–29.

3. Saslow D, Runowicz C, Solomon D, et al. American Cancer Society guideline for the early detection of cervical neoplasia and cancer. Cancer J Clin. 2002;52:342–62.

Chapter 15 – Lung cancer

1. American Cancer Society. Detailed guide: lung cancer. What are the key statistics for lung cancer? *www.cancer.org*

2. American Cancer Society. Detailed guide: lung cancer. What are the risk factors for lung cancer? *www.cancer.org*

3. Swensen S, Jett J, Sloan J, et al. Screening for lung cancer with low-dose spiral computed tomography. Am J Respir Crit Care Med. 2002;165:508–13.

4. Colditz G, Stampfer M, Willett W. Diet and lung cancer. A review of the epidemiologic evidence in humans. Arch Intern Med. 1987;147:157–60.

5. Miller A, Altenburg H, Bueno-de-Mesquita B, et al. Fruits and vegetables and lung cancer: findings from the European prospective investigation into cancer and nutrition. Int J Cancer. 2004;108:269–76.

6. Blumberg J, Block G. The alpha-tocopherol, beta-carotene cancer prevention study in Finland. Nutr Rev. 1994;52:242–5.

Chapter 16 – Colon Cancer

1. Bingham S, Day N, Luben R, et al. Dietary fibre in food and protection against colorectal cancer in the European prospective investigation into cancer and nutrition (EPIC): an observational study. Lancet. 2003;361:1496–501.

2. Peters U, Sinha R, Chatterjee N, et al. Dietary fibre and colorectal adenoma in a colorectal cancer early detection programme. Lancet. 2003;361:1491–5.

3. Thun M, Calle E, Namboodiri M, et al. Risk factors for fatal colon cancer in a large prospective study. J Natl Cancer Inst. 1992;84:1491–500.

4. Butler L, Sinha R, Millikan R, et al. Heterocyclic amines, meat intake, and association with colon cancer in a population-based study. Am J Epidemiol. 2003;157:434–45.
5. Stoneham M, Goldacre M, Seagroatt V, Gill L. Olive oil, diet and colorectal cancer: an ecological study and a hypothesis. J Epidemiol Community Health. 2000;54:756–760.
6. Lee I. Physical activity and cancer prevention—data from epidemiologic studies. Med Sci Sports Exerc. 2003;35:1823–7.
7. Cho E, Smith-Warner S, Ritz J, et al. Alcohol intake and colorectal cancer: a pooled analysis of 8 cohort studies. Ann Intern Med. 2004;140:603–13.
8. Weingarten M, Zalmanovici A, Yaphe J. Dietary calcium supplementation for preventing colorectal cancer and adenomatous polyps. Cochrane Database Syst Rev. 2004;1:CD003548.
9. Wu K, Willett W, Fuchs C, et al. Calcium intake and risk of colon cancer in women and men. J Natl Cancer Inst. 2002;94:437–46.
10. Sturmer T, Glynn R, Lee I, et al. Aspirin use and colorectal cancer: post-trial follow-up data from the Physicians' Health Study. Ann Intern Med. 1998;128:713–20.
11. Baron J, Cole B, Sandler R, et al. Randomized trial of aspirin to prevent colorectal adenomas in patients with previous colorectal cancer. N Engl J Med. 2003;348:883–90.
12. Walsh J, Terdiman J. Colorectal cancer screening, scientific review. JAMA. 2003;289:1288–96.

Chapter 17 — Breast Cancer

1. Collaborative Group on Hormonal Factors in Breast Cancer. Familial breast cancer: collaborative reanalysis of individual data from 52 epidemiological studies including 58,209 women with breast cancer and 101,986 women without the disease. Lancet. 2001;358:1389–99.
2. Colditz G. Epidemiology of breast cancer. Findings from the Nurses' Health Study. Cancer. 1993;71(4 Suppl):1480–9.

3. Breast cancer and hormonal contraceptives: collaborative reanalysis of individual data on 53,297 women with breast cancer and 100,239 women without breast cancer from 54 epidemiological studies. Collaborative Group on Hormonal Factors in Breast Cancer. Lancet. 1996;347:1713–27.

4. Writing Group for the Women's Health Initiative Investigators. Risks and benefits of estrogen plus progestin in healthy postmenopausal women: principal results From the Women's Health Initiative randomized controlled trial. JAMA. 2002;288:321–33.

5. Smith-Warner S, Spiegelman D, Yaun S, et al. Alcohol and breast cancer in women, a pooled analysis of cohort studies. JAMA. 1998;279:535–540.

6. Bernstein L, Henderson B, Hanisch R, et al. Physical exercise and reduced risk of breast cancer in young women. J Natl Cancer Inst. 1994;86:1403–8.

7. Dorn J, Vena J, Brasure J, et al. Lifetime physical activity and breast cancer risk in pre- and postmenopausal women. Med Sci Sports Exerc. 2003;35:278–85.

8. Cho E, Spiegelman D, Hunter D, et al. Premenopausal fat intake and risk of breast cancer. J Natl Cancer Inst. 2003;95:1079–85.

9. Newcomb P, Storer B, Longnecker M, et al. Lactation and a reduced risk of premenopausal breast cancer. N Engl J Med. 1994;330:81–7.

10. Humphrey L, Helfand M, Chan B, Woolf S. Breast cancer screening. Summary of the evidence. Ann Intern Med 2002; 137:344–6.

11. Hackshaw A, Paul E. Breast self-examination and death from breast cancer: a meta-analysis. Br J Cancer. 2003;88:1047–53.

12. Kinsinger L, Harris R, Woolf S, et al. Chemoprevention of breast cancer: a summary of the evidence for the U.S. Preventive Services Task Force. Ann Intern Med 2002;137: 59–69.

Chapter 18 — Prostate Cancer

1. Kolonel L. Nutrition and prostate cancer. Cancer Causes Control. 1996;7:83–94.

2. Giovannucci E, Rimm E, Liu Y, et al. A prospective study of tomato products, lycopene, and prostate cancer risk. J Natl Cancer Inst. 2002;94:391–8.

3. Mills P, Beeson W, Phillips R, Fraser G. Cohort study of diet, lifestyle, and prostate cancer in Adventist men. Cancer. 1989;63:598–604.

4. Leitzmann M, Platz E, Stampfer M, et al. Ejaculation frequency and subsequent risk of prostate cancer. JAMA. 2004;291:1578–1586.

5. Johansson J, Holmberg L, Johansson S, et al. Fifteen-year survival in prostate cancer, a prospective, population-based study in Sweden. JAMA. 1997;277:467–71.

6. Ross K, Carter H, Pearson J, Guess H. Comparative efficiency of prostate-specific antigen screening strategies for prostate cancer detection. JAMA. 2000;284:1399–405.

7. Eastham J, Riedel E, Scardino P, et al. Variation of serum prostate-specific antigen levels, an evaluation of year-to-year fluctuations. JAMA. 2003; 289:2695–700.

Chapter 19 — The golden years

1. Age-related eye disease study research group. A randomized, placebo-controlled, clinical trial of high-dose supplementation with vitamins C and E, beta carotene, and zinc for age-related macular degeneration and vision loss. Arch Ophthalmol. 2001;119:1417–36.

2. Seddon J, Willett W, Speizer F, Hankinson S. A prospective study of smoking and age-related macular degeneration in women. JAMA. 1996;276:1141–46.

Chapter 20 — Osteoporosis

1. Kiel D, Baron J, Anderson J, et al. Smoking eliminates the protective effect of oral estrogens on the risk for hip fracture among women. Ann Intern Med. 1992;116:716–21.

2. Turner R. Skeletal response to alcohol. Alcohol Clin Exp Res. 2000;24:1693–701.

3. Trivedi D, Doll R, Khaw K. Effect of four monthly oral vitamin D3 (cholecalciferol) supplementation on fractures and mortality in men and women living in the community: randomised double blind controlled trial. BMJ. 2003;326–469.

4. Bischoff H, Stahelin H, Dick W, et al. Effects of vitamin D and calcium supplementation on falls: a randomized controlled trial. J Bone Miner Res. 2003;18:343–51.

5. U.S. Preventive Services Task Force. Screening for osteoporosis in postmenopausal women: recommendations and rationale. Ann Intern Med. 2002;137:526–8.

6. Wolf S, Sattin R, Kutner M, et al. Intense Tai Chi Exercise Training and Fall Occurrences in Older, Transitionally Frail Adults: A Randomized, Controlled Trial. J Am Geriatri Soc. 2003;51:1693–1701.

7. Watts N. Bisphosphonate treatment of osteoporosis. Clin Geriatr Med. 2003;19:395–414.

8. Writing Group for the Women's Health Initiative Investigators. Risks and benefits of estrogen plus progestin in healthy post-menopausal women: principal results from the Women's Health Initiative randomized controlled trial. JAMA. 2002; 288:321–33.

Chapter 21 — Osteoarthritis

1. Dawson J, Juszczak E, Thorogood M, et al. An investigation of risk factors for symptomatic osteoarthritis of the knee in women using a life course approach. J Epidemiol Community Health. 2003;57:823–30.

2. Ruane R, Griffiths P. Glucosamine therapy compared to ibuprofen for joint pain. Br J Community Nurs. 2002;7:148–52.

3. Reginster J, Deroisy R, Rovati L, et al. Long-term effects of glucosamine sulphate on osteoarthritis progression: a randomised, placebo-controlled clinical trial. Lancet. 2001;357:251–6.

4. Cleland L, James M, Proudman S. The role of fish oils in the treatment of rheumatoid arthritis. Drugs. 2003;63:845–53.

5. Lo G, LaValley M, McAlindon T, Felson D. Intra-articular hyaluronic acid in treatment of knee osteoarthritis: a meta-analysis. JAMA. 2003;290:3115–21.

6. Moseley J, O'Malley K, Petersen N, et al. A controlled trial of arthroscopic surgery for osteoarthritis of the knee. N Engl J Med. 2002;347:81–8.

7. Sohn R, Micheli L. The effect of running on the pathogenesis of osteoarthritis of the hips and knees. Clin Orthop. 1985;198:106–9.

Chapter 22 – Memory

1. Gustafson D, Rothenberg E, Blennow K, et al. An 18-year follow-up of overweight and risk of Alzheimer disease. Arch Intern Med. 2003;163:1524–28.

2. Seshadri S, Beiser A, Selhub J, et al. Plasma homocysteine as a risk factor for dementia and Alzheimer's disease. N Engl J Med. 2002;346:476–83.

3. Shumaker S, Legault C, Rapp S, et al. Estrogen plus progestin and the incidence of dementia and mild cognitive impairment in postmenopausal women: the Women's Health Initiative memory study: a randomized controlled trial. JAMA. 2003;289:2651–62.

4. Ott A, Andersen K, Dewey M, et al. Effect of smoking on global cognitive function in nondemented elderly. Neurology. 2004; 62:920–24.

5. Wilson R, Mendes de Leon C, Barnes L, et al. Participation in cognitively stimulating activities and risk of incident Alzheimer disease. JAMA. 2002;287:742–748.

6. Verghese J, Lipton R, Katz M, et al. Leisure activities and the risk of dementia in the elderly. N Engl J Med. 2003;348:2508–16.

7. Engelhart M, Geerlings M, Ruitenberg A, et al. Dietary intake of antioxidants and risk of Alzheimer disease. JAMA. 2002;287: 3223–29.

8. Morris M, Evans D, Bienias J, et al. Dietary intake of antioxidant nutrients and the risk of incident Alzheimer disease in a biracial community study. JAMA. 2002;287:3230–37.

9. Petot G, Debanne S, Riedel T, et al. Use of surrogate respondents in a case control study of dietary risk factors for Alzheimer's disease. J Am Diet Assoc. 2002;102:848–50.

10. Mukamal K, Kuller L, Fitzpatrick A, et al. Prospective study of alcohol consumption and risk of dementia in older adults. JAMA. 2003;289:1405–13.

11. Alsen P, Schafer K, Grundman M, et al. Effects of rofecoxib or naproxen vs placebo on Alzheimer disease progression, a randomized controlled trial. JAMA. 2003;289:2819–26.

12. Solomon P, Adams F, Silver A, et al. Ginkgo for memory enhancement, a randomized controlled trial. JAMA. 2002;288: 835–40.

13. Bars P, Kastz M, Berman N, et al. A placebo-controlled, double-blind, randomized trial of an extract of ginkgo biloba for dementia. North American EGb Study Group. JAMA. 1997; 278:1327–32.

14. Mitchell S, Teno J, Roy J, et al. Clinical and organizational factors associated with feeding tube use among nursing home residents with advanced cognitive impairment. JAMA. 2003;290: 73–80.

15. Finucane T, Christmas C, Travis K. Tube feeding in patients with advanced dementia, a review of the evidence. JAMA. 1999; 282: 1365–70.

Chapter 23 – Advance directives

1. Finucane T, Christmas C, Travis K. Tube feeding in patients with advanced dementia, a review of the evidence. JAMA. 1999;282: 1365–70.

2. McCann R, Hall W, Groth-Juncker A. Comfort care for terminally ill patients. The appropriate use of nutrition and hydration. JAMA. 1994;272:1263–6.

Index

ACE inhibitors, 139
advance medical directives, 321-330
  common dilemmas, 327-30
  do not resuscitate order, 326-7
  feeding tube, 328
  health-care power of attorney, 325-6
  history of, 323-4
  hospice, 329-30
  living will, 324-5
  pre-hospital directive, 326
Alzheimer's disease, 305-9
  alcohol and, 312-3
  behavior problems and, 317-9
  caregiver support and, 317
  causes, 308-10
  comfort care and, 320
  definition of, 306
  feeding tube, 319-20
  ginkgo biloba and, 315-6, 318
  medications for, 317-9
  prevention of, 310-16
  statins and, 313
  treatment of, 316-20
  vaccine for, 315
aging
  active, 261-72
  living longer, 262-3
air
  pollution, 6, 8, 76-7
  quality, 8
alcohol, 11, 59-71
  aging and, 63-4
  Alzheimer's disease and, 312-3
  breast cancer and, 240
  cancer and, 197
  colon cancer and, 228
  diabetes and, 168

  driving and, 69
  health benefits of, 61-3
  health risks of, 64-5
  history of, 59-61
  hypertension and, 133-4
  impairment charts, 71
  measuring, 61
  osteoporosis and, 279
  women and, 66
alcoholism, 67-70
  CAGE questionnaire, 68
  screening for, 68-9
allergy triggers, 8
aneurysm, abdominal aortic, 184-6
  causes of, 184-5
  screening for, 185-6
angiotensin receptor blockers (ARBs), 139
anorexia nervosa, 111
antioxidants, 23, 25, 311-2
apolipoproteins, 146
arteriosclerosis, 93
arthritis, 289-303
  definition of, 290-92
  exercise and, 40, 293-4
  fish oil for, 296, 300
  osteo (see osteoarthritis)
  prevention of, 292-6
  rheumatoid, 290-91
aspirin
  colon cancer and, 228-9
  colon polyps and, 228-9
  heart disease and, 99-100
atherosclerosis, 93
atrial fibrillation, 180
BMI (body mass index), 110, 112-13
beta blockers, 138-9
beta carotene, 27

bladder control, 268
blood pressure
    cuff, 137
    high (see hypertension)
    medication, 137-40
blood-sugar monitoring, 171
bone health, 275
breakfast, health benefits, 15
breast cancer, 235-48
    alcohol and, 240
    animal fat in diet and, 240-1
    breast self-examination and, 245
    breastfeeding and, 241
    chemoprevention of, 246
    estrogen therapy and, 239
    exercise and, 240
    family history of, 237
    frequency of, 236
    hereditary, 238
    mammograms and, 241-5
    obesity and, 238-9
    prevention of, 237-41, 246
    screening for, 241-5
    treatment of, 247
C-reactive protein, 102-3
calcium
    colon cancer and, 228
    daily requirements of, 280
    hypertension and, 132
    osteoporosis and, 280-82
    sources of, 280-2
calcium channel blockers, 140
cancer
    alcohol and, 197
    causes of, 191-92
    common types of, 190
    death statistics for, 190
    definition of, 189-90
    diet and, 193-95
    exercise and, 196
    prevention of, 16, 192-99
    prevention tips, 194
    screening for, 203, 216
    sun exposure and, 198-9
    tobacco and, 74, 197-8
    warning signs, 199
carbon-monoxide
    alarms, 7, 8
    poisoning, 8

carcinogens, 191-92, 197-8
cardiac risk assessment,
    for men, 96
    for women, 97
cardiac risk factors, 94-5, 150
carotid artery blockage, 182-84
    screening for, 182-4
    transient ischemic attack (TIA)
        and, 182-3
cataracts, 265
cervical cancer, 201-12
    human papilloma virus (HPV),
        203-05
    PAP smears and, 201-3
    prevention of, 205-6
cervical dysplasia, 205-10
    natural therapy for, 205
    prevention of, 205-6
    treatment of, 208-9
cholesterol, 102, 143-58
    definition of, 144-5
    diet for, 153-4
    dietary, 22
    drug treatment of, 154-58
    exercise and, 154
    goals for, 148, 151-2
    HDL, 145, 148
    LDL, 145, 148
    lipid profile, 144-146, 148
    treatment of, 149-58
cholesterol drugs
    ezetimibe, 157
    niacin, 156
    resins, 157
    statins, 155-6
colon cancer, 223-234
    alcohol and, 228
    aspirin and, 228-9
    calcium and, 228
    diet and, 225-7
    exercise and, 227
    fiber and, 224-27
    high-risk factors, 232-3
    polyps and, 224
    prevention of, 225-9
    red meat and, 227
    risk factors for, 224-5
colon cancer screening,
    223-4, 229-33
    average risk people and, 233

Colon cancer screening (continued)
  barium enema and, 231
  colonoscopy and, 231
  fecal occult blood testing
    and, 230
  high-risk people and, 232-3
  recommendations for, 232-3
  sigmoidoscopy and, 230
colon polyps, 224
  aspirin and, 228-9
colonoscopy, 231
  virtual, 231
coronary artery disease, 92-3
  diabetes and, 175
  prevention of, 98, 103, 105
death, causes of, 2
dementia, 306-10
  causes of, 308
  diagnosis of, 307-8
  vascular, 307-8
depression, 50
diabetes, 159-176
  A1C test, 168
  adult-onset, 159-60
  alcohol and, 168
  blood-sugar monitoring and, 171
  complications of, 161-2, 173-5
  definition of, 160-1
  diet and, 166, 169-70
  exercise and, 169
  eyes and, 173-4
  feet and, 173
  heart disease and, 175
  kidney disease and, 174
  medications for, 171-2
  metformin and, 171
  prediabetes, 162-3
  prevention of, 164-7
  screening for, 163-4
  sulfonylureas and, 172
  treatment goals for, 167-8
  type 1, 160-1
  type 2, 161
diet, 10
  breast cancer and, 240-1
  cancer prevention and, 193-5
  colon cancer and, 225-7
  diabetic, 169-70
  Mediterranean, 23-4
  pills, 118-20

prudent, 14
  strategies, 123-24
  tips, 118
  Western, 14
diets
  Atkins, 117
  fad, 116-17
  low carb, 117-18
diuretics, 138
driving
  safety of older drivers, 270
  seat belt use and, 3, 10
eating disorders, 111
emphysema, 75
environment, health impact of, 5
estrogen
  breast cancer and, 239
  memory and, 313-4
  osteoporosis and, 287-8
exercise, 11, 31-45
  aerobic, 43-4
  arthritis and, 40, 293-4
  assessing your level, 35
  benefits of, 31-3
  blood pressure and, 133
  breast cancer and, 240
  cancer prevention and, 196
  cholesterol and, 154
  colon cancer and, 227-8
  diabetes prevention and, 165-6
  heart rate and, 45
  injury prevention, 40-1
  longevity and, 34
  osteoporosis and, 278-9
  overweight and, 36
  programs, 42
  safety and, 37-41
  starting, 32-3
  strength training, 44-6
  treadmill stress test and, 39-40
fall prevention, 286
fats, 21-22
  cholesterol and, 22
  monounsaturated, 21, 22, 226-7
  polyunsaturated, 22
  saturated, 22, 226-7
  trans fats, 21, 22
feeding tube, 319-20, 328
fiber, 17-21, 195
  cancer prevention and, 195

Fiber (continued)
  colon cancer and, 224-7
  definition of, 17
  health benefits of, 18, 195
  recommendations, 18-9
  sources in foods, 20-1
fibromyalgia, 291-2
fish oil, 22, 101-2, 296, 300
Five-a-day fruits and vegetables,
  16-7, 193-4, 226
folic acid, 25, 100-1, 103
foods
  fiber in, 17-8
  healthy, 14
  junk, 13, 14
  processing, 13, 18
fracture prevention, 286-8
genetics, health impact, 4
ginkgo biloba, 315-6, 318
glucosamine, 294-5, 298
gout, 291
hearing loss, 266
heart attack,
  aspirin and, 99-100
  prevention of, 98, 103, 105
  risk assessment for, 95-98
  risk factors for, 94-5, 150
  tobacco and, 73-5
  warning symptoms of, 103-4
heart disease, 91-106
  arteriosclerosis and, 93
  coronary artery disease and, 92-3
  definition of, 92-3
  diabetes and, 175
  folic acid and, 100-1
  homocysteine and, 100
heart failure, 92-3
hemochromatosis, 28
hemoglobin A1c, 167-8
high blood pressure
  (see hypertension)
home safety, 271-2
homocysteine, 100
hormones (see estrogen)
hospice, 329-30
hypertension, 127-141
  alcohol and, 133-4
  baby boomers and, 129-30
  calcium and, 132
  classification of, 129

definition of, 128-9
diet and, 132
exercise and, 133
magnesium and, 132
medication for, 137-40
NNT (number needed to
  treat) and, 136
potassium and, 132
prevention of, 131-34
risk factors for, 131
stress and, 134
stroke and, 179
systolic, 130
treatment of, 135-40
white-coat, 136
hypertension drugs
  ACE inhibitors, 139
  alpha blockers, 140
  angiotensin receptor blockers
    (ARBs), 139
  beta blockers, 138-9
  calcium channel blockers, 139-40
  diuretics, 138
human papilloma virus (HPV),
  203-05
  treatment of, 204-5
  vaccine for, 205
incontinence, urinary, 267-8
infections, 268-9
influenza vaccine, 268-9
iron, 28
junk food, 13, 14
lifestyle, healthy, 1-3,10-2
lipid profile, 146, 148
living will, 324-5
  common dilemmas of, 327-30
lung cancer, 213-221
  CT scan screening for, 217-18
  causes of, 214-5
  chest x-ray screening for, 215-17
  diet and, 220-1
  natural course and, 214
  prevention of, 219-21
  smoking and, 214-5, 219-20
macular degeneration, 264-5
magnesium, hypertension, 132
mammograms, 241-5
medical
  care access, 7, 9
  history, 5

medications, adverse reactions, 269-70
Mediterranean diet, 23-4
memory, 305-20
  antioxidants and, 311-2
  ginkgo biloba and, 315-6, 318
  preserving, 310-6
metformin, 171
NNT (number needed to treat), 136
niacin, 156
nicotine replacement, 86-7
non-steroidal anti-inflammatory drugs, 298-9
  memory and, 314-5
obesity, 115-16
  BMI (body mass index), 110, 112-13
  breast cancer and, 238-9
  cancer risk, 109
  community action and, 125
  fat location and, 109-10
  health crisis and, 107-8
  health risks of, 108-10
  heart risk and, 109
  waist size and, 111
omega-3 fatty acids, 22, 101-2
osteoarthritis
  definition of, 290
  exercise and, 293-4
  glucosamine and, 294-5, 298
  injections for, 300-1
  medications for, 297-300
  prevention of, 292-6
  sports and, 293
  surgery for, 301-3
  treatment of, 296-303
osteoporosis, 273-88
  alcohol and, 279
  bone health and, 275
  brittle bones and, 273-4
  calcium and, 280-82, 286
  DEXA scan and, 283-5
  definition of, 274, 284
  estrogen and, 287-8
  exercise and, 278-9
  fracture prevention and, 286-8
  frequency of, 274-5
  medications for, 286-8
  prevention of, 278-83
  risk factors for, 275-8

screening for, 283-5
  smoking and, 277-8
  vitamin D and, 282-3, 286
overweight, 114-15
  community action and, 125
  health crisis and, 107-8
PAP smears, 201-3
  abnormal, 206-9
  after hysterectomy, 211
  atypical, 207-8
  guidelines for, 210-11
  high-grade, 207-8
  low-grade, 207-8
panic attack, 50
peripheral vascular disease, 186-87
  risk factors for, 186-7
  screening for, 187
  treatment of, 187
pneumonia vaccine, 268-9
pollution
  indoor, 6, 8, 76-7
  outdoor air, 6, 76-7
polypharmacy, 269-70
potassium, hypertension, 132
prediabetes, 162-3
  diet and, 166
  exercise for, 165-6
prostate cancer, 249-260
  frequency of, 249, 251-2
  fruits and vegetables and, 253
  Gleason score and, 259
  metastatic, 260
  natural course of, 250
  PSA recommendations and, 256-7
  PSA test and, 254-6
  prevention of, 251-4
  radiation treatment of, 258
  risk factors and, 253
  surgery for, 258
  tomatoes and, 252
  treatment of, 257-60
prostate gland, 249-50
radon gas, 8
screening tests
  blood-sugar, 163-4
  cancer screening, 216
  chest CT scan, 217-18
  chest x-ray, 215, 217

Screening tests (continued)
  colonoscopy, 231
  DEXA scan, 283-5
  fecal occult blood testing, 230
  lipid profile, 145
  mammogram, 241-5
  PAP smear, 201-3
PSA test, 254-6
sigmoidoscopy, 230
seat belt use, 3, 10
sedentary lifestyle, health risks
  of, 34, 37
selenium, 27
skin cancer, 199
sigmoidoscopy, 230
smoking,
  cessation of, 80-89
  ex-smokers and, 78-80
  low tar and nicotine and, 77
  lung cancer and, 214-15, 219-20
  osteoporosis and, 277-8
  second-hand, 75-8
  teens and, 79-80
surgery,
  hip replacement, 301
  knee arthroscopy, 320-3
  knee replacement, 301-2
  prostate cancer, 258
  weight-loss, 120
statins, 155-6, 313
sterols/stanols, 22
stress, 11, 47-58
  blood pressure and, 134
  causes of, 54
  definition of, 48
  effects of, 47-9
  life events and, 51-3
  managing, 54-6, 58
  measuring, 51
  self-relaxation and, 57
stroke, 177-81
  atrial fibrillation and, 180
  causes of, 178-180
  definition, 178
  high blood pressure and, 179
  prevention of, 181
  Woodrow Wilson and, 179

sulfonylureas, 172
sun exposure, 198-99
tobacco, 12, 73-90
  addiction to, 80-85
  cancer and, 74, 197-8
  chewing, 77
  emphysema and, 75
  heart attack and, 73-5
  history of, 78
  lung cancer and, 214-5
  nicotine replacement and, 86-7
  second-hand smoke and, 75-8
transient ischemic attack (TIA),
  182-3
triglycerides, 145, 148
urinary incontinence, 267-8
vaccines
  influenza, 268-9
  pneumonia, 268-9
vision loss, 264-5
vitamins, 23-29
  A, 27
  antioxidants, 23, 25, 311-2
  beta carotene, 27
  C, 26
  D, 282-3, 286
  E, 26
  folic acid, 25, 100-1, 103
  niacin, 156
waist size, 111
weight
  normal, 114
  obesity, 115-16
  overweight, 114-15
  underweight, 114
weight-loss,
  advice, 122-3
  diet tips, 118
  goals, 121-22
  strategies, 123-24
  surgery, 120
workplace safety, 5

About the Author

Marvin Moe Bell, M.D., M.P.H. received his medical degree from the University of Southern California Medical School in 1981. In 1984, he completed a residency in family practice, a specialty that stresses prevention and healthy living for family members of all ages. Dr. Bell is currently associate director of the Scottsdale Healthcare Family Practice Residency in Scottsdale, Arizona and medical director of Scottsdale Healthcare's Community Health Education and Outreach Program. He is also a clinical associate professor in the Department of Family and Community Medicine at University of Arizona College of Medicine. Dr. Bell recently completed a master's degree through the Arizona Graduate Program in Public Health to gain additional knowledge and skills in preventive medicine.

In his more than 20 years as a practitioner and teacher of family medicine, Dr. Bell has always emphasized his prescriptions for wellness. "It's much better for doctors to teach patients how to stay well, rather than merely treat them once they are sick," he says. Dr. Bell lives a healthy lifestyle with his wife and two children. During vacations, he enjoys hiking 14,000-foot peaks in Colorado and California. In 1999, Dr. Bell climbed to the top of Alaska's Mt. McKinley, completing his quest to reach the highest point in each of the 50 states.